Genii of the River Niger

GENII OF THE

Translated by BETH G. RAPS

RIVER NIGER

Jean-Marie Gibbal

With a Foreword by PAUL STOLLER

THE UNIVERSITY OF CHICAGO PRESS • CHICAGO AND LONDON

At the time of his death in 1993, Jean-Marie Gibbal
was research director at the Centre National de la
Recherche Scientifique, Paris. He published four
ethnographies and five volumes of poetry in French.

The University of Chicago Press, Chicago 60637
The University of Chicago Press, Ltd., London
© 1994 by The University of Chicago
All rights reserved. Published 1994
Printed in the United States of America

03 02 01 00 99 98 97 96 95 94 5 4 3 2 1

ISBN (cloth): 0-226-29051-4
ISBN (paper): 0-226-29052-2

Originally published as *Les génies du fleuve: Voyage sur
le Niger,* © Presses de la Renaissance, 1988. The
English translation has been published with the support
of the French Ministry of Culture.

Library of Congress Cataloging-in-Publication Data

Gibbal, Jean-Marie, 1938–
    [Génies du fleuve. English]
    Genii of the River Niger / Jean-Marie Gibbal ;
translated by Beth G. Raps.
        p.   cm.
    Includes bibliographical references (p.   ) and
index.
    ISBN 0-226-29051-4. — ISBN 0-226-29052-2
(pbk.)
    1. Cults—Mali.   2. Mali—Religious life and
customs.   3. Niger River.   I. Raps, Beth G.
II. Title
BL2470.M35G4813   1994
966.2—dc20   93-24889
                                        CIP

CONTENTS

A gallery of photographs follows page 70.

FOREWORD

Most Anglo-American readers are probably not familiar with the works of Jean-Marie Gibbal, none of which have been translated into English. Gibbal, who died much too young in February of 1993, was one of many French anthropologists who publish fine ethnographies that remain unknown to Anglophone readers. Most of the French material translated and published in the Anglophone world is more theoretical than ethnographic, part of the "French wave" that has swept over North American and, to a lesser extent, British shores. The works of Lévi-Strauss, Bourdieu, and Godelier are cases in point. The translation of these and other similar works have profoundly influenced scholars in North America and Britain. They are worthy of translation. So too are some of the lesser known French ethnographic works that also raise major questions about theory in anthropology. *Genii of the River Niger* fits into the latter category—admirably so.

Like the noted author Jean Favret-Saada, Gibbal was part of a small group of French scholars whose aesthetic response to ethnographic worlds compels them to write highly innovative ethnographies. Gibbal was a highly regarded author who published four ethnographies as well as five volumes of poetry. His last volume, a book of literary criticism, is a highly personal portrait of Georges Perros, his poetic mentor. In his spare time, Gibbal organized avant-garde art exhibitions, whose catalogues he authored. He also directed a books series that publishes ethnographies.

My mention of Gibbal's poetry and his involvement in the avant-garde art scene is not gratuitous, for they have a direct bearing on how he conceptualized and wrote his ethnographies. *Genii of the River Niger* is the third book Gibbal wrote on possession ceremonies and magical rites among the peoples of Mali. His first book about Mali, *Tambours d'Eau* is an ethnography of the *djiné don* possession rites of the Bamana people; it is text that plays with the conventions of academic representation. The first part of the book is, as the French say, a *carnet de route,* a logbook or journal that describes in vivid, sometimes poetic prose the ecological, climatic, social and historical conditions that formed the context of Gibbal's research. The second part, which draws heavily on the contextual foundation already established in the preceding pages, is Gibbal's more formal analysis of the *djiné don,* an exposition that derives its inspiration from Michel Leiris and Roger Bastide. Indeed, *Tambours d'Eau* was a partial model for my book on Songhay possession, *Fusion of the Worlds.* Gibbal's second Sahelian volume, *Guerisseurs et Magiciens du Sahel* consists of the life portraits of three Sahelian healers, a Bamana, a Soninké, and a Songhay. Here Gibbal combines his poetic descriptions of the Sahel and its people with substantial characterizations of the three healers. Both of these volumes won praise in the French press and in the major social science and literary journals of the French academy.

Gibbal's first two books on Mali laid the foundation for this third and best ethnographic work, *Genii of the River Niger,* which explores with historical depth and poetic evocation the Ghimbala possession rites performed between Mopti and Timbuktu in eastern Mali. From the moment of its publication in France in May of 1988, *Genii of the River Niger* enjoyed great success. It was enthusiastically reviewed in the major outlets of the French press. Many reviewers compared favorably Gibbal's poetic efforts in this book to those of Michel Leiris in his monumental *Afrique Fantôme.* Writing in *Le Magazine Littéraire,* Paul Loubière says that *Genii of the River Niger* was not only the story about Gibbal's voyage on the Niger River, but also a voyage to the edges of the human imagination. In 1989 the book was awarded an Alexandra David-Neel literary prize.

This ample and deserved success is due to the fact that Jean-Marie Gibbal's books, including, of course, the present volume, can be appreciated by a wide range of readers—specialists and nonspecialists alike. For many readers, *Genii of the River Niger* will be enjoyed as a particularly evocative *carnet de route.* For students of Africa, the anthropology of religion, and literature, the book will stimulate much felicitous debate, for in this work Gibbal probes the fuzzy boundary between anthropological practice—fieldwork—and the poetic imagination. What can poetry and the artist's gaze teach us about spirit possession? about religion? about social life? By posing these kinds of questions, Gibbal's latest work traces its descent not to the arid analyses of Anglo-American studies of possession, but to the innovative French school represented by Michel Leiris, André Schaeffner, Roger Bastide, and Gilbert Rouget. Like these scholars, Gibbal considered possession a kind of "pretheatre," to quote Schaeffner, which can best be observed and comprehended from an aesthetic vantage point. Such a vantage point frees possession studies from the narrow consideration of class-conscious "cults of affliction," in which the "afflicted" become the "afflictors" during possession ceremonies. This transformation, we are told by scholars such as I. M. Lewis, is a corrective mechanism for the social imbalances between the haves and have-nots of stratified societies. Studies like Gibbal's are much more philosophical in scope; they consider how spirit possession has helped to shape a group's historical, social and cultural consciousness—*their* aesthetic reaction to *their* ever-changing world.

In this context, then, *Genii of the River Niger* is Jean-Marie Gibbal's aesthetic reaction to the Malian aesthetic reaction to change in their own world. The framework of Gibbal's aesthetic reaction to the Ghimbala, the possession cult he learned about, is the aforementioned *carnet de route*. In the first chapter, Gibbal takes the reader to the special world of the Niger River between Mopti and Timbuktu, a world in which the great river cuts a tangled swath through the arid mesas and towering dunes of the Malian Sahel, a world whose dense deep green vegetation makes one forget the desiccated fields only a few meters beyond the shore. The motif of "the voyage" is felicitously maintained throughout the book. From Gibbal's poetic perspective, the reader sees and smells the inland delta of the Niger River. The reader feels lost in the vast expanse of Lake Debo. Gibbal's poetic sensitivities are transformed into many lyrical passages. But the book is much more than a lyrical volume of travel literature. Like Lévi-Strauss in his *Tristes Tropiques,* Gibbal uses the metaphor of the voyage to write about philosophical matters: history, ecology, poetry, fiction, the incomprehensibility of otherness, surrealism and the nature of ethnographic experience.

Gibbal's poetic sensitivities enhance rather than limit his ethnographic exposition. Although readers may be carried away by Gibbal's lyricism, which is well maintained in Beth Raps's fine translation, they are continuously brought back to the ethnographic subject of the book, the Ghimbala spirit possession rites that are performed in a polyethnic region of eastern Mali. This is parched, hungry land in which the majority population is Songhay, a people who also inhabit large tracts of western Niger. There are vast sociocultural differences between Malian and Nigerien Songhay, and these are evident in the substantial disparity between the Ghimbala of Mali and the Holey Hori, the possession rites of Songhay in Niger. The rites described by Gibbal have been much more profoundly influenced by Islam. Songhay in Mali were thoroughly subjugated in the early nineteenth century by the Muslim reformer, Sheikou Hamadou, who was a Fulan. For the Songhay in Niger, the subjects of my ethnographies, the impact of Islam is less significant. Given the polyethnic situatedness of the Ghimbala in contemporary Mali, *Genii of the River Niger* brings into sharp relief the multicultural construction of a religious phenomenon. The exposition of this intercultural interference also underscores the central importance of spirit possession—at least in Africa—as a mechanism of cultural resistance to pernicious outside influences as well as a stage of cultural creativity on which peoples articulate the struggle to maintain their cultural identity.

Genii of the River Niger is an eloquent testament to the considerable cultural resilience of the people of the Ghimbala region of eastern Mali. Born of many years of fieldwork, it is also a respectful portrait of these proud people. It is the kind of ethnography that more of us should aspire to write.

Paul Stoller

TRANSLATOR'S NOTE

Two of the most important words in this book gave me pause as I considered how to render them in English. They were *genie* and *culte,* extremely important words, as the reader will see, because of the book's subject.

What concerned me with *genie* was mainly which of the word's many different correct spellings to use. Each has its own special flavor and color. I opted for the simple anglicized *genie* in the singular, but its more Arabic plural, *genii,* in part simply because of the plural's synesthetic appeal, and in part because of the author's discussion of the word's permutations in spelling and meaning between Arabic and French in a note to the introductory section (note 10, to the section entitled "Preparations"). The reader should know that in French, the word "genie" also means "genius," and thus that the title could also be understood as "Geniuses of the River Niger." My sense of the author's admiration for the Ghimbala certainly does not preclude this interpretation.

Culte required a lot more inner questioning, as I am aware that in English it often has a pejorative, trivializing connotation—while we will refer to someone else's faith as a "cult," we seldom use the word about our own. In French, however, this is not the case. One commonly hears "*la culte catholique*" or "*la culte protestante.*" The word is not pejorative, and the author certainly does not employ it pejoratively. I chose to echo his respectful use of the word, so different from "faith," "spirituality," and "religion," each of which I considered. I further felt compelled to use "cult" because of a desire to reclaim what is its unique meaning among all other synonyms. "Cult" is related to the Latin word encompassing both *cultivation* and *worship.* The accuracy of this connection was too auspicious to lose. In addition, "cult" connotes a highly participatory religion, *home-grown* by its followers. This is a vital and particular aspect of the Ghimbala faith, in contrast to so many others.

GLOSSARY

Badji-foula	Priests' ritual cap (literally, "beer/wine hat"; figuratively, hat that brings an altered state upon one's head)
Batou	Cult ceremony
Béné	Lands above the floodwaters (literally, "sky" or "above," as contrasted with *ganda*, "below")
Bomboutou	Water drum used in ceremonies, consisting of calabashes floating within a larger vessel
Boubou	Long, flowing robe
Bourgou	Nutritious grass that grows in marshy shallows
Bundi	Black billy goat; Baana's preferred sacrificial animal
Canaris	Generic term for any fairly deep piece of pottery
Dina	Kingdom of God on earth, according to Islam
Dionieri	Sheep with three horns offered as a sacrifice
Djerkélé	Single-stringed harp
Djinarou	Term meaning "genie" used by gaw of Bambara origin
Djiné	Term meaning "genie"
Djiné don	Cult of possession among the Bambara of western Mali
Djini	Term meaning "genie"
Djiribéré	Genii's annual feast day
Fogno	Fine grain eaten on feast days and often offered to the genii
Ganda	The Niger, its branches, and the lands it floods (literally, "below")
Gangi	Term meaning "genie"
Gassou	Calabash used as an instrument in ceremonies
Gaw	Priest of the genii (literally, "genii-knower"; pronounced "gao")
Ghimbala	Simultaneously refers to the river-genii, the lands they inhabit, and the cult dedicated to them
Gourgoussou	Mound (literally, "empty hill")
Kaendi	Intermediate ritual in the cure of a possessed person

Kafir	Pagan
Kanji	Final ritual in the cure of a possessed person
Karakorey	Sheep with golden eyes offered as a sacrifice
Kobiri	White sheep with black eyes offered as a sacrifice
Koubour	Small, three-stringed guitar
Malé	The master (the priest)
Malé bania	The follower (literally, "the master's slave")
N'jarka	Single-stringed Songhay violin
Rimaïbe	Songhay descendants who have become Fula captives
Sessey	Cloth band decorated with a talisman and worn around a priest's forehead during ceremonies
Shaytan	Devil
Sohanci	Songhay magician-sorceror
Sombé	Ceremonial weapon held by gaw
Sorko	Songhay fisherperson
Taba yessi	Annual contribution made to a gaw by all followers he or she has healed
Turki	Loincloth made of two triangles and worn by possessed people during ceremonies
Wakando	Elongated, black pods; the genii's food
Wakorey	Descendants of the earliest Soninké inhabitants of the Niger's upper bend
Yaré	Ritual involving the giving of a gift to the genii by the family of a possessed person seeking a cure

Genii of the River Niger

Preparations

My first encounter with the Ghimbala, genii of the waters of the Niger's upper bend, dates to 1972. It was at Koulikoro, near Bamako, in Mali. In a trance, the dancers beat the air with arms outstretched, rising and falling over the land in their full robes like great white birds. The eerie charm of their nightly ceremonies entranced me. I found them again eight years later at Mopti, the eastern Mali metropolis, and it was at this time that I began to visit them frequently.[1] Their priest Bouba, who is now deceased, transmitted part of his knowledge to me and then advised me, if I wanted to know more, to go to the cult's birthplace: beyond Lake Débo, where the river's fan of fingers unfolds—where the genii of the waters reside. To do so, I had to make some serious preparations; this isolated world is not approached lightly.

Opening

My memories of this period are anchored with a few strong stitches—sutures, to be precise, for indeed my next trip began with surgery. The operation required was to open and strengthen a faulty abdominal wall that had for six years made each return to the Sahel increasingly tricky. At my own request, the surgery was done under local anesthetic; thus I largely remained conscious. When the analgesic effect of the drug began to fade, I started to feel the surgeon's final movements at my core as dull thumps, cords pulled taut inside me. The part of me still thinking found itself elsewhere. My situation and the pain almost imperceptible, distant, then rising above the numbness, engendered a parade of hallucinations culminating in the request I seem to recall making—a kind of divinatory self-sacrifice—that the surgeon consult my smoking entrails. This experience of dreaming while awake, of having a psychic double, proved to be an

---

1. See Jean-Marie Gibbal, *Tambours d'Eau (Journal d'Enquête sur un Culte de Possession au Mali Occidental)* (Le Sycomore, 1982), 22, and *Guérisseurs et Magiciens du Sahel* (A.-M. Métailé, 1984). The last section of this work (111–51) is a monograph on the Mopti Ghimbala.

excellent introduction to the world of magicians and seers I was soon to penetrate.

Readings

I occupied my convalescence by perusing works by the few authors who might have spoken of the Ghimbala. The travelers of the past—René Caillié, Heinrich Barth, Captain Hourst—traversed this region without knowing it, so intent were they on discovering the arch of the Niger, which lies far to the north before the place where it finally swoops down toward Timbuktu. Caillié barely mentions the Ghimbala as a land situated vaguely to the south of the city, which he describes as mythic and disappointing although it was the goal of his trip.[2]

Lieutenant Desplagne, in his turn-of-the-century journey between the edge of the Dogon plateau and the northern part of the inner delta, stayed long in the lands where I wanted to travel but does not mention water-genii worship. Nor does Dupuis-Yakouba, the erudite white priest who lived so long in Timbuktu: though he spoke fluent Songhay and reports the legend of the hunter-gaw, he seems unaware of the priests of the genii, who are also called *gaw*. In his retelling of the legend of Faran, mythic ancestor of the Sorko, the Songhay fisher-magicians according to Desplagne, there is likewise no mention of the Ghimbala genii.[3]

Finally, Hampaté Ba, in his enthralling *L'Empire Peul du Macina*, clearly details the limits of Fula expansion, which in the first half of the nineteenth century included most of Ghimbala. He also mentions the merciless struggle of Sheikou Hamadou, founder of the Fula state, against local paganism. Yet he does not mention the water-genii cult recurrent throughout the northeastern part of the new empire.

Thus I realized that the region bordered by Sebi, Niafunké to the north, and Ngouma-Corrienzé to the east—the heart of Ghimbala country, where I wanted to go—had seldom been visited, and that

2. Here is what René Caillié says in *Voyage à Tombouctou*, vol. 2 (François Maspero–La Découverte, 1982), 227: "In the southern part of Timbuktu, there is a land called 'Ginbala.' [*sic*] It extends deeply into the interior; its inhabitants are all Muslims, I am told. They seldom come to Timbuktu because the Touariks [*sic*] they fear are close by. They are very industrious, grow much millet and a little rice, are very hospitable toward strangers and have many herds of cattle, sheep and kids. They grow cotton, with which they make material to clothe themselves. They prefer to go to Jenné to trade, where they have nothing to fear."
3. The titles mentioned here can be found at the end of this volume in the bibliography of works on the Niger's upper bend and the Malian possession cults.

those who wrote about the region had not stayed long. As for the water-genii cult, they had written not a word.

Carried Off

Then there were the material preparations as such, which have a certain importance because of the means of transportation I had chosen. The Niger is the ancestral path into this region. In addition, my goal was to deepen my understanding of a cult whose most faithful servants live on the banks or in the immediate vicinity of the Niger, its distributaries, and the lakes fed by it. Thus I decided to travel in a medium-sized pirogue, which would be built in Mopti.[4]

So I needed to equip the craft-to-be with an outboard motor. I had made preliminary arrangements with a company representing the coveted make with offices on a wharf on the Seine at Boulogne, near Paris. That day the summer heavens wove bright spells into my dreams for calm and wide-open spaces far away on another river. When I returned less than two weeks before my departure to pick up the twenty-five-horsepower motor, June's entrancing light had given way to November's rains. The drops impregnated the air and made the banks of the gray-flowing Seine wet and heavy. I arranged the motor and its accessories with difficulty in the old car, whose seats I had to remove to slide in the cumbersome package. It still stuck out of the trunk's wide-open door as I drove along the highway ringing Paris—traffic nearly stopped by several accidents—to the Algerian-owned travel agency that would ensure my travel at the lowest cost. There, three clients lent a hand to two employees and disengaged my package, which in so many arms suddenly seemed quite light. Then I found myself alone to count the days and nights still separating me from over there.

Just Before

Having tended to the final formalities, run the last errands, and said good-bye to the last friends, I emerge into the period of awaiting departure. It generates a certain anxiety, because all action stops. In the past I have sometimes avoided it by spontaneously having a few obligations at the last minute. This time, the trip's uncertainties multiply my questions: Will the pirogue be ready? Will the river be navigable the whole length of the journey? Will the crew I expect to accompany me be ready?

Pursuing the Ghimbala to their birthplace will allow me to visit that

4. The one I ordered was eighteen meters long, capable of transporting three thousand kilos safely.

land of severe and imposing riverbanks again. I have a wondrous memory of my first incursion into the confines of the upper bend and the desert. Now I will have to live in a place I have only passed through in a dream—a vision of the absolute, born of a brief, tense trip, which led me to construct an ideal of beauty probably very different from the daily reality of the local people.

I can glimpse this reality quite well from my vantage point at the end of November 1984. It seems the region is threatened anew by famine. I am going to stay at length in a disaster area, amid people overwhelmed by poverty, to begin new research rather than slip back into the protective mold of acquired habit and established relationships in the kind of spots people return to over and over. The near future frightens me, yet it will also be a time when personal becoming is erased by the eternal present of long stays in Mali. I love and seek to melt into that eternal present through a certain concentration of being and the relative deprivation imposed by circumstance.

ONE FINDS ONESELF ON THE PATH ALREADY TRAVELED AND ONE FORESEES WHAT REMAINS TO BE DONE
Ibrahima's Pirogue

I found myself in Mopti at the beginning of December 1984 standing on the port's breakwater. In this spot a little over a year ago I had bargained for the construction of my craft with Ibrahima Djenepo, master pirogue-maker of the Bozo people and descendant of a family that has long devoted itself to this activity. I discovered with relief that the skiff's manufacture was almost complete.

So I rode around in one of the long, black pirogues, covered in part by an arched hood called a *hangar*. These craft are made using techniques that have hardly changed for a century and a half. The boards are still curved at the fire, and only recently have they been constructed with nails rather than assembled with ropes, as they were long ago when Caillié took pirogues from Jenné to Timbuktu. The spaces between the boards are caulked with old rags soaked in karite nut butter. Leaks are nonetheless inevitable, although they stop after several days afloat when the wood has swollen from permanent contact with the river. The crew spends a good deal of its time scooping out the water that slides to the rear between the flooring and the hull of the pirogue.

Ibrahima and his family had only to finish the painting on mine, decorate the poop and the prow with the traditional geometric polychrome motifs, and cover the arches of the central shelter with matting.[5] A few more days of work would be enough, giving me time to purchase the last provisions in town and assemble my crew. Its members were my Fula friend Almâmi from southeastern Ghimbala as assistant and interpreter; Alkaya, the Koroboro guide, born in Niafunké at the top of the bend, who knows the river's maze perfectly; and two young Bozo pirogue hands: Ali, Ibrahima Djenepo's nephew, to handle the cooking and his friend to serve as our engineer.[6] We can soon get under way.

Ghimbala

I left, then, with the aim of learning more about the cult of the genii of the river Niger, whose extremely dramatic and violent possessions had so impressed me in each past encounter.[7] From west to east in Mali, in the upper Sahel near the desert, cults have been created by the local peasantry in response to the growing hegemony of Islamic monotheism. I already knew the *djiné don,* a cult born of the ancient Soninké civilization.[8] I wanted to know, among other things, whether a connection existed between this group and the mysterious Ghimbala. At the same time, I knew I had to beware of feeling I had seen and heard it all before.

The term *Ghimbala* comprises three realities: natural, religious, and human. In the first, it refers to the northeastern part of the inner delta of the Niger, beyond Lake Débo. More precisely, it refers to the region between Issa Ber to the north—the river's main arm until it reaches Koriomé, Timbuktu's outer harbor—and Gourma to the south. This edge of the central Sudanese plateau is just a hair's breadth beyond a line running roughly from the Ngouma to the Sah regions on the Bara Issa, the arm of the Niger that flows to the heart of genii country.[9] Next, Ghimbala is the name of the genii of the waters,[10] who

5. The geometric motifs differ from one builder to another. Ibrahima's nephew, Ali, was the one who drew them on my pirogue.

6. For each journey, I call on the same collaborators except for the pirogue engineer of my first trip, who has returned to an old employer, a great marabout from the Mopti region.

7. See the Postscript for definitions of the terms *trance* and *possession.*

8. The djiné don (genii's dance) or Ji-dunu (water drums), are of the Malian west.

9. The country of the genii straddles the regions of Mopti and Timbuktu, that is, Mali's fifth and sixth administrative regions. The 1987 census lists 1,261,383 inhabitants for the former and just 453,032 for the latter.

Ghimbala is traditionally composed of the ten following subregions: Dirma (from Ambéri to Youvarou); Dongo (Sebi); Ndyodjiga (Sah); Korumbana (Corrienzé); Soungadio (Andiam, Singo); Soukaré (Koumaïra); Fitouga (Saraféré); the canton of Sariamou; Binga (Boyo); and finally Yaptodji, to the east at the edge of Gourma (the

people the lowlands and shallow inclines where the river fans into a multitude of arms, lakes, and pools and once covered the ground almost entirely during the flooding season.[11] Finally, the cult dedicated to these genii and its members are also called Ghimbala. In fact, the cult's roots stretch beyond the strict geographical boundaries of the region that witnessed its birth.

My approach to this multiple reality parallels the stages of a river journey. Thus I want much to evoke the physical rhythms of a trip that owed its unity to the Niger itself—the great artery of life that runs through Ghimbala country—before penetrating the river-genii's world.

Ngouma region). The right bank of the Niger in principle forms the northern border of Ghimbala, but certain informants add Farimaké, the region that extends north of the river and Lake Débo all the way to Léré, although it is not traditionally a part of genii country.

All these names are of Fula origin. A Fula griot reported the following tradition to me: There was a pond near Sah in Ndyodjiga named Ghimbala. The Fulas who occupied the approach to this place were Bari, and they married with the Sidibé of Kounari. The two clans called this alliance Ghimbala from the name of the pond.

10. I keep the term *genie* because it seems to me the best to refer to spirits of the places to which the people of the upper bend devote a cult. Followers call them *gangi* (in Songhay), or, yet again, *djiné, djini,* or *djinarou*. These latter names, derived from the Arabic, go back to the *djinn* of the Koran (see its sūrah entitled "Al-Djini," dedicated to them), to which the genii of the Ghimbala have been assimilated by Islamic propagandists. These people are willing to believe in the existence of the genii on the condition of a small slip in meaning that makes them negative creatures, in any case inferior to the Divine—whence, in the upper bend, the use of the word *diable* [devil] to identify them in French. But in the beliefs and practices of the cult faithful, the genii retain the natural ambiguity of pagan divinities and are as capable of protective, reparative, and even creative actions as of aggressive acts.

In addition, the word *genie* introduces the idea of a person's double, whom the entity thus designated besieges. And this is indeed in question in many cults throughout the world in which the possessed, in ritual trances, incarnate certain characteristics of the genii astride them within the configuration of their own psyches.

11. There is a variation in level of only about thirty meters over more than five hundred kilometers of the Niger's course according to Jean Gallais, *Hommes du Sahel* (Flammarion, 1984), 8.

1 / On the River Niger

The river Niger and its multiple arms constitute the natural means of access to the countries of the upper bend, which they irrigate as they drive northward into the sands.

Once our material and provisions are loaded, the pirogue comes away from the breakwater at the port of Mopti. We weave our way between the sandy banks of the Bani and the dense traffic of small craft, quickly reaching the place beyond the governor's seat where the Niger meets its tributary and takes the muddy waters into its own blue-green torrent under the brilliant Sahel sky. We enter this world of the river and melt into its crowds. We become part of the group of long, narrow, punted pirogues whose conductors transport passengers short distances from one village to another on market days, squeezed together like rows of onions; of heavy transport pinnaces used for long trips, packed almost higher than the waterline; and of frail fishers' skiffs shaken by our own wake.

On this as on all my departures, I feel exaltation at entering a peaceful kind of time, smooth after all the trouble and delays of preparation: rainy Europe, where I assembled the many accessories impossible to find here, without which this trip would become impossible; time in Bamako, brief but necessary for the required formalities and a few new purchases; sending baggage over seven hundred kilometers on a borrowed vehicle, hypothetical each time; and, finally, Mopti. There, the busy days in this swarming metropolis of the upper bend where all the peoples of the region rub shoulders, where northern refugees collapse in successive waves, fleeing the famine of recent years. From morning to evening, the crowded city pours into its streets a continuous wave of people, making their difficult way amid the intense traffic of taxis, carts, and two-wheeled vehicles, first from the residential sectors toward the port and business district, and then, at twilight, in reverse toward the same places left at dawn, where rest is found at last. Final errands, checking the material, pulling the crew together again.

After several days spent either in the dusty streets or the confinement of the concessionaires' cubical, tiered houses—wrapped around courtyards that shelter their closed, silent life in contrast to the activity outside—space is simplified, the river's horizon spare, air suddenly purified, and one knows one has escaped. Life lightens, emptiness settles in, there is nothing to do but let oneself glide along, and for an instant everything seems easier. In the passage from closed to open on the banks, the Macina—Fula country—is cleansed by the sun. Already the first flights of water birds mark the journey's rhythm with their movements like writing on the sky.

The journey is a slow climb upward to the area to be studied, where we will arrive—if all goes well—two or three days after we get to Lake Débo. It is nothing like the violent jolts of automobile trips on ruined roads that leave one panting at each stop, covered in dust from head to toe, thirsty, and exhausted. The long, black pirogue slides quietly, sometimes straight, sometimes tacking to avoid the shallows and the blustery northeast wind, which rages and shunts strong waves ahead of it. At those times we scrape the protected bank to keep from taking on a cargo of spray.

On a pallet of vegetal cushioning, shielded from the sun by the arched arbor at the center of the craft, I settle into the hours' rich monotony, barely interrupted by minute events foreseen or unforeseen along the way. Purchases of fish involve a floating bargaining from pirogue to pirogue, though sometimes we pull up alongside one to choose from the pots of live prey. Sometimes beautiful Fula women approach, who with age begin to look like old Pueblo women under their hair, braided every which way. They offer us fresh or curdled milk, depending on what time of day it is. A sudden stop when one or the other of us absolutely has to "go into the bush," to use the time-honored expression. Mint tea in the afternoon, while we are gliding over water after our lunch break. Meeting a pirogue crewed by friends our young hands hail joyously.

On the Niger, the same situations recur in no particular order but always similarly, an expression of the laws and dangers that rule navigation of the river: The cast net we are alerted to by the cries of the fisherpeople; to avoid destroying it, our engineer must cut the motor and make it pivot sharply upward on its axis. Herds swimming across the river, driven by their Fula herders—a veritable flotilla at water level of lowing heads—forcing us to slow down. In earlier times, these animals risked attack by caimans, which have now almost completely disappeared from the upper bend.

Gusts of wind cause the enormous, overloaded pinnaces either to capsize or to run aground on the sandy banks, providing the same display of shipwrecks they did many years ago when Caillié went to Timbuktu along the same path. An accident unleashes intense activity on board the shipwrecked craft, whose perishables must be salvaged from the cargo with great haste. The trip will resume after hours, if not days, of immobility—but here, time is not money. In many ways, the material lives of these peoples have not changed, and along the river one finds in daily use the same objects described in earlier travel narratives: trifooted earthen ovens; small, neolithic grain mills, used by generations of housewives; bread-ovens for baking delicious *ta-koula,* unleavened durum-wheat wafers.

At the beginning of the trip, the river makes its path between banks of dried mud; the large Fula or Marka villages gather closely around their mosques of rammed earth, finding refuge from floods on the rare hills that break the landscape's uniformity. A few large trees shelter the approach to each of the villages, their bright green attenuating the austere geometry of the houses' ochers and grays, their rounded, earthen angles. The villages are restful to the gaze: Bargodaya, Nan-taga, Kami, Madina, Saya, Komio, Batamani—often an evening's stopping place.

A few small islands arise in the waters, covered with young grasses or full of big stones on which loons and cormorants meet, with the hieratic silhouette of a tall, blue-grey heron like an epigraph. An eagle skims, then turns sharply in the wind. The pirogue goes around a rocky bank just before the village of Bouna, the last permanent town before Lake Débo and the rival of the Marka village of Diantaka up-stream on the other side for control of this part of the Niger. Beyond this point, there is nothing along the river except the temporary en-campments of the Bozo fisherpeople, which appear larger and larger as one journeys up the bend. Behind the bank lies the desolate expanse of the Sahel, its lunar landscape extending as far as the eye can see, enlivened slightly by a few bushes at the water's edge. Then the main pathway of the water begins to snake between deeply embanked tribu-taries after sending out several unnavigable branches that go nowhere. As we near Lake Débo, the Niger narrows in a deeper riverbed, while herds come larger and bird flights more numerous, different species of ducks and snipes predominating.

After one last bend, the bank drops and we emerge into the vastness of the lake, always a moving experience. Several hills stud the path from west to east along the southernmost bank, the nearest one easily climbed. Tondi Kaïna is a tiny mountain of ferruginous rock, from whose tip the climber embraces the entire horizon. In the foreground, the lake stretches languidly into multiple bays, which are the first to go dry, and then extends into infinity to the north and west. The melancholy, tuneful cries of the water birds, seagulls among them, heighten the seaside feeling one gets in this place, while clusters of waders skip along the gravel at the water's edge as if at low tide. Herds of humped oxen stand, still and gleaming, clearly visible against the short, tender grasses left by the shrinking river. Above, brown and white fishing hawks skate through the air on unknown missions. The sandy banks form islands and then isthmuses as the waters retreat during the great but temporary fishing period that they host.

Only the branch of the river that we have taken remains navigable to the larger pirogues; the smaller ones—thin, black lines on a net of water—thread their way into the lake using branches that have become mere visible fords. *Bourgou* fields yellow in the sun and the wind blows over Tondi Kaïna, which Caillié baptized "Marie-Thérèse" as he passed by. He had dreamed of erecting a small fortress there to patrol entry of Lake Débo.[1] Toward the east, the red hill of Goura, striped with black at its foot by the receding waters, closes the horizon, answering Soroba Hill to the southwest.

In the middle of this broad, calm place, where water finally balances the teamed force of arid earth and sun, I imagine that the ancient sages came to meditate in solitude on these three peaks. If this was ever the case, no buildings remain to attest to it in the surrounding areas. The people here today have modestly accepted the precariousness of their stay: a few small Fula encampments; some Bozo straw huts at the foot of Tondi Kaïna; two hamlets on Goura's sides, with a frail mosque set into the rock amid three tufts of green, protected from the floodwaters. Bulls converse in bellows from one herd to another, a cock sings, a few goats climb the slant of a hill. And the sun, slightly veiled today, envelops this peaceable present in a mist of heat.

Lake Débo is always considered heavy with legend and thick with dangerous surprises for river travelers in overloaded, poorly maintained boats. Thus, despite the well-kept state of our own pirogue, the crossing creates a moment of tension for the crew. Each member speaks of the dangers of getting lost at night after leaving the channel inattentively—the brutal tempests in which wind and waves catch crosswise at boats, push them off track, and thrust them down toward the sludgy shallows or, worse, toward the traitorous sand banks, which rip brutally into floorboards and pull apart poorly assembled hulls.

Despite these fears, it is at this hour, when the sun is about to begin its descent, that I love to be in midlake. The declining star turns the water's surface to copper, blurs the banks to a nearly invisible line, and

---

1. In Caillié's time—although his trip was not made until April, when the river is now no longer navigable—Tondi Kaïna hill was surrounded by water. Thus he considered it an island: "I named it 'Marie-Thérèse' in honor of H.R.H. Madame la Dauphine" (Caillié, *Voyage,* 182).

hangs us between sky and water in a purifying golden light that turns the occasional pirogue trembling far off into a surreal apparition. Gulls catch our wake in their nostalgia for the ocean, skewing our perception of the world a little more by their squalling flight. Then the lake shrinks, the banks draw closer, and other birds reappear as colors and form begin to turn to shadow. At this hour, one can sometimes distinguish a compact bank of pelicans in the distance, a living relief of feathers, feet, and beaks.

Always on these journeys, and usually at nightfall, we arrive at the Diou-Diou encampment, a little way from Youvarou, a little downstream of Akka on the other bank. Before the last drought cycle, this was a prosperous stopping place. Since then, such exchanges have slowed, fish and travelers are rare, and numerous houses are in ruins. Only a handful of fisherpeople remain in this place, related to and dependent on Diou-Diou, a tall, handsome old man who fulfills his role of patriarch among them with dignity in memory of his past splendor.

As it leaves the lake, the Niger splits into three branches: the Bara Issa to the southeast; the Issa Ber to the northeast, the widest and for the past several years the only branch that remains navigable all year long; and between these two, the Ambéri. A little interior sea, and a great reservoir of genii, Lake Débo marks the border between Fula and Songhay country along the river's course. At this point, Songhay becomes the dominant language, though groups of all the peoples of the upper bend continue to live together beyond this point.

Here we enter the sandy lands. The desert descends with the river, and we go toward it along banks on which villages are scattered, houses bedecked with the lacy earthenwork that lightens their heavy, massive architecture. They are often supported against great mounds, the *gourgoussou* (empty hills), which bear witness to towns extinct, enshrined in the dunes, the only landscape relief before Goundam. Heirs to the population waves that have washed over this land through the centuries, today's peoples live here as conquerors and conquered together, almost without memory of those long-ago times— as do most of the peoples of the planet, with few exceptions.

And the present is sufficiently difficult to engage their entire attention. The presence of water softens the Sahel landscape and can give a false impression of ease to the newcomer. In fact, the Niger here drives into a land where, since the 1970s, people have endured increasing poverty following the draining of the hydrographic system and accompanying desertification.

Seen from a distance, these sites that so beautifully marry the diverse elements—pure background lines, villages with their lovely architecture—inspire calm and peace. The simple act of mooring changes this vision terribly. Beyond the few sparse gardens that sometimes ring the villages, one enters extreme poverty. There is no trash on the ground that cannot be used—quite a difference from the wealth of garbage discharged by our Western societies. The imposing earthen houses offer up a view of interiors emptied of all everyday objects save a few large beds on sculpted daises, vestiges of earlier grandeur. Their heavy hangings, the rugs in shimmering colors, and the elaborately worked vessels of old have disappeared. This inescapable material destitution is often accompanied by a physical poverty that strikes young children and old people in particular.

In 1984–85, the situation was at its worst: the Niger was emptied of fish; livestock, for which there was no pasture, starved to death; farmers had been deprived of harvests for several years. In 1986, the situation is less desperate after a more abundant rainy season and a somewhat more normal flood season, which allowed the river to overflow its bed, feeding some of the ponds and flowing into swamps, bourgou fields, and rice-growing areas. Starvation and its accompanying parade of epidemics receded. Fish reappeared, herds grew again, and farmers harvested rice, especially in the Koriomé plain near Timbuktu. On the other hand, in contrast to the situation in the rest of Mali, the millet harvest was almost nil, thwarted by still-too-irregular rainfall and negated in areas such as Niafunké by flights of migrating crickets. Even in the best of cases, it will take a long time to erase the effects of the last drought. The upper bend of the Niger has become one of the poorest regions on the planet.

But we float painlessly on the peaceful, easy waters of Issa Ber beyond Lake Débo, safe in our travelers' bubble. Some African dogfish with silver, tapering flanks and red side fins leap from the surface to land in the pirogue, their menacing faces thrust forward armed with fangs. Attara, Bia, Sebi, Dabi, Gombo, Sibo, and Waki—the old men of every village crouch in small groups, first under the trees and then right on the beach as the day advances into evening. They keep their gaze turned toward the river, from which they await any event that might come to break the implacable cycle of their lives.

The Niger enlarges a little in the reach of Niafunké, where we again cross hippopotamuses, the last of the fabulous beasts that people the river since the disappearance of caimans and manatee. Once we pass Niafunké, a small island of pale greenery against the charred plain and the first of three towns along the rise of the bend to Timbuktu, the river becomes thin again between the black rocks of Tondi Farma, cutting with sudden hardness into the softness of the sandy slopes.

Then, toward Tonka and Diré, the two other townships, the low banks give way to steep sandbars blocking the northern horizon.

In these places where the river and the desert meet, the crest of Balla Mahoudé is one of the most bitter and grandiose to be seen. Toward the northeast, studded with spiny plants, the sandy plain extends to the mountain of Goundam. On the opposite side, the wide meanderings of the long, sinuous, liquid path gleam, backlit by the full afternoon brightness, only to disappear in a haze of heat at the horizon. In the foreground, a little Songhay village is nestled at the bottom of the slope against a sharply turning branch of the Niger. A herd of fawn-colored goats descends the light dune to the water. The goatherd comes to crouch some distance away from the lone white man the better to observe him, all the while humming a song in which the name of this place recurs over and over. Then I head back down toward the pleasure of a restorative bath in the river—very deep at this point—after the furnace of the upper dune. To get there, I cross a beach littered with pottery debris come from a nearby necropolis. The river and everywhere, silence; wind and sand.

The Niger widens, narrows, strikes a difficult course across the Sahel's aridity, the earth increasingly denuded. The plain crouches under a sky veiled at times by light cirrus clouds like giant ripped sheets, whose filter turns the river's waters green. The walls at Danga, right on the river between Diré and Timbuktu, are painted with the hot colors of the setting sun. This evening we stop at the edge of a damp shallow that is vibrant with insects. Offshore, a band of hippotamuses hold an all-night jubilee—complete with trumpeting, groans, and enormous smacks of sound—to the great displeasure of the local fisherpeople, who fear for their nets.

After this stage, the river swings slowly to the east. The fisherpeople in their great white turbans look like the desert peoples who made the river's claw into the exhausted earth even heavier. Here and there, the occasional grove decorates the top of a furrowed mound and blends into the phantom trees and puddles rising up from the mirages produced by the air as it vibrates under the sun's apogee. We pass Toya, famous for the defeat of the Fulas of Macina at the hands of the coalition of Tuaregs and Arma in the first half of the nineteenth century. Then come the pirogue moors at Koriomé, the outer harbor of Timbuktu, whose access is by road. We must go there to have our papers examined and to replenish our fuel supply.

Timbuktu. Despite the kindness of its excellent governor and the director of the Amed Baba Center, the "mysterious city" (to use the phrase of the signboard on the road to the airport) no longer weaves the magic it did twenty years ago, when I discovered it at the same time I discovered Mali.[2] Then, lightweight pirogues came up the river from Kabara to the foot of the hotel encampment by a narrow canal, which has since become covered with sand and transformed into the periphery of a market garden. The backcountry had not yet been ravaged by drought, and life was good in the depths of the shadowy courtyards and on the high earthen terraces in the neighborhoods of Saré Kaïna, Sankoré, and Sidi Yaya.

Nonetheless, in the evening the mosque of Jinghereber—the oldest one in the city, built by Emperor Kankan Moussa on his return from Mecca—still gleams a little with light in jewel tones of ocher and rose. The place embodies the tired calm of a town grown sleepy from too much history, while the setting sun flares in promise of better days. It's the end of the harmattan and the cold season; the sky will be purified for several weeks. For an instant at this hour when the world trembles, the past comes to the surface of walls covered in fine cracks. What of the state of things, the present situation. Timbuktu has known far worse! Then the tremor stops with the onset of night, the place falls back into its lethargy, and a choked life drags through its streets of sand.

The town right now is dusty and a little rotted by tourism that lately, because of the difficulties of transportation, comes only in dribbles, or rather in abrupt cargo loads of foreigners dressed like explorers in a musical comedy. They visit this site as quickly as possible, since walking is made difficult by the sandy soil. A tightly gathered group makes its way through the city, the tourist hunters go crazy, and then the manna disappears and the level of street animation returns to the daily vehicular dance. Leading it are cars belonging to experts and to the members of international humanitarian organizations, some of whom take themselves for new crusaders from the West, invested with the mission of redressing wrongs, or for good Samaritans, disdaining to know the long and difficult history of this country and the bitter fruits it has produced, which must be tasted before forming an opinion about it. The others, happily in the majority, are content to go about their work conscientiously and with no grand, useless theories. In any case, let us quickly regain the good Niger to return to its great spaces and our river wanderings.

The trip continues. As we advance, it becomes impossible to tell if we are gliding along water or time. Minutes and hours are layered,

---

2. One must be the guest of a Timbuktu family to measure the subtle local art of living, which unfolds as unfailing hospitality. This was the case in 1971, as I reported in *Tambours d'Eau,* xx. In February 1988, I carried on this tradition thanks to my friend Saleck, and once again my point of view changed.

erasing any memory of differences in the continuous band of the river. Void is added to void; we only pass, incapable of retaining anything of our passing. These moments of abandon—are they not the finest? And then to let oneself be overtaken, drunk with useless movement.

UNMOVING BANKS / THE PIROGUE GLIDES / MOVING VOID

Only our stops manage to stem the flow of this loss of perception. When they occur, perspective inverts from the bank to the river, almost unmoving. Each strip of land becomes a stage on which daily rituals are played out in slow rhythm, bringing the people face to face with earth, sky, and Niger.

Strip 1

I am leaning against a mound, my back to the river, facing the setting sun at Dondoro, an encampment of fisherpeople on the northern bank of the Niger between Sebi and Dabi, near Niafunké. I watch a young teacher, who has brought us two bags of fresh vegetables in exchange for some seed packets I gave him, return to the neighboring village. He's no longer riding a moped as he was yesterday. He must have run out of gas and thus came on foot, walking several kilometers with his heavy load in order to keep our meeting.

The sun disappears, a formation of ducks makes an imprecise gash across the sky, shapes begin to darken. A pirogue with a big, square sail glides silently down the river on the other side, pushed along by the evening wind.

Strip 2

On our return from Diré we stop at the beach of the village of Alvalidji, which slumbers at the foot of a gourgoussou that looks like a gigantic spoil heap, one of the most remarkable sites in the region. Something is almost always happening on this vast arena of fine sand that borders the Niger. Toward noon the Gaïrama peasants come together to wash after a hard morning of redigging the canal, which will allow the floodwaters to rise to the level of their village pond several kilometers away.

Two Tuaregs in turbans with their long, supple walk—one all in white, the other in long, flowing, emerald veils and a sword at his side—head toward the furnace where Ali is preparing our meal ration and, without permission, take a bit of ash to mix with the tobacco they chew to soften its bitterness. Mocking my discomfort, they tell me to try some, then walk off at a rapid pace singing, arms around each other's shoulders.

Small shepherds and their animals replace these two. Goats and sheep stand in two separate groups while their masters kneel on the sand in prayer. With a spare gesture from one, the herd moves off again. Heavy pinnaces pass along the river, filled to their brims, roofs garlanded with human beings. A cameleer perched high up on his camel crosses the strip and stops at the river's edge before a group of laundresses. His feet never touching the ground, he asks them for a little water. A young woman stretches a tiny calabash up to him. He empties it in a single movement, returns it, and trots off nonchalantly on his camel. Already the sun has turned, colors deepen, the afternoon proceeds toward its end.

Strip 3

The oblique light of evening expands and transfigures the low bank, where one can make out the wretched shanties of the encampment at Gombo; it hangs on the smallest outcropping and turns it immense. Last year, at this stopping place, the harmattan blew onto this desolate place a haze of sand that infiltrated everything. At a certain point, the other bank of the river disappeared, and I felt I had taken shelter at the edge of a gray northern sea.

Today the rays of the setting sun cast a halo of glory around the poor fisherpeople of the encampment, sitting squarely in their old, patched pirogues. Behind them lies the village of Dabi between dunes of red and beige.

Strip 4

Near Tonka a brief procession of dunes creates a rampart between the backcountry and the strand and then becomes a soft beach, where we are drawn up. I stay on the pirogue for an entire day, absorbed in checking my information with the great genii-griot Mahaman Tindirma, who has accompanied us up to this point; transcribing the tapes recorded last week; or just dreaming, turning first toward the dunes, then toward the river, trying to protect myself from the sun that tramples the shadows under the pirogue's covered arch as it descends.

The Niger has goosebumps under the wind's caresses; laughing and singing, the graceful laundresses with their bare breasts take advantage of their labors to go swimming. Why, all over the world, do laundresses laugh and sing while they beat their laundry? Sky and sand fade under the light; the rare trees in this place crouch over their shadows; the air is burning hot, even under the matting stretched over the pirogue's arch. The hours flow by, sequences follow sequences: tea, the quiet of our afternoon break, a poem read aloud.

Toward evening, a pirogue heads slowly toward the other bank, carrying its cargo of beasts and humans pressed tightly against each other. This is the only one today to cross the river. Yesterday, on market day at Tonka, a great many pirogues even more heavily charged went over at sunset toward the neighboring villages in a swarm of color, murmurs, and cries. When the crafts reached the middle of the river, fear of tipping over imposed silence, broken far off on the other bank by the hoarse, muted calls of kneeling camels awaiting their masters' return.

I return from my absence renewed and fresh. The full moon is already high in the sky, and I decide to climb the sharp edge of the dune, from whose peak I can see the river like a mirror under the light of a world midway between day and darkness. At this height, the strip comes into relief, and I can distinguish the shapes as well as the colors of the objects filling it, projecting their pale shadows onto sand bleached by the lunar light. Travelers from two fat craft moored near the beach have chosen this site to spend the night and dispersed into several groups. Some are certainly well-to-do, judging from the quality of the rugs they have settled on, the richness of their clothing, and the power of their radio-cassette machines sending *koubour* and *n'jarka* music—probably recorded within the region—into the air. They gaily pass glasses of tea during their animated conversation. Other sailors on the long haul, those who make the Mopti–Koriomé run, prefer to use this night-without-night to continue their travels, and their pinnaces cruise offshore at low speeds, shadowing the Niger for the space of a moment with their long, black mass.

I straddle the sandy crest for a long time and then let myself slide down to the gravel, where perspective again flattens out into the blue tent of the liquid world beyond dreams.

♣

This crossing and these stopovers in Ghimbala country should give a sense of the milieu in which genii-worship has bloomed: the enormous area of flooding lowlands, shot through by the Niger and its multiple arms, riddled with ponds and lakes fed by the floods they then hold in reserve; great, flat expanses that barely break up the bars of dunes descending from the threatening desert or from mounds planted with trees set there by nature or by ancient inhabitants (one can never tell which at a distance); nests of green, an oasis of sleepy towns on the fawn-colored sands. And all the while, making its way through an impalpable maze of air, wind, sun, and night, the emaciated Niger River regenerates this old country less than before, when for more than a thousand years earthen cities were born of the soil, took their walls from it, grew across its surface, and returned to it.

The old travel histories and more recent accounts from the first half of the twentieth century testify to the inexorable draining of the river system. Caillié's huge craft navigated the Bara Issa in April without encumbrance between Guidio Saré on Lake Débo and Issa Faye near Diré. In early February 1985, taking the same path in the opposite direction, we came up the arm with difficulty and ran aground several times. Entering Lake Débo, the Bara Issa was but a thin, muddy rivulet; it took almost two hours of effort by about twenty villagers from Guidio Saré to portage our boat over sand and silt to the ready waters of the lake. During the colonial 1930s, that lake was still traveled by great ships and barges at the height of the hot season in late March and early April. At the end of January 1986, despite satisfactory flooding compared to earlier years, a boat ran aground in the middle of the lake and had to wait for the next high water to get free.

Even in its shrunken state, the Niger is no less the axis of life in this region to which it gives meaning, history, name. The peoples of the upper bend live by the rhythm of the floods and falls of the river and despair, emigrate, or hang on to their dunes when flooding is not sufficient. This is the crucible of their common history, for they have been subject to close or distant domination by one great empire after the other in this part of Sahelian Africa. First, the region found itself on the periphery of the two early empires that controlled it at their apogees: the empire of Ghana in the ninth and tenth centuries, whose capital, Koumbi Saleh, was to the northeast in Mauritania; and the empire of Mali in the fourteenth century, whose even more distant center was in the Mandingo mountains to the west of the present nation of Mali. This region was also an integral part of the Songhay Empire, which lasted from the end of the fourteenth century to the final decade of the sixteenth under the Sonni, and then of the Askia dynasties. The capital then was Gao. The upper bend became the central section of this immense nation, which at its height extended from the kingdom of Tekrour on the Atlantic coast to Hausaland in the east.

The Gao empire was invaded and destroyed in 1591 by the troops of the sultan of Marrakesh. On its remains grew a vassal state of the invader pashalik of Timbuktu, whose zone of influence included Ghimbala. The Arma of Timbuktu, descendants of these Moroccan conquerors, were then themselves severely beaten and subdued in 1833 by the troops of Sheikou Hamadou, founder of the Fula empire of Macina fifteen years earlier. This Fula state controlled the whole upper bend of the Niger until it was in its turn destroyed after 1860 by El Hadj Omar, the Toucouleur conqueror from Fouta Toro. The advent of the Dina, the Fula theocratic empire, constitutes one of the key events in the development of worship of the Ghimbala, as we will see farther on.

The present-day peoples of this region are products of the mix brought about by this tormented history: Songhay peasant communities descended from subjects of the Gao empire; Bambara people from the chieftaincies of Sah, Saraféré, and Nbétou who have taken refuge here since the seventeenth century; Fula herders who have become sedentary in part since the Dina; Bozo fishers and ferrypeople; Somono and Sorko peoples; and finally Moorish and Tuareg nomads. The ethnic points of reference translate partly into demographic and cultural realities. Thus can one say that there is a majority presence of Fulas, Markas, and Bambaras to the west and south and of Songhay and Tuaregs to the north and east; however, social divisions remain more pertinent.

Local society is strongly hierarchical and marked by a recent feudal past perpetuated in the daily reality of the peoples of the upper bend. Power is in the hands of heterogeneous ruling groups: descendants of nobles and princes of long ago; Muslim religious authorities and great merchants, often confused by outsiders; and finally representatives of the Malian state. The base of the hierarchy is made up of a peasantry highly dependent on these different powers and of the masses in the cities and towns. The representatives of this numeric majority are often of servile or low-caste origin, as the populations of ancient empires included a number of slaves and low-caste people who performed agricultural, domestic, and craft tasks.

In contrast, representatives of the different powers live in the larger towns and small cities of the region, ensuring domination by these centers over the neighboring countryside within this predominantly rural society. Farmers, herders, and fisherpeople do not, however, make up a single, undifferentiated mass but rather live in individual village communities. These villages maintain a certain cohesion despite human, economic, and cultural impoverishment following the drought of the last fifteen years and the resulting social crisis and emigration.

In these population centers, neighborhoods correspond to economic specializations that follow ethnic lines: the Fula herders' neighborhood; the Marka, Songhay, or Bambara farmers' neighborhood; the river-peoples neighborhood. Each of these groups is included in the council of notables that brings together representatives of the powerful families in the area with the village chief, who is descended from ancient power-holders, unless he is the *chargé d'affaires* appointed by the lords of the nearby town.

While the members of the ruling groups officially profess their attachment to orthodox Islam, priests and clients of Ghimbala worship are recruited from the ranks of rural communities and the city masses. Being a perfect Muslim and believing simultaneously and openly in the Ghimbala reflects and reinforces the existing social divisions. From this perspective, Ghimbala-worship looks like a true popular religion, bringing together clients, practitioners, and sympathizers of the same social condition from all the region's peoples.

Among them, the Marka, distant descendants of the Soninké of Ghana and probably the first inhabitants here, maintain their identity within the multiethnic villages and sometimes have their own neighborhoods. They refer to themselves as "Wakorey" in the Songhay language, although they have not spoken Soninké for a long time.

The Marka are traditionally perceived as propagandists for Islam and as businesspeople who prefer to live in towns and small cities. The fact that the Wakorey groups frequent the Ghimbala suggests a subtle change in their image, because among them one meets many farming families. In addition, as the oldest inhabitants of the place, the Wakorey are often given the role of interceding with the genii. Thus they are frequently found in the role of master of the waters, which they share with the Sorko and the Koronghoy. We will soon see that the tales of the mythic and historic origins of the Ghimbala make reference to them.

The product of a diverse history and a specific natural environment, the water-genii cult is deeply rooted in the traditions of societies that arose one after the other in the Ghimbala basin. The bells and chains used today by the *gaw*, the Ghimbala priests, faithfully reproduce the ones exhumed from the tombs of long-ago magicians and healers and help us to imagine much of this past. The cult of today expresses the region's unity and continuity by connecting the amalgamation of peoples that live in the region. Beliefs surrounding the Ghimbala mark their daily and seasonal activities, organize their perception of the universe, and offer explanations of certain misfortunes that strike them.

2 / The Emperor and the Magician

WAADA SAMBA'S EXPLOIT

On the advice of the marabouts and ulemas of his council, Sheikou Hamadou, founder of the theocratic Fula empire of Macina, decided to eradicate the remaining traces of paganism that incessantly resurfaced in the populations he had conquered and to establish at last the kingdom of God on earth. All the gaw, the priests who claimed they were of the local genii, were to have their throats slit if they did not renounce their beliefs. But as Sheikou Hamadou was a just man, he wanted first to determine "whether the gaw were lying," as his counselors suggested to him, or "if they told the truth."

The most famous among the gaw was named Waada Samba. He lived on an island in the great pool of Awgoundou near Ngouma, three hundred kilometers to the northeast of Hambdalaye, Sheikou Hamadou's capital. The tale of the feats this gaw had performed reached the emperor's ears, and he begged Waada Samba to come to him immediately so he could know more. Waada Samba was already a very old man. He had heard the rumors that were traversing the country, so he was rather circumspect and waited to be solicited. When Sheikou Hamadou sent along a gleaming cavalry to serve as his escort, the gaw finally allowed himself to be led to Hambdalaye.

On his arrival, the emperor invented this trial to test him. He had his personal advisers capture a guinea fowl with great secrecy and enclose it in a *canaris*. Then he called everyone together to see which of the groups—the marabouts and ulemas or Waada Samba and his followers—could divine the truth. He warned the onlookers solemnly, "He who lies will have his throat cut." The marabouts spoke first. They consulted among themselves and made their own divination. One of them said, "The animal enclosed here has four paws." Another added, "It has large ears." A third concluded, "It's a hare." Then it was Waada Samba's turn. He began to dance, surrounded by the gaw who had accompanied him up to this point; entered into a trance; and, inspired by his genie, declared, "What is in this canaris has two feet, wings, and black and white spots all over—it's a guinea fowl!"

Sheikou Hamadou knew the gaw was right, but if he allowed

Waada to triumph, the conquered peoples would revolt and the Dina's power would be finished. He quickly made this prayer to God: "If the gaw has told the truth, men will turn from Thou to follow him in his beliefs. Do something to make him have lied, so that White triumph over Black." Then Sheikou raised the lid of the canaris and a hare leapt away. The gaw cried out, "Waada Samba told the truth, but God is always right!" and after getting about ten meters, the hare again became a guinea fowl, which it had been in the first place, and flew away.

Waada Samba performed other feats at Hambdalaye. Sheikou Hamadou had an only daughter, Balkissa Sheikou.[1] She had been attacked by genii, who had driven her mad, and all the marabouts and the pagan healers nearby had tried in vain to free her. Sheikou asked Waada Samba, "If it is true that you are allied with the genii who have driven my daughter mad, can you heal her?"

Waada Samba answered him, "Of course! I have only to organize a *batou* in the city." But the marabouts became indignant: "What? You will again allow this pagan to dance in the holy city of Hambdalaye and make all his devils descend?" They wanted Waada Samba and his followers to go far into the bush to have their ceremony, the batou. The gaw refused. Finally, a compromise was found: the batou would take place outside, but very near, the city.

On that evening, Waada Samba's people began to sing and dance before the house in which Balkissa was held. When she heard the music and chanting, she broke through the door of the room in which she was sequestered. Screaming, she threw herself into the middle of the ceremony and dragged herself up to the feet of the gaw. Then she was possessed by her genie and entered a trance. Waada Samba healed her in one night. As the daughter of a pious Muslim, she could no longer dance with the Ghimbala. That is why the gaw chased her genie away for good by having Balkissa undergo the *kanji*.

Sheikou Hamadou recognized the good results of the gaws' activities and decided to stop persecuting them. He became a great friend to Waada Samba. He gave the magician many blessings and entrusted to him his own genie, Ali Soutouraré, who always accompanied him into battle and ensured his victory. From that day on, Ali Soutouraré split his time between Doundé, Waada's village, and Hambdalaye. Sheikou also asked the gaw to bring all the other genii of the Hambdalaye region with him. The gaw returned to his village loaded down

1. I have chosen one of the names given to the emperor's daughter, but this name can vary from one tale to another.

with gifts and honors. Sheikou Hamadou's blessings on Waada Samba are passed on to all gaw to this day.

Therapeutic Vocation and Religious Dependence

For all tellers, this more or less legendary meeting of the emperor and the magician constitutes the beginning of the Ghimbala cult of worship in its present form. Without exception, and despite the multiple variations of their tales, they all mention the delicate relations of the first known gaw to the Islamic authorities of the period, as well as his successful cure of the emperor's daughter. Thus in this founding story are forcefully affirmed the two dominant traits of the Ghimbala cult: its therapeutic vocation and its dependence on Islam.[2] The Ghimbala cult is tolerated by the Muslims because of its therapeutic successes. The gaw exist first of all to put order back into the relationships between genii and humans. This aspect will be developed at length further on. But it is useful to discuss now the constant, obsessive, threatening presence of Islam, which haunts the conscience of followers torn between their ancient pagan beliefs and their obedience to the dominant religion.

BETWEEN ISLAM AND PAGANISM

Around Ngouma, Lake Débo, and Timbuktu, many versions of the legendary meeting of Waada Samba and Sheikou Hamadou can be found. In mine I have been faithful to the middle ground of meaning found within multiple tales gaw and griots chant in an epic mode to the rhythms of the koubour (the three-stringed guitar), the *djerkélé* (a kind of small harp), or the n'jarka (the single-stringed Songhay violin). In some versions Sheikou Hamadou encloses a guinea fowl in the canaris, in others a hare—the direction of the transformation reverses, but the moral of the story remains the same. Certain variants remain on one side of the tradition's middle ground and are favorable to the pagan religions; others are in frank collaboration with Islam.

2. The legendary tale of the meeting of the emperor and the magician also emphasizes the divinatory capacities of the latter. It is while in trance that Waada Samba perceives the secret of the canaris prepared by Sheikou Hamadou. Possession by the genii favors the appearance of exceptional abilities—among them, divinatory gifts. The therapeutic practices of the cult take this into account, as we shall soon see. Let us simply clarify for the moment that the identity of the healer-priest to whom the sick person goes and the knowledge of the type of cure to undertake and the items to use often appear as a form of revelation articulated by the possessed, in whom the genii inspire these messages during public sessions of the cult.

The tradition hostile to Islam supplies a tendentious origin for the illness afflicting Balkissa, Sheikou's daughter. According to this version, Waada Samba was crying on the bank of the Awgoundou pool when Baana, the most powerful genie of all the Ghimbala, came out of the water and asked him, "Why are you crying, my favorite gaw?" "Because Sheikou Hamadou wants to cut the throats of all the gaw," answered Waada. "I'll take care of that," said the genie. He flew off for Hambdalaye, attacked the emperor's daughter, and made her insane. None of the treatments administered by the emperor's marabouts could cure her. It was then suggested that the emperor call the gaw, Baana's priest, who came to Hambdalaye.

The divination session takes place as in the usual tale until the moment of the cure. Then, according to this version, the gaw demanded that a black rooster be sacrificed—Baana's color. Yet there was only one winged creature like this in all the city, and it belonged to Sheikou Hamadou. He was very attached to the animal and hesitated to give him up. ("At that time, there were neither clocks nor watches," according to one of the tellers, "and Sheikou Hamadou needed his rooster to wake him in the morning for the first prayer.") The emperor offered a black sheep and even a black bull, but Waada remained firm: "A rooster is what is needed. If you do not offer yours to Baana, your only daughter will not be healed." The emperor gave up the rooster, the sacrifice took place, and at the end of the ceremony the young woman recovered her wits.

The tradition favorable to Islam insists, on the contrary, on Waada Samba's respectful attitude toward the revealed faith and on his desire for conciliation. In this version, not only was the gaw a good Muslim who prayed and accepted God's law, but he had a knowledge of the Koran superior to that of the average Muslim. He recited a well-known mystic poem in honor of Sheikou Hamadou; Sheikou, enraptured, damned his detractors and became the gaw's friend. When Waada left Hambdalaye, Sheikou gave him his blessings and asked him to bring all the genii of the region with him.

The divergences between the versions favorable to Islam and those favorable to the religions that preceded it are not peculiar to the Ghimbala oral tradition. Similar divergences can be found in tales tracing the history of Mandingo society in the west of Mali. In particular, these stories offer differing analyses of the reasons for the fourteenth-century pilgrimage of Kankan Moussa, the first African monarch to go to Mecca. Waada's legendary chronicle tells us—and herein lies its interest—of the antagonism between Islam and paganism inscribed in the cult's oral tradition. This antagonism remains the primary obsession of the present genii-worshipers.

In the legend, conflict is resolved through official recognition of the genii cult and an alliance between the emperor and the magician. In reality, it is not altogether thus, as we will soon see. Recognition of the Ghimbala by the Islamic authorities in the legend was based on the Ghimbala's therapeutic and divinatory efficacy. The founding story delimits the cult's range of action in the context of a hegemonic and conquering Islam, which can be braved if it must be but whose superiority cannot be contested. "God is right!" cries Waada Samba amid his trials. Present conditions for the genii cult's practice have not changed qualitatively: they still must recognize the superiority of the Prophet's religion, whose believers in exchange accept the cult as an efficacious therapeutic institution. But these conditions have simply gotten worse under the double impact of endemic famine and the rise of an increasingly intolerant Islam.

LEGEND AND HISTORY

For today's faithful, Waada Samba was the first gaw of the Ghimbala. As a contemporary of the founder of the Fula empire of the Macina, he lived early in the nineteenth century. Tradition has the cult beginning in this period because there is no trace in collective memory of what might have existed before Fula expansion. However, among the objects exhumed in digs of the ancient magicians' tombs are spears, necklaces, and little bells that are similar in every way to instruments used by the gaw of today in their functions. Perhaps the Fula conquest produced a unifying effect by gathering the multiple territorial cults of worship that surely already existed under a common name with similar forms of organization. These cults must have been brought together in resistance to the force of an Islam that sought to take root in the smallest villages. Before this time—much before the nineteenth century—Islam had been the religion of princes and had been contained in the larger urban areas.

In Waada Samba's Village

Trying to learn a little more, I undertook a visit to a descendant of Waada Samba who still officiates at Doundé near Ngouma, in the east-southeastern part of Ghimbala, not far from the edge of the central Sudanese plateau. It has been a long time since the region of Ngouma was navigable, so as soon as I arrived in Mopti in January 1986, I decided to go there by land on a market day, when the gaw and his followers would surely be there. We left in a rented vehicle, turning our backs to the river and taking the sandy trails that lead to the village, birthplace of the cult. We arrived at Ngouma, the district's small seat, a poor marketplace crouched under the ferocious sun of the Sahel. Life seemed to have withdrawn from these places like the water that at one time must have been abundant, as attested to by the two hippopotamus skulls completing their demise in front of the headquarters building of the seat. There the young administrator received us with much warmth and put a corner of the administrative encampment at our disposal.

We had hardly settled in when I learned that Oussou Kondjorou, the gaw, had just left his village for an indeterminate period. The harvest was still so catastrophic that year that he had gone to make the rounds of those he had healed in the past to get a little millet from them. Fortunately, Almâmi and Alkaya, who knew everyone in the area—the former because he had relatives there, the latter because he had often traveled there in his work as a transporter—each brought me someone close to the gaw with whom I spoke in turn. I discovered first of all that contrary to what I had learned from the other gaw of the upper bend, Waada Samba's people don't call themselves Wakorey but "Rimaïbé," that is, "Fula captives." I also noticed that, unlike the gaw I'd met before, Oussou had a special room in which the instruments of the cult of Baana, his genie, were stored. The room seemed to conceal an altar, something else I had never seen before.

At the end of the afternoon, I decided to go to Doundé, the birthplace of Waada Samba's descendants and the mythical and perhaps historical birthplace of the Ghimbala. Some time ago it was a tiny hamlet planted on an island in the Awgoundou pool. The pool still spreads its wide, blue spot on the map, which dates from the 1950s. But the last flood stopped kilometers away from it, and the island became an earthy mound dominating the dried pool bottom, which was invaded by Sahelian vegetation. Doundé, a poor village like the others, clung to its ungrateful bit of land. Long ago, Waada Samba lived there alone with his followers, amid the hippopotamuses and the genii. Today, one has to go very far to find a residual underground water level, all that remains of the great pool of earlier days. I never had better measure of the tragic draining of the Niger's interior delta than I did here.

Ousmane Waada, Oussou's brother, led us through the usual labyrinth of alleys toward the absent gaw's compound as several men struggled to contain an amazing swarm of kids that threatened to engulf us. I was shown the room of cult mysteries at a distance, but of course there was no question of visiting it in the absence of the master of the house, even though our guide was the keeper of the keys. When it grew late, we returned to Mopti toward the setting sun, which illuminated the desertifying savanna's flat ground, inhabited by skinny herds pushed along by half-starved nomads. Thirty years ago the re-

gion was still covered in thick brush. Indeed, it had been very dangerous to travel there at night as we did because of the elephants and
lions, who have now fled far to the south because of the drought.

Escapade at Arrham

The Ghimbala seem to have a distant Soninké origin. Their extended
area also corresponds to the western part of the old Songhay lands.
Many followers either are Songhay or—where they are of Bambara,
Fula, or Soninké origin—have become Songhay, in that they use a
variant of the language spoken at Gao, the old imperial capital. It was
important for me to learn whether the genii cult of the upper bend of
the Niger was inspired by the classic pantheon of the center and east
of the Songhay lands: the Tooru, their allies, their dependents. On this
subject, Jean Rouch and Adam Konaré, both great Songhay history
specialists, advised me to go to Arrham, where neither one had had
the chance to travel. For the Songhay, the name Arrham is linked to
that of Dioumou Mangala, its founder, leader of the western group of
Sohanci magicians. Askia Mohammed relied upon this group at the
end of the fifteenth century in overturning the Sonni dynasty, which
was supported by the Sohanci of Wanzerbé to the east.

Arrham starts to sound like one of those mythical villages that inhabit the contemporary Malian imagination. The place can, it seems,
hide from an undesirable visitor's gaze—that of the tax collector,
for example. It evaporates into space. Those not born there do not
like to go there. One never knows what will happen in such a place,
whose inhabitants possess, it is said, strong occult powers. This reputation preserved Arrham from the Fula wars. Tuaregs and Arma, who
fought the Macina empire, came here to take refuge.

During a stop at Diré, I abandoned the river and pirogue for a day
and went to Arrham, east of a trail leading to Goundam. I discovered
a village more than half-emptied of its inhabitants. The chief, Ibrahima Gareï Maïga, was surveying the establishment of a durum-wheat
field not far from there, irrigated according to a technique new to the
region. He lost no time in coming to us and putting himself amiably
at our disposal for several hours. A modest functionary in retirement,
but a direct descendant of Dioumou Mangala, he had taken on the
chieftaincy at his father's death. He had left the village at an early age
to learn to read and write and returned only occasionally. Thus had he
inherited the political power held by his family but not the Sohanci
magical tradition.

He now admitted regretfully that he had not become interested in
this legacy until his father was dying. "My son," his father had said,
"you want to know who you are and you want to know the history

of Arrham. It's a very long story to tell you and it's a little late, as I've begun to lose my wits." And it was too late; his father died without transmitting most of his knowledge. He nonetheless had the time to teach his heir that the village's present site is recent, dating from approximately the beginning of the century. The historical site is several kilometers to the northeast: both the griots and blacksmiths of Arrham required the Sohanci to go down closer to the Niger, to a place where water was less scarce. Every year at the end of Ramadan, the chief still goes to the abandoned site to converse with his ancestors at the spot protected by all of Dioumou Mangala's buried talismans.

Gareï Maïga then stopped his tale. At the moment, he was more concerned with modernizing his land than conserving the past. He had just established an irrigated sector of three hectares, and he hoped to do better next year. To help me, he brought in his brother, a strange, old magician fine of face and full of trickery but perhaps also of formidable charms. He was accompanied by the last two griots of the family remaining in the village. A hesitant and painful debate ensued: the old man and the griots had apparently forgotten everything. The partners made tremendous efforts nonetheless, but were not very competent and were even a bit pitiful. It seemed that the best one among them had left the region when poverty descended.

On the other hand, I was not altogether sure that the old sorceror wasn't trying to obstruct the process, feigning a bout of amnesia. Or maybe it was his advanced age. But I scarcely gleaned a few bits of information about the absence of the water-genii cult locally. The old man mentioned several great names, such as Djini Samourrous, Djini Yacouba, and Djini Souleymani—genii who never descend into people anymore but instead belong more to the general and vague system of Ghimbala references.

I tried to have them tell me the legendary story of their great ancestor, Dioumou Mangala, but the tale was chaotic, laced with contradictions and frequent lapses: the two griots really remembered nothing. Aggravated by this confused slowness, Gareï Maïga decided to tell me the legend of his ancestor himself, helped by Almâmi, who knew it well because he had in fact heard it from the mouth of the famous griot who had emigrated far away.

When the Askia Mohammed undertook his pilgrimage to Mecca, he asked all the Songhay who followed him to abandon their idols, destroy their magical instruments, and forget their beliefs. Some time after the pilgrims' return, a very beautiful horse, which had been given as a gift to the Askia's son, disappeared. The people found its tracks, which led to an anthill and ended there. The genii had taken it. The people did not know what to do.

The Askia sounded his *toubal* to gather everyone.[3] All the Songhay came immediately. They asked the Askia, "Why are you calling us together?" "My son's magnificent horse has disappeared. I must ask you to help me find it." "It is you who have complicated our lives. You forced us to abandon our magic; you said it was a pagan thing. We abandoned everything and you are responsible for our abandonment. You must suffer the consequences."

The Askia began to interrogate those present, one by one. They knew nothing. Only Dioumou Mangala suggested assistance. He brought out his magic snuffbox and performed a ritual smoking of the area. Then he set his ingredients [literally, *safari,* "medicines"] on the anthill. It opened immediately. He saw Samourrous Al Djini, the immense, leprous devil with whom he "worked."[4] Dioumou went down into the hole. Samourrous asked him, "Why did you call me?" "It's about our horse that has disappeared." "Well, that's not hard."

Samourrous led Dioumou around in the subterranean genii city. They found all the genii gathered around the horse. "Who made this horse disappear?" asked Samourrous. The genii pointed out the thief. "Why did you make it disappear?" "I was under a *garboy* with a friend when the man tied up the horse.[5] Then he killed the friend I was playing with. That's why I stole the horse after the man left." "When he killed your friend, what form were you in?" "We were two snakes; we were playing and fighting, so he wanted to strike us. I was able to escape." "When you leave the city, you mustn't take on the shape of animals because people may kill you. I forbade you this a long time ago. Too bad for your friend, who did not obey me." Samourrous then gave the order to put the horse back in his harness and to lead him to the exit of the anthill.

When the Askia saw Dioumou return with the horse, he said to him, "I see that you have kept your pagan practices, and that your Songhay heritage has not yet been lost. If you abandon it,

3. A toubal is a big drum, a sign of supreme power. It is also the drum struck to announce war.

4. That is, "of whom he asked help on the occasion of the magic he performed."

5. The garboy (*Balanita aegyptiaca*) is known as *tanni* in Fula and the *dattier du désert* in French (thorn tree or zachun-oil tree). A small, thorny tree with persistent foliage, it is one of the plants the genii like very much (see appendix 4).

our "way of being Songhay" is lost, but the country is not yet purified.[6] A Songhay, even if he has made the pilgrimage, cannot abandon magic. *Korti* will never cease in these lands!"[7]

When Dioumou died, the power of the Songhay crumbled. But while he was alive, the Songhay were powerful, thanks to the genie who helped Dioumou personally.

Back to Doundé

I returned to Doundé in mid-March 1986, almost two months after my first visit. I had more luck this time: Oussou Kondjorou had just returned from his tour. Faintly flattered that I had made a second Mopti–Ngouma journey for him, almost five hundred kilometers round-trip and half of it on exhausting roads, he received me with nobility and reserve. Oussou and the brother I already knew greatly resembled each other. They were men of imposing appearance with faces both large and refined, as though the more than thousand-year history of their Soninké ancestors had come to rest in the hollows of their cheeks, the wrinkles of their foreheads, and the depths of their eyes. Oussou led a group of followers, mostly men, who seemed to me to be very close to him, very available. He led them with authority and simplicity. Since his return, the courtyard of his compound had returned to a state of great animation. Three patients, one in chains, awaited his care. I immediately felt I was in the presence of a great gaw.

Oussou gave me the longest and most detailed version of the meeting of his ancestor with Emperor Sheikou Hamadou. It ranked among those that are not hostile to Islam but rather establish the basis for a collaboration with it (see appendix 1). One point of the tale intrigued me nonetheless: Waada Samba's predictions at Hambdalaye were made in Songhay because he spoke that language very well and Fula very badly. Today the opposite is true: his descendants know only a few Songhay words and have become Rimaïbé, Fula captives. But the gaw could not or would not tell me how they got this way. He responded evasively to my question: "We became Rimaïbé in contact with the Fulas, but we call ourselves 'rimaïbé-rimbé' or 'free rimaïbé,' that is, 'without masters.'"

At least there was no longer any doubt about Waada Samba's existence. Up to this point, I knew the tale of his mythical life; on this day

6. Which means, "There are still many magical pagan objects."
7. Korti or *nkorté* (*koroté* in the Malian west) is fatal poison that is magically administered at a distance.

I discovered the line of his descendants that leads directly to Oussou. It is not certain, however, that relations between the first great gaw of the Ghimbala and the emperor at Hambdalaye were as good as legend would lead us to believe.

I then attempted a few questions about the world of the genii. Oussou answered that I would find what I was seeking in the chants of his cult. But I had to wait until evening to hear them, to allow the gaw time to assemble all his people. A long wait culminated at teatime, with tea taken beneath a light shelter under the full Sahelian sun, already very strong in this season. I was pulled rather suddenly from my euphoric torpor by the arrival of the Fula chief, who demanded to meet me. I received him with his large retinue. Introductions. Exchanges of courtesies. I finally understood the purpose of his visit when he told me in an insistent manner that the entire population of the village is under his jurisdiction, including "those with whom [I] ha[d] spoken," that is, Oussou Kondjorou—whose name he did not even mention—and his followers.

At the end of the afternoon, we gathered in the overheated room where the morning's interview had taken place. Oussou sat surrounded by a group of followers, all men, who began to chant and strike calabashes turned over on the ground before them. Everyone sat directly on the sand. The chants merged in the relaxed, good-natured atmosphere, though the air was rendered stifling by the crowd obstructing the only two openings. It seemed as though the whole village had gathered in the courtyard behind the wall. Oussou and his followers took no notice and pursued their friendly evocation of the genii. Singers and musicians smiled at each other between verses, exchanging jokes.

Oussou was backed up by a griot, a kind of medium, who was extremely attentive to the least injunctions of his chief, high-strung, his face highly sensitive. I expected him to enter into trance from one minute to the next, but instead a large, fat man dressed in a dull *boubou* was suddenly taken with violent trembling and began to rock from side to side. As the possession increased, Oussou took the man under his arm, rocked him softly, without haste or worry, and then made him swallow something quickly.

The possessed dropped into a deep sleep: the session continued in the same bantering vein. Oussou and his griot gaily took snuff and chewed tobacco, all the while unfurling their story. When everything finally stopped, I came out into the crowd, stupefied from the heat and dust. We went off in the deepening night toward Mopti, our lower backs aching from the trail.

SOME SHADOWS OF CERTAINTY

These detours from the river were not useless. At Arrham, I discovered that the ancient Songhay source was surely not determinative in constituting the Ghimbala as a possession cult, though it had clearly played a role. At Doundé, I saw that the Fula domination of the last century, a memory still strong in followers' minds, had probably not been as pacific and conciliatory toward Waada Samba and his followers as legend would lead one to believe.

From the day spent at Arrham, I retained the notion that the Ghimbala cult is not connected with the tradition and power of the Sohanci, magicians of the Songhay, even though the reconstructed legend of Dioumou Mangala reveals the dealings his descendants have had for a long time with the pre-Islamic world of the genii. Nonetheless, in the northern part of the Ghimbala area of influence, from Niafunké to Timbuktu, a good number of gaw are Songhay; few of them are Sohanci. In Tindirma, the last historically Songhay site toward the west, for example, the Sohanci play no role in the local genii brotherhood. In addition, the Ghimbala pantheon has little to do with the Tooru pantheon, the genii of the classical Songhay tradition, even though it is sometimes possible to establish correspondences between certain members of the two families. Ghimbala antecedents are better researched elsewhere, especially among the Wakorey, descendants of the Soninké. We will soon discuss these when we sketch portraits of the principal cult priests and agents encountered along with the Niger and its genii.

In contrast, the relatively recent impact of Fula domination appears more obvious in the cult's development. The present condition of Waada Samba's descendants is proof of this influence. In tales gathered among the priests in villages far from Doundé, Waada Samba and his followers are considered Wakorey. Yet the gaw Oussou Kondjorou and his brother immediately called themselves Rimaïbé, captives of the Fulas, whose language they speak to the exclusion of Songhay while the majority of their colleagues speak both.

The Ngouma region has thus been completely fulanized.[8] Ousmane Waada, the gaw's younger brother, in fact declared calmly, "Once we were Wakorey; then we became Songhay; now we are Rimaïbé." Yet it is well known that Sheikou Hamadou reduced to servile status those populations that did not accept conversion to Islam when faced with the advance of the Fula armies. It seems probable that Oussou Kondjorou's ancestors and those of his people resisted conquest

8. That is, become Fula.

and that they were forced to renounce their beliefs and convert, whence their present condition of Rimaïbé. But here, as in Arrham, I remain in the realm of conjecture, using deductions from present-day observations because there is no trace, among the Fula or the Rimaïbé, of what might have been a conflict that ended in the taking of Doundé.

It is certainly an advanced hypothesis, however, that the descendants of certain of Waada Samba's companions who went with him to Hambdalaye remained Wakorey—Aïssata Boureïma and Hamadoun Boureïma, for example. Both have as their ancestor Alfa Mahaman, one of the gaw's followers, cited many times in the tales. The first lives in Sebi and is the sister of the second, who lives on the other side of the river at Mékorey. The two villages are in the northern part of the Ghimbala extension area, which endured lighter Fula domination for a shorter period. The priests of the genii there were able to pursue their cult without losing their Wakorey identity.

In contrast, when I went back up the Bara Issa to return to Mopti in February 1985, I met several gaw who called themselves Rimaïbé. They lived in the territory near Doundé that extends between that arm of the river and the Gourma. They, too, were probably descended from families that had been forced to convert and reduced to captives. But they kept their pagan background, expressed through the genii cult.

♣

From Doundé to Arrham, the multiple tales gathered at the various stages of river travel offer the image of a cult whose modern traits have been shaped by the warrior expansion of Islam under Fula domination—a source of trauma to the old peasant populations of the Niger's upper bend, who must have kept their territorial gods up to that point. Thus the Ghimbala verify once more the general hypothesis that the origin of possession cults often coincides with periods of difficulty and change during which people seek to draw closer to their gods, whom they then bring down upon their own heads. Or perhaps the present cult, under the impact of Fula oppression, was simply content to gather diverse possession cults already existing locally. One thing at least seems certain: the Ghimbala genii are profoundly anchored in the soil and society that gave birth to them.

3 / Between Above and Below

A STORMY CROSSING

After three days' stay in Niafunké, we decide to take to the river under the setting sun to get back to the little encampment at Gombo, near Dabi, where we can spend the night quietly. We advance under a heavy sky. To the west, the sun disappears under dense clouds. Dull twilight succeeds it, then nightfall, thick with insects falling on the pirogue. For the weather is already hot, two days after torrents dumped from the sky on their way up the Atlantic coast from southeast to desertified northeast. We advance carefully in the dense darkness at indecision's whim. This night-navigation without markers creates the feeling of being in a nonplace, becoming oppressive over time. A sandy, rainy squall sped along by lightning unfurls itself on us, transforming our wide canal—quiet just moments before—into a raging mass of water. We get to shore as quickly as possible to allow the squall to pass. It is unusual at this time of year, perhaps the result of rapid climate change.

Now the whole crew is shivering, stretched out on the pirogue's bottom under the shelter of the hangar at its center, while the wind strikes, saturated with the faint smell of brine and carrying the cries of birds gone astray in the gale. Above our heads the dark and desolate bank seems to await the apparition of some terrifying specter as the storm rips the sky. This is the time Baana could emerge—Baana, the greatest and most feared of the Ghimbala genii, who follows the thunderbolts and unleashes lightning; Baana, whose slogan is "the unconquerable captive," whose laughter mixes with the thunder's groans; Baana, whose name also means "rain" in Songhay.

We stay here until the tempest moves away, and then we return to the still-agitated river, crossing through leaping, swirling schools of African dogfish. About ten fall into the pirogue, ensuring us our coming meal. After passing the village of Sibo while detouring around a bend, we arrive at a place in the river where it seems there are always a few hippopotamuses—our last danger spot before stopping. Our unexpected trial moves toward its close on a wave that grows more peaceful as we pass several other craft, which look as ghostlike as ours surely does to their crews. The smell of the water; the slap of the waves against the hull; the softened wind full of insects' music arising from the nearby earth, regenerated by the rain.

I think this powerful, stormy evening helped me understand from the inside the world of the river genii—how familiar their relationships are with the people of this land, their central importance to the most essential concerns of these peasants, whose existence is inextricable from the Niger's caprices. Thus, when floods give new life to the river's branches and dried-up pools, the masters of the Ghimbala's waters and of the whole upper bend wear hope on their faces as well as the danger manifest in these mounting waves, heavy with the genii said to animate them. Each man watching over his assigned territory meticulously observes the waves' progression and describes it to the village chief, sometimes every hour. He then returns to this moving border between earth and water and moves with it, accompanying it along the bends in the terrain, stopping at critical points. Thus does each appease the genii, who have come to take possession of their seasonal homes, so that they will not threaten people. Each then tries to earn the favor of the genii with the appropriate offerings and sacrifices. I think of all these men, alone but simultaneously confronted with the forces of the river, as we come up to the beach at the Gombo encampment, still moist from this recent shower.

BAANA, THE UNCONQUERABLE CAPTIVE

Baana was a young captive, son of Samourrous, and a slave. Although his father was a prominent genie, king of all the genii, Baana was of no account in his family because his mother was a slave. The genii called him good-for-nothing and even a little crazy, and they bore him no consideration until the day he saved them from disaster. Here is how.

> The genii were gathered at Taoussa, upstream of Timbuktu, around Moussa, Moussa Al Djini, for a batou during the night between Thursday and Friday. In this time, a great genie named Gangikoy existed who lived in Walo, near Hombori. Samourrous was dead, slaughtered by a lion, and the genii wanted to ask Gangikoy not to remain above but to descend into the water to become their chief, below. In the middle of the batou, they decided to choose one of their own to go to Walo.
>
> Moussa rose and said he wanted to go. He took his horse, he took his golden war chains, and he left Taoussa. When he came to Gangikoy's home, he cried out, "I will bring you to the river with me!" The other answered him, "It won't be you who forces me to descend into the river!"

Moussa tied one end of his golden chain to Gangikoy's neck, the other end to his ankle. He tried to drag him and ended up losing his leg. He also tried to take him into his arms and drag him that way. After a while, one of his hands became paralyzed. Now he only had use of one arm and one leg. He returned to the batou, where he fainted dead away.

So Baana rose and began to dance next to the batou, and then entered the circle of genii gathered. "You must give me the golden chain! Give it to me! I will go to Walo and I will bring you back Gangikoy." All the genii thought him crazy and came to him one by one to spit the cola they had been chewing in his face. But as Baana was bigger and stronger than all of them, he jumped over them, he took the chain, and left, saying he would bring back Gangikoy of Walo. When he got there, he told the genie, "Get up! Let's go!" The other answered him, "You can do nothing! Moussa came here, he tried, but he wasn't able to make me descend. It won't be you who succeeds!"

So Baana jumped on him, grabbed him, and put him over his shoulders. He transported him this way from Walo to Taoussa. He met up again with the other Ghimbala who were carrying on the batou. He threw Gangikoy into the middle of the dancing and then spoke to Harakoy: "Here is the *gangi-bibi*.[1] If he moves, I will kill him!" In this way, Baana made Gangikoy descend to Taoussa, where he lives to this day.

After this, the genii held another batou, again on the night before Friday. Baana then declared to them, "I want to marry Awa." At that time, Arouna was courting Awa; he spent his time playing the koubour for her. The genii stood, scandalized by these words they so disliked. "What? A captive like you—you want to marry Awa?" Then Harakoy said, "The night Baana went to Walo to bring the gangi-bibi back among us, I thought he was stronger than everyone. It remains for him to give one more proof that he can marry Awa, my daughter. All the young men gathered here will fight Baana. Him alone against all of them. If he can beat them, I will give him Awa; if he is beaten, he will not have her!"

Baana agreed and even asked in addition that they build six houses on top of him. He added that if the genii laughed it would be fine with him, but if Awa laughed, he would come out from

---

1. *Gangi-bibi* literally means "black genie" in the classical Songhay pantheon. From Gao to Niamey, the gangi-bibi are the slaves of the Tooru, the noble genii.

under the six houses. He remained like this until about five-thirty in the morning. During this time Arouna played the ge-nii's songs with his koubour. When he came to Awa's song, she began to laugh.[2] So Baana leapt from the ground, making the six houses crumble. But as for Harakoy, she did not want to believe this feat without proof to the contrary. She made all the young men come and had many mats placed on the ground.

Now Baana was ready to fight. His first meeting was with the one who was courting Awa. There were six thousand mats on the ground. Baana took his adversary, threw him to the ground and walked him over the mats until his back poked through them all. The loser ran away; he became Kumbaré, the crowned crane. Baana did the same thing to the second; he became a *jungu* [small rodent]; the third became a *miney* [anteater]. The fourth genie he faced was his future mother-in-law. He took her, threw her down, and made her go through the six thousand mats. She cried out that she would disappear underground. But Baana held out his hand to help her up. So Harakoy gave Awa to him. . . .

War was approaching at the edge of Lake Oro. The Ghimbala feared being beaten. They had found no solution yet, so they began to play the koubour. When Baana's song came, he said to them, "What's the matter? Don't you see what is coming toward us? We don't have the means to resist; we may be beaten."

So Baana transformed himself into rain, into wind, into sun that burned so hot that the enemies fled, terrified. It was at this time that he planted a tree in Lake Oro. (No one has seen the top of this tree above the water's surface to this day.) After this time, Baana became chief of the genii's army.

Baana bragged that he was a captive who had married his mistress. He had taken Awa, thanks to his strength, and brought her to Birinia Doundou.[3] There he lay with her and they ended up having a child named Diarahilou. This child grew and there were none like him, neither above nor below. When Huruleyni saw Diarahilou, she said she had never seen anyone like him. Diarahilou answered that he had never seen a woman as beautiful as Huruleyni. She did not respond to young men's advances. In

2. To show she was pleased.
3. There are several Birinia Doundous. First, there is the mythical place found in the Koulikoro rapids downstream of Bamako, far from the lands of the upper bend. There is also a great water hole in the Diré region, situated exactly between the villages of Koura and Kirsamba.

the same way, Diarahilou did not concern himself with any young woman other than Huruleyni; there had never been such a beautiful woman.

One day [Diarahilou] wanted to go above to see her, and by misfortune he was killed. Awa was braiding her hair when she learned of her son's death. She always used a big needle to untangle her hair; now she took it and began to kill all the genii she passed. She met her elder brother Moussa, who caught her by the hand and said to her, "You are massacring all the genii because of the death of one of them?" And he prevented her from continuing. The genii went to warn Baana about his son's death. Baana gathered them all and then began to scream. All the genii killed by Diarahilou's mother and by Diarahilou himself were brought back to life.

Some say that Baana is a captive; others say he is a nobleman and all that comes from what precedes. Here is where Baana's story stops.

This story, which I have hardly retouched,[4] was obtained at the end of January 1985 from Oumar Kontao, gaw of Koriomé, and it illustrates well Baana's slogan—the unconquerable captive. He is the central figure in the Ghimbala pantheon, although he ranks only third in the songs used when the faithful invite the genii to descend upon them. He comes after Moussa, the old, disabled chief, and his sister Princess Awa, who became the wife of her former captive.

But once the rules of protocol that rank the Ghimbala in order of birth have been satisfied, one must consider their actual strengths. Baana is the strongest, without contest; it is he who holds the greatest powers. In another tale, he takes Awa from her rivals because he is able to dig the Koli-Koli, a branch of the Niger that flows toward Corrienzé, allowing its waters to go far into the south and enlarging the genii's domain. No other genie had dared try his luck because Mama Kyria, who had organized this trial, had set a limit of seven days to accomplish it and "everyone knew it was impossible." Yet Baana pulled off this colossal task in three days.

GREAT AND LESSER GENII OF THE GHIMBALA

Awa, Moussa, and Baana together form the dominant trio of the Ghimbala world. Beside them exist three equally important genii:

---

4. While retaining the meaning, I have edited the repetitions, flashbacks, obscure parts, and, in places, digressions.

Mayé, another war chief; Samba Poulo, the Fula shepherd; and finally Mama Kyria, the pious old leper. The others count less, while these half-dozen major genii possess marked personalities and appear in a wealth of stories in people's minds, such as the one told about Baana by his priest Oumar Kontao, who of course had a strong penchant for valorizing his protective genie.

Moussa

A priest of Moussa will likewise draw a rather triumphant portrait of *his* personal genie and will show him, too, as capable of besting his enemies by force, by ruse, and by a decisive spirit (see appendix 2). Moussa nonetheless recognizes Baana's worth—his family's former captive, now accepted as an equal because of his courage. Moussa's slogans and praises especially emphasize his warring valor, his bravery, his nobility: "We have never seen anyone so strong as you!" "There is not another like you in your father's lineage!" "There is not another like you among your mothers!" "None is your equal in your generation, in your village!"

Moussa is called "the genie who takes people; the genie who does not fear poison, because it is not poison that will make him die." If Moussa's story is told in its entirety, we also hear, "As a child he was already very strong. When he grew old, he lost arms and legs, he lost arms and legs." Moussa has a dual personality: he is very strong, but he is found in situations of extreme weakness; he is noble and majestic, but he is sometimes impulsive and full of anger; he is supposedly Muslim, and yet sometimes he seems quite the opposite. "Moussa, when he fights, looks like a *kafir;* when he sits back down, he regrets his savagery."

Awa

The princess of the Ghimbala has a patrician beauty. There are other beautiful women among the genii, but she has a royal bearing and eclipses all the others. In a country in which a woman's walk is an integral part of the canon of femininity, hers is without peer, and it incites the enthusiasm of those who sing to her, "You are as beautiful when you approach as when you go away!" "You are as beautiful when you come forward as when you go backward!" The genii take great pains for her and react to her moods: "When Awa smiles, the *gangi* are happy. When she laughs, they laugh too."

She possesses great knowledge. "She sees what the other genii see, but she also sees what they cannot see. This is the exceptional knowledge that God has given her." Awa is very wealthy: she wears white veils woven with golden threads, a gold belt, and many jewels. She is a fervent Muslim. She shows a sweet and well-balanced character, unless she gets angry. She can fight like a man, in fact. Hence these slogans: "Awa, a wrap-skirt is better than pants," "the spindle's tip is better than the spear," "the *bijuri* is better than the shield."[5]

Samba Poulo

He is Fula [*Peul*], as his name indicates. Shepherd of the genii and their animals, clothed in a yellow boubou, he dances with the shepherd's long stick. Ghimbala followers also call him "shepherd" of the fish, who follow when he wants them to desert a pond whose owners he dislikes. On the other hand, the person who wins him over will have fruitful fishing. But if the fisher abuses the alliance with him and catches too many fish, Samba Poulo takes those remaining and carries them to shelter in another part of the river. (In passing, I note a modern and somewhat maleficent avatar of Samba Poulo: Samba Diom Torchi, a genie armed with a flashlight. With one of its rays, he can sweep the surface of a watery area and immediately empty it of all piscine species. He also uses his instrument to misguide laggard and careless travelers at night by drawing them with his luminous call toward dangers of the river or its banks, rocks, bogs, or water holes.) Finally, Samba Poulo walks both above and below, creating communication between the earthly and the watery worlds.

Mayé

"His mother is a genie, his father is the *shayṭāns'* blacksmith," goes his first slogan. "You, too—you are son of genie and son of blacksmith," the recitant embellishes. A pagan genie, stuttering and irascible, Mayé is especially dangerous. The possessions he provokes are very violent. One taken by him rolls on the ground screaming, tears one's clothing, dashes toward the *bomboutou* (the water drums in the possession ensemble, overturned calabashes floating within vessels filled from the neighboring river), and rolls them over. As all Ghimbala possessions are convulsive, those of Mayé must be particularly excessive for people to distinguish them from others.

Mayé is, like Baana, one of the war chiefs of the genii. Because of this, he possesses a weapon, the *sombé,* a kind of scepter armed with a long, two-headed point apparently representing a pelican's beak. It is an instrument possessed by priests who count Mayé among the genii of their cult, even if he is not their personal genie. Mayé hurls himself on his enemies with his weapon and makes it whirl above his head,

---

5. *Bijuri* is a small piece of leather on which the point of a spindle is set.

facing every side to return the blows. "When he enters into battle, he looks to one side, he looks to the other; he strikes a blow on one side, he strikes on the other. He strikes ahead, he strikes behind; he strikes all those he meets."

Mayé is also the genie of the floods; he is found wherever the water begins to rise. Far more than Samba Poulo he is the genie of the Sorko, the fisherpeople of the Songhay area. A pagan genie, he is associated with the elements in motion. He shares this privilege with Baana, the greatest kafir genie, whose portrait I must now complete.

Baana

"He is afraid neither of God nor of the Prophet." In brief, he is a great pagan. Neither is he afraid of lightning bolts nor of lightning, because he is their master and unleashes them at will. He comes during times of storm, dressed all in black. He announces the tempest following him. When the storm explodes, he is crazy with happiness. He screams facing the sky, against which he is seen in profile, his two arms outstretched. One of his favorite slogans is, quite naturally, "Baana, if the sky rumbles, it is because you have unleashed the lightning by beating your chest." And, people add, "If the rain falls, it's also thanks to you, Baana." This is why sacrifices intended to ensure a good rainy season were once dedicated to him.

Baana, the "genie of a hundred pair of wings," of legendary strength, is the most powerful of all the Ghimbala, as we already knew. His possessions are extremely violent like those of his crony, Mayé. He is the most feared of all: "Baana, all the gaw, despite their knowledge, are afraid of you!" "The genii are afraid of you!" "Poison is afraid of you!" "The shaytāns are afraid of you!" "Sorcerors are also afraid of you!"

Mama Kyria

The leprous old genie completes the group of great genii. He moves about slowly and with difficulty because of his illness. His possessed retract their fingers and lips and limp and hop about, imitating their master's look. But this genie commands hidden resources. "Mama Kyria's hands and feet are sick, but the way he walks is astonishing. If the genii go on a trip and leave him behind, they find him seated ahead of them, awaiting their arrival."

Though originally a captive, he is chief of all the genii above—those who live only in the bush and in the dry places. He is also the genii's messenger, the one who warns humans, even during the fast,[6]

6. That is, during the period of Ramadan, when the genii are supposed to disappear

of serious news—an approaching death, for example—and who gathers the genii for a ceremony. He is an excellent Muslim and fulfills the functions of a *kadi,* that is, a judge. When he makes a decision, the other genii cannot ignore it. His piety puts him in the first row during prayer and gives him the title "imam of the dunes." There is also a hellish version of Mama Kyria, an underhanded old genie who camps in cemeteries, among ruins, and on garbage-heaps, ready to strike hard with paralysis those who come to meet him inadvertently.

♣

Some great genii of the past are still alive but no longer descend into people. The gaw are content to invoke them in their incantations and still "work" with them, as they say. Of the best known, I will note Ali Soutouraré, the warrior genie whom Sheikou Hamadou and Waada Samba shared; Daouda, a marabout genie; and Djini Arouna, also a Muslim, Baana's unhappy rival.

Harakoy, the old woman who is first in the classical Songhay pantheon of the Tooru and their allies and dependents, has a more marginal importance among the Ghimbala. Each time I asked if she were taken into account in the cult, the gaw answered me affirmatively: "Of course; she is the mother of the river." But in fact, I never saw Harakoy embodied during the numerous possessions I attended. At Mopti, she descended into Bouba, the asthmatic gaw now dead, whose brotherhood was open to external influences.[7] (Thus even in the middle of the Ghimbala there are *haouka,* the modern genii of fire, strength, and change, whom Jean Rouch filmed admirably in *Les Maitres Fous.*[8] Never do they present themselves in ceremonies of the villages of the upper bend: "They are afraid of the Ghimbala," people say.) While Harakoy is mentioned in Niafunké, Tonka, and Diré, the region's small cities, and especially in Koriomé, Timbuktu's cosmopolitan outer harbor, and while some of the gaw spontaneously invoke her seniority and importance, the great goddess of the Niger plays no role in daily affairs of the cult.

The six great genii of the Ghimbala are the most powerful and most

---

from humans' lives out of respect for God. Mama Kyria benefits from favor in this regard.

7. See the description in Gibbal, *Guérisseurs et Magiciens,* 111–14, of a ceremony within Bouba's order.

8. The haouka, the last genii in the pantheon of the eastern Songhay, are a symbolic creation of the peasantry from the region of Niamey in the 1920s. They were invented by the possessed of the period in response to multiple traumas born of colonization.

present interlocutors of people, and only rarely is a gaw priest of none of them. I have met some exceptions, however. Séry, one of the gaw in the village of Sumpi, is possessed by Badji-Badji, a frivolous young woman who is nonetheless received with much honor everywhere because she is noble. Yero, an old, blind gaw who lived in Dabi near Niafunké, had as his genie Dia, a woman who is "what you think and what you don't think." She is a genie of multiple avatars—calabashes, rings, and so on—who even transforms herself during flood season into an aquatic monster that attracts children to the bottom of watery abysses in order to devour them. It must be noted that these exceptions are infrequent and that they concern gaw who are certainly respected but of relatively modest rank in the unofficial hierarchy of reputation.

But many other genii descend into people, beginning with the greatest avatars, in particular those of Baana, Awa, and Moussa. Less powerful than their leaders, they are part of each one's clientele. Then there exists a crowd of more modest genii, subordinate to the first, who incarnate in those cult followers who will never become gaw. While biographical details abound about the half-dozen prominent personalities who dominate the Ghimbala, the genii subordinate to them are only noted by a few stereotyped traits and some bits of history, with the exception of those who are related by family to the first group: Djini Maïrama, Komaïga's wife; their daughter, Gassikoy-Mariama; her fiancé, Kodal Djini, who is also Moussa's son; Kokota Djini, a rather lazy sometime journalist. The personalities of all these remain rather vague in the minds of followers, who nonetheless know precisely where in their region each one has elected to reside (see appendices 2 and 3, in which a certain number of these secondary genii appear).

ABOVE AND BELOW

The Ghimbala followers share their lands with *béné*, which means "sky" but also "above," and *ganda*, "below." Below: the river and its network of branches, lakes, and pools, but also all the lands the floods invade, the shallows and temporary pools connected to the principal course of the river by narrow canals that turn to dusty entrails during the dry season. Above, béné begins where the floods end, with all the lands that never flood: the dry bush; the spots the villages attach themselves to, sheltered from the high waters; the dunes; the ancient gourgoussou. Both parts of the world are peopled by genii. But Awa, Moussa, Baana, Mayé, and even Samba Poulo belong to the below. Mama Kyria is the only prominent genie to come from above, although many genii of lesser importance exist, whom the old leper governs.[9]

Genii, like people, go between above and below, according to the hour of day or night and the seasons. The genii from below—Mayé in the lead, armed with his sombé—follow the head of the flood. Normally those of above, including Mama Kyria, never descend into the water. The former, especially the key trio of Awa, Baana, and Moussa, possess both aquatic and terrestrial homes. As the waters rise, they move into places farther and farther distant from the riverbed, occupy temporary pools and intermittent arms of the river, and then turn back with the fall of the river to take refuge during the hot season, when the water is lowest, in the shadowy grottoes of permanent holes. Thus they live like the people, according to the rhythms of the Niger. And the great gaw and the genii-griots who know these various, remarkable places do not fail to enumerate them during ceremonies to flatter the genii and get them to descend upon their followers' heads.

The importance accorded to the genii of the below reflects the concerns of people for whom the Ghimbala are the emanation of the land. In this country of very low relief, floodwaters fill places slowly and with majesty, covering everything little by little. They are the element of life; they regenerate arid soil and, when they pull back, reveal the fertile shallows. But they are also an ungovernable source of danger. They cover expanses that can only be perceived at their mere surfaces. So the genii incarnate this infinity, this sacredness—so near, melted into what is not mastered but sometimes tamed.

We can imagine that water has often in the past offered possibilities for protection and escape from invasion, a danger that almost always came from above. From the south, Sheikou Hamadou's riders came from the Séno, the unfloodable Fula steppe; from the north, the Moorish and Tuareg nomads imposed their laws until the beginning of the twentieth century; much longer ago, the Moroccan columns descended across the desert to destroy the Songhay Empire. Perhaps the tendency to value what is low-lying—water and the genii who represent it—as more powerful than terra firma comes from all this history. Is it not these genii who always manage to dominate those from above—in contrast to human history, in which what came from

9. To the north of the extended Ghimbala area, in the regions of Niafunké, Tonka, and Diré, another important genie from above exists. He is Sourgou Al Djini, also called Mahaman Sourgou, a genie of Tuareg origin. His presence reminds us of the worries of the sedentary populations, caused by the nearness of those nomads who once pillaged them mercilessly.

on high (Gao, Timbuktu, the old nations, the nomads) rather dominated the lower (the peoples of the river's lower delta)?

The great genii of the waters give order to the world, and simply by the nature of their actions, they connect the two primordial elements. This seems to be intended by some slogans of the three first among them: "Baana: one of his feet is above, one is below." "Awa: one of her feet is in the water, the other is on the dune." "Moussa: one of his feet is on the rocks in the river, the other is on the trees."[10]

More specifically, the Ghimbala live in different places of note in the territory they share, attributed to each of them preferentially: to Moussa, the river's great holes and its principal arms; to Baana, the lakes and large pools; to Mayé, the great isthmuses, the canals through which the floods reach the interior, and those natural reservoirs, the great pools such as Tenda and Kabara to the northwest, Lakes Oro and Fati to the north, Awgoundou and Niangay to the east. Samba Poulo contents himself with large puddles and temporary ponds but can also descend into the river, where he possesses certain holes as well as the rocky fords he shares with Moussa. Mama Kyria and his followers haunt the dry places: the heights of the dunes and the gourgoussou, extinguished hearths abandoned in the bush. But above is not reserved for these genii: those from below can get there, too. The Ghimbala of the water like the great trees along the river very much, especially those sacred to them (tamarinds, bastard mahogany), as well as anthills and termite hills—especially Moussa, who hides his gold there sometimes.[11]

Finally, Awa possesses some prestigious holes in the river and especially in immense Lake Débo, at the foot of Goura hill, whose peak she colonizes as well—whence the title Awa-Goura sometimes used to refer to her. She prefers to divide her time between her religious obligations—her elder brother and her husband, Baana, at times living with one in the river, at times living with the other in the ponds and lakes. In other words, she is very busy and not often in the company of her husband, who in fact complains about this. The cult's sessions remain the place they can be together. This is why when one of the two comes into a person during a batou, the other does not stay away long. However, her familial and Islamic constraints keep her from Baana and constitute one of the points of debate that we will take up

---

10. We are talking about not just any trees but those the genii prefer. Their names are associated with the praises sung them. Their leaves, their bark, and their roots are used in the diverse preparations intended to heal the illnesses the gangi provoke (see appendix 4).

11. The tale of Douré, a gaw from Sadjilambou, mentions this; see chapter 7.

shortly. Until then, let us remark that the least hole in the river, its rocks, its lakes, its pools, large trees along its banks, dunes, gourgoussou, termite hills, and anthills are classed as homes of the genii throughout the whole of Ghimbala country.[12]

THE BLACK AND THE WHITE

The main genii wear specific clothing whose colors correspond to their sacrificial objects. The coats of the animals to be sacrificed range from immaculate white to absolute black, including all possible combinations of these two fundamental colors and between them, red and its many variants, from light ocher to dark brown. The major opposition between black and white symbolizes the antagonism between the Muslim and pagan poles, made explicit by the main characters in the legend of Ghimbala origins. During the confrontation of first great gaw, Waada Samba, with the Dina marabouts at Hambdalaye, Sheikou Hamadou, the Fula emperor, cried out, "The marabouts did not lie, nor did Waada Samba lie, but I will say the marabouts are right because white must not be beaten by black!" To which Waada Samba, magnanimous and diplomatic, responded, "God is always right!"

In the Sahel, white is the color of Islam, the color of the Friday prayer, and the one preferred by the marabouts, disseminators of the cult. The fetishists (kafirs) rally around black, and it recalls the aggressive magic for which animals the color of night are sacrificed. Black genii are considered by people to be much more dangerous than white genii.

Baana, the gangi-bibi par excellence, is blackness and paganism incarnate. The Muslims have tried everything to convert him, but he has never let them have their way; he has always refused. More-

---

12. Over the overt geography of the region is superimposed the secret geography of the Ghimbala. The holes of the river considered most important are those that kept their water during the great drought at the turn of the century. This drought was so terrible that even the Niafunké reach went dry and people cultivated millet in its bed. So the genii took refuge in the holes in which water remained. They continue to frequent these more than the others. These great holes are said to be connected to each other from one branch of the river to the other through subterranean passages. Thus, according to Sina Kala of Sokoura, a hole on the Bara Issa near his village communicates with one on the Ambéri branch of the river and with a third facing the village of Bia on the Issa Ber, the river's main course.

The genii's places also bear evocative and precise names that situate them immediately in local space: "the great tamarind tree near the pile of cow dung," "the hole near the sandbank with the hippopotamuses," "the hole where the sweetest tamarind tree is."

over, he is stronger than the Muslim genii. His priests wear dark cottons, and the animals sacrificed to him are of his color exclusively: hens, sheep, and especially the *bundi,* the black billy goat, his favorite animal.

The sacrificial colors of the other great genii are less important. They tend more toward red for Mayé, who is also a blatant pagan and wears brown clothing. The animals offered to Moussa are sometimes the same as the ones offered to Baana, although people prefer to offer him a white sheep with black eyes (the *kobiri*). This animal corresponds to the color of his *turki,* a loincloth made of two triangles and held together at the base with a hole in the middle for the head to pass through, which the possessed put on when they dance. The fluctuation in Moussa's sacrifices sheds light on the ambiguity of his position in relation to Islam. In principle, he is a Muslim, but his faith often vacillates. Is there not a slogan of Moussa's that proclaims, "At Mecca, he is in the first row for prayer, but when he takes someone he completely forgets his faith"? Moussa oscillates between the two poles and shows himself to humans sometimes under one, sometimes under the other aspect. He is, of course, more dangerous when he gives in to his pagan propensities.

Awa, always in white, is the guarantor of Islamic purity. Her favorite sheep, the *karakorey* with golden eyes, has an immaculate coat. She nonetheless accepts lightly spotted animals (the *herdi,* for example) on condition that their coats are more white than not. Awa and Baana's marriage is thus the alliance of opposites. Perhaps it signifies the understanding necessary between Islam and the old territorial cult, transformed into a cult of possession through contact with the Islamic invaders? However, Awa's Islam separates her from her husband, with whom she sometimes fights. This detail is furnished by some tales of the probatory tests Baana had to pass to marry the Ghimbala princess. And it is Baana who triumphed. Awa uses the very great knowledge God has given her, but Baana, beyond his legendary physical force, possesses occult powers superior still. This most powerful of the Ghimbala is a black genii. When he descends, he attacks Muslims, whether human or genie. The popular religion of the region's inhabitants does not lean in favor of Islam, although the immense majority of followers claim they are believers, make their daily prayers, and respect the fasting period, even if they don't follow it by abstaining from any cult activities during this time. Awa and Baana's antagonistic marriage is one of convenience. In fact, they are not often together because the one must respect Islamic taboos and the other those of the kafirs, but this did not impede their marriage.

THE GENII AND PEOPLE RESPOND
TO EACH OTHER

The world of the genii and that of people are similar, even if the former's extraordinary capacities cannot be measured against normal achievements. Magic bridges the gap, and because of it the border between the normal and the exceptional is always porous. Thus the genii reproduce human traits and the organization of the human world. The Ghimbala embody the whole range of human sentiment. According to circumstances and the individual concerned, they are by turns good, peaceful, and brave or angry, lying, and violent. They form a feudal society, with its nobles, marabouts, servants, captives, and people of low caste, just like local society. In this the Ghimbala closely resemble the djiné don of western Mali, with whom I worked previously.

The great genii behave in ways much marked by their positions of dominance. They are impulsive and move easily from their impulses to criminal acts, such as when Awa heard of the death of her son and massacred all in her path. They sometimes commit monstrous acts, as when Komaïga and his wife stewed their own daughter and served her up in pieces to suitors who would have been happy to have just her hand (see appendix 2). In this, they are hardly worse than the great ones of this world who enjoy boundless, unrestrained power—such as Dinga, dark hero of the legend Dupuis-Yakouba obtained at the turn of the century in the Ghimbala region.[13] In the legend, we see this great criminal raised to the rank of a prince who kills, pillages, robs, and betrays shamelessly. Invincible, he dies a natural death. The definition Julien Gracq gave the Shakespearean hero seems to apply to both of them: "A crowned beast remains a beast with the power to kill and constrain immensely: nothing but a man with a belly, a money-bag and a fly, brusquely full of lightning, immediately, naively, tranquilly monstrous."[14]

But in a way the genii are more just, their actions more predictable. One can make their domination, their violence, stop by appropriate acts because there exists a law, a set of rules. One has to apply them during rituals, to know the incantations, to establish debate with the genii from which ruse and peasant good sense are never lacking.[15]

13. See Dupuis-Yakouba, "La Légende de Dinga," in *Essai de Méthode Pratique pour l'Etude de la Langue Songoï,* Leroux, 1917.

14. Julien Gracq, *Lettrines 2* (José Corti, 1978), 83.

15. This is an attribute of Africa's pagan religions, land-based religions, peasant religions. See what Marc Augé has accurately said in *Génies du Paganisme* (Gallimard,

With luck, those who know them well—the gaw, for example—can make an equitable deal between the two parties. The genii, alerted by the reminder of their slogans, flattered by the repetition of the usual praises, overwhelmed by the offerings and sacrifices, let up their pressure, stop tormenting people, return to their homes. But the right words must be spoken and the animal sacrificed must be attractive and healthy. The genii are basically just, whereas human arbitrariness is limitless.

The genii continue to explain the world in the making. They embodied and still embody the conflict between Islam and paganism. Their existence gives meaning to what occurs.

In colonial times, people also called on the genii to account for the troubles caused by these changes. For example, during the 1920s, Lake Oro was developed by a series of hydraulic projects. On several occasions, the breakwaters and dams broke. People saw the intervention of the local genii in this. The ultimate success of the enterprise was attributed to the victory of the Europeans over their adversaries, who were captured—except for Ali Soutouraré. Here is the story told about those troubles by Amadoun Coulibaly, a gaw who comes from the Bambara village of Nbétou to the south of Niafunké:

> After the deaths of Waada Samba and Sheikou Hamadou, Ali Soutouraré settled in Takadji pool toward Tondidarou, near Niafunké. When the Europeans dammed Lake Oro, he demolished their work. So a white man came from France and demanded that all the genii be caught, or else their efforts would not work. There were three genii—one in Lake Fati, another in Takadji, the third in Lake Oro. The white man was able to lay hold of the one in Fati, Baroutou Djini, after capturing Moussa of the

---

1982) about the relationships people establish with their gods in polytheistic societies.

He expands on his thinking in *Le Dieu Objet* (Flammarion, 1988), in which he writes in particular, "People and gods resemble each other and need each other: people need the indulgence and favor of the gods, the gods the offerings and sacrifices of people" (22). But these manipulations are dangerous: "It would be better to say, so as to eliminate the ambiguity of the term 'instrumental' (as one does not do what one likes with the gods), that they are manipulable, as electric or atomic energy may be, but at the manipulator's own risk: the chain reactions unleashed are not always controllable" (94–95).

What Augé has written about the *vodu* of the Gulf of Benin, who also often incarnate in ritualized possessions, applies to the genii of the Ghimbala. The genii are nevertheless more circumscribed spatially, more separate from people, perhaps because of Islamic influence. Yet sessions of possession are the occasions on which people and gods draw closer together, and even sometimes the occasions for a certain confusion, dangerous indeed when the official meaning conferred on these public events crumbles.

Oro.[16] Here is how they were caught: the men saw the genie in their binoculars, they used their secrets, and they dove into the water with their magic to seize the genie.

They put Moussa of the Oro in a bottle. They put the stoppered bottle in a house. When the white man who had come from France left, the genie got out of the bottle. Each time the white man returned, he found the genie before him. He said, "If I shut you up in a trunk, will you get out?" "Yes," said the genie. The white man opened a trunk and the genie went into it. The white man closed the trunk and took the key. The genie wasn't able to get out of the trunk. "You told me you could get out of the trunk. Why couldn't you?" "Because you betrayed me." "Well, someone has to betray someone."

So the white man took Moussa of the Oro to France and also took the genie of the Fati. The white man came back, but the genii remained prisoners in France. Then the whites went to Takadji to catch Ali Soutouraré. They did everything they could to catch him, but they didn't catch him. They saw the genie in their binoculars and tried to take him, but he always escaped them. So the white man built a house on the shore of Lake Takadji and said, "I won't go away until I've captured that genie!"

Ali Soutouraré was tired, the white man too. The genie went to confide in a marabout from Tondidarou and asked for his protection: "There is a man who has taken all my friends; I'm the last one left." During this time, the whites were following the genie's trail with their binoculars and saw him go into the marabout's house to hide. They came to this man's house and asked him whether he had seen someone come to hide there. The marabout asked, "Who is this someone?" "A certain genie."

The marabout said he hadn't seen him. [At this point in the story, Amadoun brought out two bells, sounded them, and set them down in front of himself for protection.] One of the whites then said, "Let's go. When we come back, if you haven't opened the door so we can find the genie, you'll see what will happen to you!" After their departure, the marabout took sand from their trail and said over it, "May they never come back to my house!" And they never came back. Ali Soutouraré remained a while with the marabout. . . .

16. Moussa of the Oro is an incarnation of Moussa but not the great Moussa himself.

In the middle of 1985, the flooding of the Niger was satisfactory for once: the waters violently reached even branches and pools that had lain dry for a long time. So the people of the river, seized by fear of seeing the elements upset in reverse excess, sacrificed numerous black billy goats to appease the anger of Baana, the unconquerable captive. People thus continue to ask the inhabitants of their river, lakes, and dunes to soften the rigors of their existence. But Baana and his followers do not always respond in the way they hope and sometimes even assault the faithful. People are not all equal in these confrontations; some, the gaw and certain others, have privileged relationships with the genii.

4 / Children of the River

THOSE WHO KNOW THE GENII

Gaw means "one who knows." A great fisher is a fish-gaw; a great hunter, one who knows the animals in the bush, is a gaw of the hunt. When you master your work, you become gaw. We are the genii-gaw; a marabout is the gaw of God."

This is how Kola Gaba describes it. A genii-priest of Dabi village, near Niafunké, he is a large, dry man of about sixty; spare and laconic, yet precise; lively and imperious in word and gesture; his gaze goes deep. With his mere presence, he conveys mastery and authority. His direct influence extends from the west and northwest of Ghimbala to the lower part of Farimaké, towards Léré, and he is well known beyond the entire upper bend of the Niger.[1] He lives on a vast piece of land at the edge of the village, opposite the mosque and the imam's home.

Kola Gaba's own house is always animated, full of numerous dependents and clients, and in marked contrast to the surrounding poverty of neighboring plots without the impression of opulence. The Gabas have held power over the Bara Issa waters between Guidio Saré and Issafaye since the time of Barakoy Souleymana, their first known ancestor. Until recently, anyone who wanted to fish these waters had to request the authorization of one of his descendants. At the end of the last century, Kola Gaba's grandfather came to live in the Dabi region, where Kola Gaba's father grew up. The genii came to his father when he was still very young.

> He was at play outside the village when he met them. "When you go home, you must not reveal that you have seen us," one of them told him. My father promised to be quiet. He went home and said nothing to anyone. Then he fell ill and remained ill for a year. Afterward, he screamed and called out the name of the *malé* [master] who was to heal him.[2] Marabouts and gaw tried to treat him, without success. He told them, "Don't worry;

---

1. Farimaké is the northwestern part of Ghimbala.
2. "He screamed" is one of the ways of naming possession, referring to the fact that the possessed screams at the moment the genie takes him or her.

the one who must heal me is close by. Her name is Fatoumata Harkoussou; she is my malé."

They brought him to this woman, who treated him until he was entirely healed. Fatoumata then told him, "I won't ask you to pay. May God grant you luck here and in the other world!" Later, when my father became gaw, Fatoumata sent sick people to him to treat. My father healed them.

One evening when my father was already in bed, the genii of the region came to find him: "We have a woman traveling who has just given birth; we cannot do anything for her, so you must take her in." He took her and brought her to his home. The genii had clearly told him, "This foreign woman will be your ally."

The genie-woman and her child stayed with him for three months. My father fed them. The child grew. One day, the genie-woman said to him, "I am leaving today. You have become one of our brothers. To the end of our race, no one will hurt you. Instead, people will do you good; they will help you; they will serve your sons, your grandsons, and all your descendants."

The woman had given birth at the bottom of a dune near the village. All of Dabi knows this story, and if you ask at the surrounding villages—Gombo, Corrienzé-Haoussa, Waki—people will tell you that it is true. The genii came to find me in turn. They made me ill. My father treated me. I got better, and then they struck me again. My father again healed me, and then he died. So they came back. Hamma Gombo, one of my father's students, had been put in charge of me. He healed me once and for all, and I married his daughter Koumba when I myself became gaw.

Bili Korongoy is an immense, gaunt old man with huge, impressive hands. At a less advanced age, he must have possessed exceptional physical strength. He still sometimes displays great energy, as on the evening I saw him dancing, leaping, and crying out when Moussa possessed him, or on another occasion when he gained control of a crazy man to put leg irons on him. His gaze reflects a certain brutal violence, mixed with trickery. He lives in Gaïrama, a village a few kilometers west of Diré. He is *dimadio*, that is, descended from a Fula captive. But he has always lived among fisherpeople in Koronghoy-Béri, near Issafaye. His father and grandfather were also gaw.

I inherited my genii from my father, who had them from his. The first time I was struck, my father was still living. I was not fully a man yet. I was paralyzed for a year and three months.

Although I could no longer walk, I continued to speak normally. During my illness, I made my n'jarka and played the genii's songs all the time.[3] I spent day and night with them. I was happy in the company of no one else; I needed no one else.

My father was already too old to handle me, for my strength was far superior to his, especially when the gangi possessed me. He put me into the care of Abacina Boureima Mahaman, near Alvalidji, who did not manage to heal me. A man came from the East who treated the genii-sickness and who could unmask witches. His name was Sobon. He healed me. It was a real miracle—I could get up, and everyone was astounded. Sobon then put me into the care of his student Bokar Sourgou. This man was my third master. I stayed with him until his death.

These gaw treated me. Bokar Sourgou took me on as an apprentice also, but I learned all the plants I use and my way of healing by myself with the one I alone could see.[4] I learned everything according to my own understanding and thanks to the help of the genii—also thanks to the help of God, who gave me the genii so that they would teach me. The genii loved me so much that they sought me all the time, like something they might lose.

Sina Kala is the gaw of Sokoura, a little village downstream from the township of Sah on the Bara Issa, one of the main branches of the river. In the beginning of 1985, he was a man with the strength of years. Medium-sized, massive, but completely muscular, he has an odd, round head with a great face on which the nose, jutting cheekbones, and direction of his gaze give off a concentrated power. He is the descendant of a line of Sorko, the people who have always been priests of the genii. They are also great fishers, and hunters of elephants, hippopotamuses, and caimans.

I was still a child when the genii struck me. I stayed paralyzed for a year; my father treated me. He held a batou;[5] I was taken by my genie and then healed. My father said that I would cry out no more until after his death. When he died, the genii came back into me; they made me sick again, and I couldn't move for three years. My mother and my elder brother called all the gaw

3. The n'jarka is the single-stringed violin whose sound is particularly effective in making the genii descend. It is called *ngoyé* in the eastern Songhay lands.
4. An allusion to his protective genie.
5. *Batou* is the generic term for any public session of the cult. Here it refers to a batou held for healing.

to try to treat me. Moussa Bokar came, Leya Moussa came, Maga Moussa came. They did smoke purifications; they asked my elder brother to slit two chickens' throats to get "the work" moving, after which they slit the throat of a white sheep.[6] Then they held batous for seven nights. . . .

The sickness went away and then returned. When there was an improvement, I began to walk again, and then I fell and lost consciousness. I moved no more than a corpse; people brought me into our yard. When I went to fish, the genii drew me into the water and dragged me down to the bottom of their holes. Then, when they had had enough of me, they sent me back up. That lasted three years.

At the river's edge, facing Sokoura, there is a place planted with three huge trees. This place is called Seitirey [as he spoke, the gaw pointed to the cluster of trees on the other bank]. Each time my illness returned I would dash over there. This happened often in the middle of the day. One day when I was over there at noon, I saw five people come out of the river. They were completely dripping with water in the strong sun, yet they did not look wet. When I saw them coming toward me, I wanted to cry out; I couldn't. I wanted to run; I couldn't.

One wore a white boubou, and that was Moussa. The other was Mayé, with a sombé in one hand, wearing a striped boubou. There also were Awa Gafouré, Samba Poulo, and Mama Kyria. When they came to where I was, the genie named Samba Poulo spit on me. I was covered with water from head to toe. Then they sat ringed around me. Samba Poulo wore an ocher boubou and also had a sombé. They said nothing to me, and I said nothing. Then they arose to go back into the water. But just as they left, they declared, "If someone is possessed, all you need do is knock your head against theirs, and they will calm down."[7]

In fact, it was Samba Poulo who said that. When they reentered the water, there was a great wake, as though a very wide pirogue had just passed. I got up after they left and dried off Samba Poulo's spittle, in which I was covered.

Before meeting them, my whole body hurt. Afterward, the pains stopped. It was a Thursday; I went to meet my big sister Aissata in a fishers' encampment nearby. I sat down next to her, and almost immediately I was possessed. The people encamped

6. "The work" (*goy* in Songhay) here means "the treatment."

7. Samba Poulo reveals to the apprentice gaw one of the expeditious ways to stop a trance—a procedure that gives tangible results, as I have witnessed myself.

gained control of me. When the possession was over, I no longer felt pains in my body; I was healed. Soon, I began to treat people. But since that time I see those people on the nights between Thursdays and Fridays.[8] I see them when I sleep; they tell me when something important or serious is going to happen.

FAMILIARITY WITH THE WATER

Almost all gaw, like those just described, are born to families who have had an intimate relationship with the world below for generations. Thus, dealings with the genii come of the families' long establishment in the inner delta of the Niger, their intimacy with the river, and their long experience with the watery universe.

These gaw are the descendants of the Wakorey, the first inhabitants of the area; are related to the old masters of the waters, as is Kola Gaba, whose Baranké ancestors held the Bara Issa; may be Sorko, and thus fisherpeople like Sina Kala; or, finally, may be Koronghoy rowers who spend their lives on the water, as is Douré, whose story is told later.[9] In the south of the region, where Fula hegemony is more marked, numerous priests are descendants of captives, probably because the heads of their lineages did not wish to renounce their privileged relations with the genii from their prior positions as Wakorey, Baranké, or Sorko water-masters.

This seems to be the case for the descendants of Waada Samba, who founded the cult during the time when the village of Doundé was surrounded by water. Oussou Kondjorou, his direct descendant, remembers that his family possessed mastery of the waters of the great Awgoundou pool and the floodplain near it. The present Malian government has abolished these ancient rights. Oussou limits his own rituals of propitiation before rainy season to the territory of his own village. The rituals are intended to obtain the protection and assistance of the genii, especially that of Oussou's master, Baana, so that abundant rains will make future harvests sufficient. "We are certainly not going to make sacrifices in areas that have been taken from us," he says. "If we did, people would believe we were casting evil spells."

A decreasing number of gaw come from above. They live in the villages beyond the flood zone and come from families that have had close relationships with genii, even if they were not the Ghimbala genii. These priests—descendants of the Bambara hunters or the Song-

---

8. "Those people" is a turn of phrase used to avoid speaking the names of the gangi too often. Otherwise they might show themselves in an untimely way.

9. See chapter 7.

hay magicians, for example—are usually less powerful than those who come from below.

How Mahaman Became a Genii-Griot

Those who live near the places the genii frequent, who pass through their lands, and who travel outside the villages and townships during the dangerous times reserved for these invisible and powerful beings meet them more often than most people. Their lives can be completely altered by these encounters, as happened to Mahaman Kontao, descendant of the masters of Lake Faguibine's waters. He tells how he came to speak the secret language of the genii one night as he passed near Issafaye, where the Bara Issa meets the main branch of the Niger.[10]

I was traveling alone at night in my pirogue. Between Issafaye and Kanayé, at Kaffa Sirati, I saw some seated people. I was facing them; I thought they were human beings. I came over to greet them. As I made my greetings to them, I lost consciousness.

When I came to again, I returned to my pirogue and left for Goundam. For a month and seven days I ate nothing, because food seemed to smell bad to me. I could only take a little rice mixed with milk. I lay down; I was sick. But when I was lying down, those I had met when I was in the pirogue came to me and surrounded me. They each told me their names. When I got better, I remembered everything they had told me. The gangi said much in front of me. They ordered me to make a little koubour; I made it.

There was a big batou being held in Tindirma.[11] I went there; I was still very young. No one could figure out how to have the village gaw possessed by his gangi. When I began to sing, everyone was astounded by my knowledge, and everyone asked me where I had cultivated it. How could a human being gain knowledge of things that had been buried for so long? So the gangi came to explain the thing before everyone who was assembled:[12]

10. It is true that Mahaman speaks in an idiom incomprehensible even to my companions when he talks to the genii. Afterward he has often translated for us the praises, flatteries, and slogans he used. Alongside words that may be purely personal creations, there exist, according to my interpreter-translators, words that sound Soninké. The many recordings that I hold of this secret language remain to be studied.

11. Tindirma is the last historically Songhay population center to the west.

12. The gangi "came to explain the thing" through the mouths of the possessed, who transmitted their messages.

"We gave Mahaman his knowledge. We want to keep this child with us to give him many more things still."[13]

From that day on, all the gaw received me, and I accepted working with each one so there was no jealousy. But ultimately I had to return to the one into whose care the genii put me, Hamadou Fofana, the gaw of Tindirma.

I made no effort to understand the genii's language; they were the ones who found means of making me understand. You have to speak this language to know what a genie likes and what it doesn't like. The teaching is like the meat in a stewpot. When it's completely cooked and you take out the juice, you can separate the meat from the bones.

THE TRUE GAW AND THE OTHERS

After his initiatory illness, Mahaman became the genii's griot, and he knows their secret language. Genii-griots are a gaw's precious familiars, though the griots are not possessed.[14] Each has knowledge complementary to the other. Griots know the sacred history and the special words of each genie, the chants that make them descend into people during the ceremonies. The gaw direct treatment, lead the faithful, and know the secret incantations that make genii favor people. They alone can bear the title gaw, "genii-know-

13. Mahaman's experience is very close to the situation of the bards of archaic Greece, as Marcel Détienne describes it: "He is privileged to enter in contact with the other world. His memory allowed him to "decipher the invisible." Memory is thus not only the material means of the chanted word, the psychological function that supports formulaic technique, but also and especially the religious power which confers on the poetic utterance its status as a magico-religious word. In effect, the chanted word, pronounced by a poet gifted with sight, is an effective word. By its own virtue it sets up a symbolico-religious world which is the real itself" (Détienne, *Les Maîtres de Vérité dans la Grèce Archaïque* [Maspero, 1967], 15). In the same way, Mahaman's inspired words possess an effectiveness that permits them to act upon the real: when he calls, the gods descend upon people.

One can extend these correspondences further. Détienne writes a little further on, concerning a divination during sleep: "On leaving the incubatory consultation, the initiate is given a memory, a gift of sight that is no different from that of poets and diviners" (47). Mahaman acquired his knowledge while conversing with genii in his sleep.

14. The griots of the genii should not be confused with the griots of humans. Sometimes the two functions are combined, but it is also very common to meet people who, like Mahaman, are not griots of rank and who are content to flatter and praise the genii rather than their peers.

ers," because their experience of the Ghimbala world is the most profound.

The Genii's Elect

All gaw are not equal; they do not all enjoy the same powers nor the same degree of intimacy with the genii. The young person who wants to become a gaw links up with a master, who passes on his or her knowledge after treating and healing the apprentice. He or she reveals to the young person the names of the genii's plants, the way to pick them, and the incantations to speak while doing so. The master explains how the treatments unfold, from the earliest smoke purifications to the most intricate therapeutic rituals; how to slit the throats of the sacrificial animals and what words one must say at that time; what to murmur over a patient's body. He or she teaches the student how to conduct a ceremony of worship, what to say and do as it unfolds, what treatment to give. If the people heal, they will call the student gaw even if she or he is still working with the master, the malé, who has not yet consecrated her or him.

In point of fact, the apprentice will have simply applied techniques while lacking the "true knowledge" that only the genii can give the student—the knowledge of the "true gaw," as Mahaman Tindirma says. Who are these "true gaw"? They are the ones not satisfied with learning under a master; a gaw's teaching has never sufficed to make a student his or her equal. The true gaw acquire their knowledge directly from the genii because "it is the gangi who make you gaw," according to Moussa Founé Nabo, priest of the Dondoro encampment between Sebi and Dabi.

The genii choose their gaw, come to them, and take them to their world. The expression of their preference takes the form of an ordinary attack. But let there be no mistake: there are those the genii simply want to make sick, and then there are the elect, those who are struck because the genii love them and take them, not out of meanness or self-interest, but to transmit their most secret knowledge.

Here, in brief, is how it happens. The gangi might tip over a pirogue and drag the one they love by the hand to the depths without killing the child, as they did to Sina Kala. When the child reappears above, among people, he or she necessarily falls ill because he or she has been in the genii's hands. The child's family then helps the local gaw to organize a batou. During the ceremony, the genii make a possessed person cry out the name of the person who must heal the child. The family cannot obtain healing of the child without taking her or him to the designated gaw. This gaw cares for the child successfully and makes a student of the young patient. Yet the gaw knows that the patient does not become gaw thanks to his or her efforts: the student's "gaw-being" is received directly from the genii.[15]

The Three Sources of Knowledge

A great gaw such as Kola Gaba, Bili Korongoy, or Sina Kala receives the benefit of a triple apprenticeship. A father wards off the genii and provides the child's first treatment, passing on the most rudimentary knowledge. But the child undergoes decisive treatment and definitive training at the side of another. Finally, throughout this entire time, those who initiate the child and are invisible to most mortals never let the child go. It is with them that the child will acquire the essential components of future mastery.

The gaw who directs the apprenticeship of such a young person knows rather quickly that she or he is working with someone whose destiny is unusual because the genii love and have come to that person. The gaw notices all this by observing the student's behavior. The student seeks to be alone, talks to himself or herself, and goes often to the bush or to the river's edge where the Ghimbala are. The gaw finds confirmation of her or his intuition from the genii themselves when they speak in dreams and trances, and understands that this one who is ill is predestined to receive an otherworldly education.

For the apprentice gaw whose family is amenable, his or her own desire to become a priest and the master's recognition reinforce the primary aspiration breathed into her or him by the genii. They impel the apprentice to discover new plants, make new instruments for worship, and invent new healing techniques. Thus do the separate heritages of the new gaw—passed on from the parent, taught by the master, and directly acquired from the genii—form an indissoluble whole.

THE GAW'S HERITAGE

First of all, the gaw's heritage includes the practice of possessive trance itself. This ability is shared with other worshipers but is made possible by the gaw's mastery. Then there is the technical know-how related to worship, which has been mentioned above and will be detailed further on. Finally and especially, there is all that allows her or him to constitute the gaw-being.

15. "Gaw-being" is my translation of the Songhay expression *sanda amaka gaw:* "how he becomes gaw."

From Initiatory Travels to Therapeutic Dreams

The gaw willingly tell about their early travels to the waters' bottom. According to some, these trips can sometimes last several years. I have even met one who prided himself on seven years of such seclusion. Public opinion echoes what they say. Down there, the genii-captors oblige them to serve in a world that so closely resembles the one above that the protected prisoners mistake one for the other when they awake in the morning: houses, places, and genii who go about their daily work. They meet other children there, also carried off from their families and transformed into small servants. One detail emerges often in all their tales: aspiring gaw and genii come very close to each other, but never touch. The genii cannot stand the odor of the humans. They hold their noses and turn away with disgust when the children hand their food to them. These trips take place at the time of the gaw's first disturbances and in their trial years, during which their vocation as gaw becomes apparent.

When they see their genii, is it in a state of aware dreaming, in the imagination, or as a double? I was never really able to find out. In any case, once the initiatory period ends, the gaw keep up these meetings through their dreams on the nights between Thursday or Friday or between Sunday and Monday, which both belong to the Ghimbala. For this they prepare with smoke purifications of plants mixed with incense, and the sleep alone, far from their spouses. Then the gangi show themselves during their sleep and speak to them. The gaw see them and receive more or less information according to the degree of favor in which they are held. The messages particularly concern treatments that are in process: which plants to use, which sacrifices and offerings to make, to which genii to turn, or perhaps to which other priest to send the patient. During these hallucinatory interviews, gaw and genii converse "mouth to mouth," to use Mahaman Tindirma's expression. Those unable to communicate with the genii after a simple smoke purification bring them on by appropriate offerings. Still others manage to see the genii but obtain only a modicum of information from them. The better beloved the gaw, the better he or she will be served, and thus the more powerful.

Alliances with Greater and Lesser Genii

Everything distinguishes the genii's elect from their mere victims. The former are the allies of a powerful genie, normally one of the six who lead the Ghimbala. The latter are simply possessed by those with the same names as the lead genii or by little-known genii and can never become gaw. Priests who want to make contact with the invisible world first speak with their personal genii. These are the ones that made them gaw by giving them the essentials of their knowledge. Then the priests invoke the other great genii who descend to possess human beings of Ghimbala territory between Timbuktu, Lake Débo, and Ngouma. Finally, gaw call the great genii of the past who never now incarnate but who are known by all.

The most powerful gaw also have at their disposal a band of genii in their service often known only to them. The ranks of this private group can be large or small and are composed of lesser genii belonging to each village. This is why they vary in number from one priest to another. They are part of each gaw's heritage. Some were discovered by the gaw, who convinced them to serve. Invoking them accompanies invoking the principal genii. The gaw who has them at his or her disposal reinforces his or her powers.

Instruments and Adornments

A gaw's apparatus is an astonishing mix of seemingly incongruous instruments and strange adornments, particularly the headdresses and diverse head ornaments worn when the priest officiates or heals. I especially know of two kinds, the *sessey* and the *badji-foula*. The first is a simple band tied tightly around the head. It is decorated with a large talisman enveloped in a leather sheath sewn onto the band, and it is set in the middle of the gaw's forehead like a spelunker's headlamp. The second is topped by an impressive mane of red wool and was once made of tanned bark; it is now made of cloth. Information on how to make it is breathed to the protégé by his or her personal genie, as Douré, gaw of Sadjilambou, explains so well further on in telling how he acquired his. Final dedication of the headdress comes from the master presiding over the apprenticeship. The gaw with neither cap nor decorated headband wears a sumptuous turban studded with different amulets.

When exercising her or his functions, a gaw always uses a weapon, which is an instrument at once of power and of protection. The ones who have Mayé among their familiar genii—whether or not they are his priests—use the sombé, emblem of the genie of the floods, a dual-pointed scepter that resembles a pelican's head. They always have it with them when they go out, even if on a long journey. Gaw who do not have the sombé substitute a spear or a chain.

Material accessories of the genii-priesthood vary infinitely: hunting whips, flyswatters, bells, necklaces made of diverse stones, pendants and talismans, and unexpected tools, such as the pair of pincers in the apparatus of Hamadou Boureïma, the gaw of Mékorey, near Sumpi. He is a direct descendant of a comrade of Waada Samba.

A student gaw attains autonomy upon taking possession of the cult instruments, which serve as receptacles of strength and power over people and genii. From this day on, the student cannot do without them. Bili Korongoy says, for example, that he must wear his cap to see his genii. Hamadou Fofana, Tindirma's gaw, is required by his genii to produce his bells at each ceremony, under pain of their refusal to come if he forgets these indispensable accessories. At the beginning of each session, the gaw speaks incantations over the spear or sombé, which he or she then drives into the ground near the musicians to protect the session against disturbance by other genii. Since Oussou Kondjorou lost the handle of Baana's sombé, which he had inherited from that great ancestor, he is satisfied with throwing the remaining metal part into the bomboutou as a precaution.

THE GAW HIERARCHY

Thus true mastery of the Ghimbala postulates a double apprenticeship, a double investiture—one by humans and one by the genii. The great gaw are those who directly experience the world of the gangi and who develop this experience. They accrue the greatest number of advantages in order to succeed. They acquire their knowledge from the most powerful genii, whom they meet often during their disturbed youth and with whom they continue to converse in their dreams. They have a large band of genii at their disposal, which reinforces their powers. Great gaw capture people's imaginations with their inspired actions, shattering divinations, sovereign attitudes, and, above all, therapeutic efficacy. Their inventiveness and success are of course attributed to the fact that the genii coddle and assist them, preferring them to their competitors.

At the bottom of the gaw hierarchy one finds all those who enjoy no gifts of clairvoyance and who keep to therapeutic activity to the exclusion of religious practices; during the course of this, they do not enter into direct contact with the genii. These gaw are often simply maintaining a family tradition. The one who has gone before—parent, elder sibling, or other relative—was able to maintain intimate relations with the gangi, for example, by being possessed or organizing batous. The heirs don't have these abilities and heal only with what they have inherited from their predecessors, without having directly seen the genii. The genii might reappear later because they sometimes skip a generation. Thus among Waada Samba's descendants there have been only four gaw who have been elect of the genii since their great ancestor. On the other hand, the ineffectiveness of a gaw may mark the beginning of a regression. Such gaw would in essence be turning away from their family heritage, distancing themselves from the Ghimbala world.

Most gaw I met move between these two levels of skill. They don't possess the great gaw's full mastery, but unlike the lower-level gaw they do possess certain gifts of clairvoyance. In particular, they share with the great gaw the experience of possessive trance, for one of the great Ghimbala genii descends into them and makes them gaw. Thus they are able to organize public sessions and direct a group of followers. The lower-level gaw do not enter into trance, are not leaders of the cult, and instead occupy the position of lay magicians: they use the healing techniques designed to reduce the illnesses inflicted by the genii without really being acquainted with the genii. These unequal relationships to the world of the genii, which differentiate the gaw, play a large role in the way treatment is conducted, and they are an essential aspect of this therapeutic cult.

Female Gaw

Women are fewer than men among the ranks of the priesthood of the Ghimbala cult. Here are the reasons the male gaw and the genii-griots give: "The gangi love purity, and a woman cannot always be pure because of her menstrual period and her birthing. So it's difficult for a woman to be a gaw, and women are fewer among us. The gangi will make a woman pure by stopping her period and making her sterile. They also love discreet people: they hate to have their secrets revealed, and that is also why it's difficult for a woman to be a gaw."

I've nonetheless noted the existence of several priestesses during my stays; I've met some and have even interviewed one of them several times. Awa Koulikoro, an energetic and subtle woman of about fifty, hair already white, is descended of a Wakorey family and lives in Sebi, a village that still holds rights over the waters and the local soil, a privilege of the first to occupy the lands. But she serves as a gaw in the neighboring village of Kormou. She sometimes goes to Sebi to make sacrifices and offerings on two black rocks that she inherited, set in a street in the village and dedicated to Baana and Awa, who appeared to one of her ancestors in this very place. She has also given birth to several children, of whom the eldest have in turn had children. Not among the first rank of the priesthood, she nonetheless enjoys a solid reputation.

A woman can thus be a gaw without being condemned to sterility, but she stops all cult activities during her menstruation because the genii distance themselves from her at that time. She doesn't gather plants, doesn't prepare powders and potions, leads no rituals, and organizes no batous, and if she happens to attend a ceremony she is not possessed by her genie. Despite these constraints, the names of certain great priestesses, elect of the genii, are passed on to posterity and still evoked by followers today, as much in private conversation as during ceremonies.

THE GENII CULTURE

The lives of everyday people in the upper bend who believe in the existence of the Ghimbala are marked by concrete signs of the presence of these genii. Has an overcharged pirogue capsized on the river? Has a retaining wall given way? Has the flood entered a pool too violently and drowned a young shepherd? Followers see in each of these events the work of their familiar genii—feared, invisible, but visibly marking the world by their actions.

Gaw and griots, who converse with the genii in a kind of delirium when they experience periods of clairvoyance, are considered not crazy but exceptional: beloved of those who govern the elements and press their laws heavily on people; different from mere mortals, whom the genii attack but never converse with privately. With these personages are also included certain great singers because of their talent.

The singers' performances nourish the vitality of the genii culture throughout the Ghimbala lands. With their songs and stories they maintain an atmosphere of legend in daily life. This they strengthen by mingling stories of the great, fabled animals that populated the Niger and its branches with evocations of the genii. The ancient, water-based fauna are also linked in song and story to the exploits of great gaw of the still-recent past. The genii had conferred upon these gaw the power to approach and tame hippopotamuses, manatee, and caimans without danger when there were still many of them.[16]

Démoudou, originally from a village near Niafunké, is a man devoured by leprosy. His hands are no more than bloodied stumps, and his face has the characteristic leonine cast the illness gives in its advanced stage: startled eyes, eroded lips, wide-open nostrils. He goes about on foot with great difficulty when he is not astride his donkey. But he possesses a vigorous voice pushed to the point of paroxysm, in contrast to his thinness and physical decay. The piercing tone of his invocations has the gift of making the gangi descend, so he is much in

16. Manatee and caimans seem to have totally disappeared, and hippopotamuses are now rapidly becoming extinct.

demand throughout the region each time a cult session is held. His repertoire greatly resembles those of other Ghimbala balladeers. He speaks of water holes, especially the one where he was kept for three years by the genii. He speaks of his nocturnal travels, during which he goes to meet the genii on his donkey. He speaks of the flood, of Baana who makes the green river waters turn black, of Moussa the blind. He enumerates the names of the great gaw of past and present. Ultimately, he says no more about them than any good genii-griot, but he sings his message in an excessive mode, with an intensity and force that transcend the words' meanings. I will speak of him again in the following chapter.

I discovered Ali Farka Touré at least ten years ago in a Mopti street when I heard one of his songs being played at full volume by a shopkeeper. I went in to hear it better and purchased a copy of the tape; it was about the genii of Lake Débo, of Lake Oro, of Lake Fati, and of course of the Niger River. But I didn't meet the singer until 1985 in Niafunké, where he comes from and spends most of his time. Farka is a big, strapping, athletic man—extremely amiable just the same—who carries off European suits and the immaculate full boubous people of the upper bend don on special occasions with the same panache. His repertoire somewhat synthesizes the culture of the rock-music generation with the genii culture in which he was raised. He once lived as part of the entourage of Kounandi Samba, his grandmother, whom he claims was a great priestess of the Ghimbala. He spent a lot of time with this old woman. She grew attached to the child and began to transmit her knowledge to him. On her death, Farka hesitated to involve himself more fully with the Ghimbala; his own mother finally dissuaded him. His inspiration was a gift from God—and from the genii, who helped him when, as he was looking for something new to add to his music, he happened to use the djerkélé, the single-stringed instrument that particularly moves them. Afterward, he recomposed the songs he had just invented on his guitar.

His conversation roams from the most modern sound-recording techniques and the process of making a record with a multiple-track mixing board in some faraway European studio to the world of the river: the manatee, a veritable floating gourd of butter, he is so fat; the crocodile who "only fights with his teeth" and who's so bad he could be mistaken for a shaytān; the hippopotamus, who is so heavy he "digs tombs" as he moves over the solid earth, though apparently there are great fisherpeople who know how to flatter him so well they make him dance on the water, as light as a calabash. Then they mount his back as they would a horse. He associates these soon-to-be-mythical animals with the Ghimbala genii, whom he has of course also met directly and whose mysterious presence around him he senses every day. In the same breath he can name both the sound technicians who taught him modern recording techniques and his country's great gaw. Of the latter he says, "Thanks to them, I have a well that never goes dry." He has also paid them homage in song: "When these people disappeared, I really had to do something in their memory on my first record."

Ali Farka Touré and Démoudou are also children of the river.

♣
S

Griots, singers, and gaw are heirs to the very old world of the water-genii, whose culture they maintain and disseminate. Among them, the best-known establish themselves as central figures in the Ghimbala cult and master a particularly complicated range of activities: conducting treatments, leading public ceremonies, directing groups of followers and diverse dependents. The components of the gaw-being of these great genii-priests make them personages who in fact recall Siberian or Amazonian shamans, beyond the phenomenon of possession.

A series of Ghimbala beliefs and practices permits me to support this hypothesis. Becoming elect of the genii resembles an initiatory illness, as noted above: flight into the bush, fainting spells, prolonged fasting. The tales of seclusion beneath the waters recall shamanic voyages. There are also instances in which gaw have to maintain mastery over what is happening to them—during treatments, for example, as we will see shortly—and instances in which they use their bands of private genii, who resemble the auxiliary spirits of the Tungus shamans of Siberia.[17]

The techniques of clairvoyance, whether in hallucination or in sleep, and the use of magical hairstyles and clothing call us to the same comparison. Conversely, shamans can be possessed by spirits, but going from shamanic trance (in societies that practice it) to possessive trance is considered an inauspicious accident that risks making the shaman lose his or her powers. The gaw, who are in the positions of

---

17. See Laurence Delaby, "Chamanes Toungouses," *Etudes Mongoles et Sibériennes,* no. 7 (1976). I have borrowed the essential elements of my terms of comparison from this lively, precise monograph, whose author shows us what Tungus shamanism used to be.

shamans, use abilities not in the least condemned by their entourage; on the contrary, their followers see in trance the expression of an even greater power. The worlds of possession and shamanism are not as separate as current anthropological theory seems to affirm.[18] In any case, the great gaw remain, as we will see, guardians of a tradition that is currently threatened.

18. The question of interference between acts of shamanism and acts of possession gave rise a few years ago to the creation of a project of "programmatic action" for which I assumed scientific responsibility, whose title was "Nature et Evolution Comparées du Chamanisme et de la Possession" (in Sahelian Africa, the Amazon basin, and northern Pakistan). Request of ASP ORSTOM/CNRS, Sciences Sociales, October 1985.

Conductors take advantage of a windy day on the Niger to hoist their large patched sail. (All photographs © M. Lerat)

A possessed person acts out a scene from the life of the genii.

Between the above and below: a narrow pirogue moving down the river.

The gaw of Sadjilambou getting ready to dance at the opening of a batou.

Oussou Kondjorou telling the legend of his ancestor, Waada Samba.

Kola Gaba, the gaw of Dabi and one of the best therapists in the upper bend.

The river, path of entry into Ghimbala country; a heavily loaded transport pirogue.

The possessed at the height of his trance rises and drops to the ground like a great night bird.

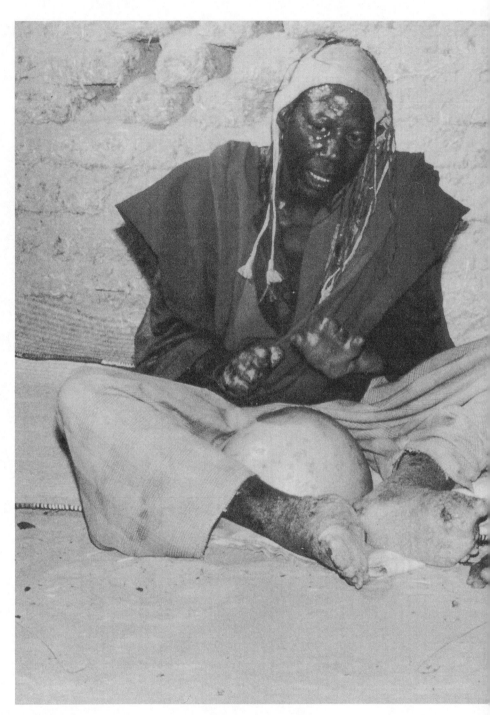

Démoudou (at left) singing while playing the gassou. He is accompanied by a djerkélé.

The priestess Awa Koulikoro between the two rocks where her ancestors saw Awa and Baana appear for the first time, now dedicated as an altar to the genii.

Friday prayer at the Sebi mosque.

Moussa Founé, the Dondoro gaw, invokes the genii before answering the anthropologist's questions.

5 / Live Devils

POSSESSIONS UNDER THE MOON

Tonight there is a full moon like others I saw here ten years ago when I discovered Songhay villages ensconced along the river for the first time. I again find myself delighted just to walk in the sandy streets of Tindirma as light-colored shadows slide along the walls of dried earth. I find Mahaman trying out his koubour before this evening's event. He invites me to sit down while he tunes his instrument, which he begins to play in a masterful way, looking happy, inspired. Soon he will accompany the possession of Hamadou Fofana, the old blacksmith and Ghimbala gaw of this town so heavy with history.

It is the end of February and the nights are already getting hotter. Around us the village is noisy with rumor, and silent shadows continue to slip softly by. I listen to Mahaman's koubour giving off its tremolo notes in the night. In a few moments the batou will begin. The site of the event is so well lit that I will be able to write a few notes without using my flashlight on the sly. The gangi detest full light. This is why they are invoked only at night in the absence of all artificial light, which is strictly forbidden. Moreover, this is the first time I can record "live" and without difficulty a ceremony's unfolding.

The present one seems extremely well organized. Two women flank the choir singers and spur them on; one of them visibly commands the group. Men contain the crowd—many people, but no disorderliness. The musicians let go into the music right from the start, and there is a harshness in it that invades everything: the dull sputtering of the sticks on the bomboutou, the water drums, with their muffled sound, overturned inside basins of water; the *gassou,* calabashes set on the ground, struck with the bare hand; and the koubour, whose voice is a little drowned out by the volume of the percussion instruments.

The genii descend very quickly into the dancing area and the first possessions happen early. Two women are taken by Mayé, disquieting genie of the ponds and holder of the sombé; another by Moussa, the noble old warrior; a fourth by Baana, the most powerful and most feared of the Ghimbala; a fifth by Dia.

71

The old gaw is seated on a mat to the left of the musicians. Draped in a large, black cloth, the sombé planted at his feet, his head held by a band of cloth bearing a talisman that looks like a big eye at his forehead, he remains impassive while the woman possessed by Moussa rolls in the dust screaming. Sometimes one of the possessed drags herself to the feet of the priest to implore who knows what aid. Then she gets up and flogs herself vigorously, as do her companions. The captain of the choir encourages these acts of flagellation with her voice and movements, making her contribution to the general flogging with the very cords she holds in her hand and with which she strikes "the mares of the gods."[1] At a given point, the possessed meet and take up their dance in a ring. The flogging leader herself is not in a trance and guides their parade, which she pulls along with one hand, shaking her instrument of punishment with the other.

As a sixth person falls to the ground screaming and wailing, taken by Awa, Fofana leaps from his seat. The great black cape raised by his running reveals magnificent white pants; a great night-bird, he crosses the dancing area briskly, almost flying. A movement of the crowd signals a new possession in a corner of the enclosed but wide-open space we occupy.

Then, one by one, the possessed are freed of their genii by hands placed on their heads, accompanied by a completely incomprehensible incantation. Moussa's servant, who does not wish to undergo this brief ritual, flies away through the crowd, which prudently moves out of her path. The women in the choir, led by the captain, chase her, catch her, and make her lie down to receive the treatment necessary for the departure of her mystical master.

Way has been made for the old gaw to be possessed, but then a man leaps up from the audience, screaming. Mahaman stands up suddenly and calls on him: it is Moussa who has descended again into one of his "horses." The god incarnate now advances toward the musicians with tense and measured steps and a theatrical attitude, one arm folded over his chest, the other thrusting toward the musicians. Then he reaches the edge of the audience and stops, beginning to scrutinize the night. "He is looking for sorcerors," my neighbor tells me. He returns to the middle of the circle, throws himself onto the sandy dance floor, and finally decides to dance, powerful, leaping, spectacular.

His impressive performance unleashes a series of possessions among the ranks of the faithful. Baana descends on one woman; another and another woman are taken, by whom I can't tell. The session

---

1. This would be rather *gangi-bari* (the horses of the genii) or *holo-bari* (the horses of madness). The second term is the most often used.

starts up again. Attention is newly dispersed, although the moment before all eyes were on the old gaw, who is now content to rock softly on his mat, waiting for this new flame of possessions to consume itself. The man whose trance changed the course of the ceremony throws himself on Mahaman, who cedes his koubour to another musician to declaim Moussa's praises more freely. The words sputter, sonorous, dizzyingly fast.

The horse of the god stops in front of the singer and the musician; he rocks, gasping, leaning forward, legs spread, hands holding his knees. A little farther on another possessed begins to hurl invectives at the possible sorcerors, threatening them with death if they do not flee. Suddenly, everyone laughs and I turn to my neighbor: "The gangi is threatening to tear off their mother's genitals." And he adds, "Tonight it's going to get hot for the sorcerors!" Indeed, Moussa's possessed runs to the street to verify that the sorcerors aren't there, then comes back into the ceremony, where Baana's possessed has begun to sing in honor of Mama Kyria. The third possessed woman begins to dance, stumbling, miming the old, leprous genie with the bloodied hands and feet. Moussa, who is coordinating this sequence, sets himself in front of the musicians and addresses the koubour player while one possessed woman I haven't yet seen goes to greet the gaw on his mat.

A rather confused agitation reigns, even more difficult to grasp now that a slight screen of clouds of variable thickness makes the moonlight capricious. On the ground, the possessed women's delirium grows. One of them rolls frenetically in the dust; she is freed of her genie. She stands up looking dazed and goes home like a sleepwalker. Mama Kyria dances [while] seated on the ground in front of the musicians, while another possessed escapes. She is pursued, belted, and brought by force back into the circle, where Moussa, who has lost his terrifying look, sings in a high, nasal voice, nearly ridiculous.

It is at this moment that Fofana's genie chooses to manifest himself. The gaw stands up, sits back down, gets up again; crosses the dancing area with huge steps, as he did earlier; then comes back to sit down. This he does several times. Finally, his whole body begins to tremble. "There it is! He has been taken!" people say around me. Several men support him now while one of them ties a fluttering cloth around his forehead over the first headband, and another gives him his sombé. During these preparations, Moussa flails himself, standing right in front of the old gaw, who has become Baana. As for Mahaman, he begins declaiming the praises of the unconquerable captive with something like emotion in his voice. The genie-man listens to him, curled in on himself. Then, after this moment of reflection, he goes off, sowing terror by running in all directions amid the crowd, whip in hand: the genii's hardheartedness is like that of humans.

Baana has thus descended into his priest despite the apparently parasitical presence of the other possessed. Now the ceremony is organized around the gaw in a trance, who slowly occupies the whole stage while the other actors in this disorganized drama draw back one by one. First the genie throws himself into a series of handshakes; my own hand is squeezed to a pulp in passing. Then comes a long sequence of quietness and restrained emotion during which the god-priest and his griot converse face to face, the first seated on a grain mortar, the second crouched at his feet. We are, I think, entering a moment of great perfection: the gaw, a great black bird with folded wings perched on his seat, and the griot all in white, stand out against the light sand. Much tenderness filters through the present confrontation, which is nonetheless very ritualized. The dialogue begun so long ago between these two beings who have known each other forever continues this very minute in the mode of a sacred conversation.

But then the quiet is over. Baana stands up, makes a tour of the dance area, plunges into the audience, crosses it, explores the edges of the ceremony behind the crowd, comes back to the front of the stage, and rests on his perch. He rocks briefly there, back to front, panting, then throws himself—despite his age—into a very athletic dance and looks as though he is taking off from the ground. The two tips of his great black cape held out at the ends of his arms like two wings, he rises and falls in place with an incessant pounding of feet.[2] I note: "The old gaw dances like a true god!" He is one, for that matter. Baana-Fofana then loses one of the bands around his forehead; two men run to pick it up and put it back on him. He makes a few more jumping steps, then crouches near his seat, which he holds with effort in order to keep himself up. He curls up to it; he will hardly move anymore. Yet the women redouble their hand claps, chanting and music grow louder, and the possessed priest begins to dance again. Seated on his mortar, throwing arms and legs into the void, he turns, turns on himself as though impaled on his axis. The moon again strongly lights the scene in a sky suddenly cloudless.

The old gaw is impressive in his thinness, and I wonder from what depths of himself the trance can draw such energy. The dialogue between Mahaman and the gaw, who has stopped his curious circular

2. The dance of the Ghimbala always resembles the phantom flight of great nocturnal birds. At the same time, each gaw makes it a point of honor to introduce small variations to denote execution of his or her personal inspiration.

dance, begins again. But not for long, as here he is jumping off again, picking up his sombé, which has sat driven into the ground for a while now in front of the musician. He makes three rounds of the floor, which he ends by planting his scepter in the same spot. It seems to me he is beginning to lose his strength and to move with less vigor than at the beginning of the possession. When he sits back down on the mortar, the other possessed try to massage his shoulders, nape, and head in rhythm, especially Awa, queen of the genii and Baana's wife.

A final exchange begins between the griot and his master while Awa administers the massage with loving gestures. Suddenly, a great cry—the genie has evaporated into the ether! The gaw lies for an instant on the ground. Then he is picked up and he tears off his own forehead band. At top speed, the choir strikes up the chant of the genii's departure, and some assistants start to free the last possessed. Already the audience is leaving. I take my leave of old Fofana, who barely recognizes me after this colossal expenditure of energy. We return to the edge of the river, where we are encamped two kilometers away, in the company of the man who replaced Mahaman at one point on the koubour.

❧

The often convulsive beauty of this batou was first of all a result of the passionate interest people had in it after having been deprived of ceremonies during the preceding years of drought and famine. It also came from the visual and musical perfection of what was achieved there, the bouquet of colors, shapes, and sounds. But how to render in writing (or by any other means, in fact) this concentrate of an experience born of the exchange between exterior perception and mental projection?

I had high expectations that the transcript of the recording I made that evening would help me to set down a bit of what had happened and to go more deeply into it. As usual, it was disappointing. The content of the words exchanged by the possessed and their interlocutors proved to me that one can produce dramatic intensity with a relative paucity of message. Moussa's and Baana's long diatribes were merely exhortations to the people to understand each other and denunciations of sorcerors in vague and allusive terms: "There are people here who wish evil to others." But none of the possessed that whole evening denounced any particular person by name, given how serious such an accusation would be. The behavior of the possessed diving into the crowd was nonetheless imprinted with a violence that went beyond their words. The people who fled—were they simply afraid of the gods incarnate, or did they indeed consider themselves sorcerors? By behaving in that way, didn't they fear the weight of suspicions of witnesses to the scene? It is difficult to grasp the meaning of the stakes revealed for a too-brief instant by these microevents.

A DISCREET AND EFFECTIVE ORDER

Between this immediate perception, impossible to grasp in its totality, and my deferred, disappointing understanding exists a middle ground recurrent from one event to the next. Making the genii descend among people and then celebrating the encounter of the two worlds is one of the goals of each public ceremony. From this emerges a progression and an underlying order that are not readily apparent in the primordial level of meaning of the evening in Tindirma. The order of the ceremony and the rituals that precede it are about the same from one time to the next.

The Descent of the Genii

The genii ordinarily live in their aquatic or earthly homes. Their coming among people is made possible by a series of acts that leads to possessions, which are the culmination of the ceremony and the privileged means of communication with the genii.[3] As the genii's presence is at the same time desired and feared, the faithful cover themselves with diverse precautions and begin with sacrifices and offerings so as to gather in the genii's favors.

During the night preceding the batou, the organizing gaw goes above and below to the places the great genii live on the village's periphery. Above is on the termite hills, on the anthills, and in the great trees elect of the Ghimbala. Below is at the edge of the river or a pool. At these different spots, the gaw distributes first blood and pieces of a sacrificed animal (long ago, when life was simpler, a sheep or a billy goat; now just one or two chickens), then the consecrated offerings: milk, millet porridge, and *fogno* mixed with the gangi's favorite plants.[4] She or he addresses the most important of those genii who incarnate and enjoins them to come without disturbing the ceremony. He or she also asks them to summon the lesser genii subordinate to them and to intercede with those of great renown who no longer possess people but are still invoked in the ceremonies and simple rituals of the cult, so that all will be present the next day. Going to consecrate

---

3. The definition of the phenomenon of possession can be found in the Postscript.
4. For a list of the gangi's main plants, see appendix 4.

the dancing area, she or he disperses seven *wakando* pods, each of which holds seven seeds.[5]

The evening of the ceremony, when everyone has gathered, the same gaw moves to close the musical calabashes in the band. Up to this point they have been simply set on the ground on their convex side, open to the sky. The ritual consists of turning them over—some right onto the ground, others into their recipients full of water. The gaw simultaneously speaks incantations in which he or she reiterates the recommendations of the night before: "Come one, come all, but do not disturb the batou!"

The session can then begin. The participants make an approximate circle around the dancing area. The musicians and the choir are put on the eastern side; the gaw, in the company of the genii-griot and certain intimates among the faithful, crouches over a large mat close to the first group, most often on their left side. The public, which includes the other followers, occupies the remaining edge of the circle, with the exception of an opening created facing the musicians.

The first chant is a general call to all the genii sprinkled with invocations of the places they haunt, the trees and plants they like. This enumeration of the whole, a short version of the knowledge of the Ghimbala, which will be reprised and detailed later on, has the advantage at this time of making the genii descend into people, thus completing the beneficial effects of the prior sacrifice and offerings. The verb *descend* is taken literally. In effect, people picture the genii as having wings.

Overwhelmed by the gaw's sacrifices and offerings, shaken by his or her promises and threats, the genii leap from their homes at the first calls of the choir and begin to whirl above the batou. In fact it is their flight that the faithful imitate as they venture out into the dancing area. At the end of the chant, the genii settle one by one not in the middle of but outside the ceremonial circle, close to the opening created, which is the manifestation of their invisible presence. Using this point of entry, they can throw themselves on the one they want to take without dangerously upsetting the mere spectators. In fact, this is the reason no one sits near the genii's doorway. The batou brings people closer to their mysterious interlocutors, but any anarchic and prolonged contact with them would be dangerous. This is why the

---

5. Wakando—a long, black, crackly pod—is the most used seed in the cult. It is called *ghile* in Fula; I don't know its scientific name. An aromatic seed, it is used as a condiment in cooking and is commonly found in all markets. Its color makes it the vegetable element preferred by Baana. Is it in homage to him that followers crunch them during ceremonies?

gaw takes all the successive precautions: so that an untimely attack can not be imputed to his or her possible carelessness.

Possessions

Now possessions can take place at any time, as the women of the choir and the griot again name the great genii whose praises and slogans they sing. If one of them incarnates, the singers redouble their efforts, the percussion increases in volume, and the griot leaps up to be near the possessed and accompanies his or her trance with emphatic, vigorous declamations. Sometimes the gaw sets aside her or his reserve to join in the operation. After the beginning of a trance, which is often disorderly and extremely violent, the possessed take on the stereotyped roles of their genii.

But the coding of behaviors is much less developed than in other possession cults. For example, it is far from the extremely complicated etiquette which presides over the *orixas'* descent in the *candomblé* of Salvador de Bahia in Brazil[6] and even from the relatively elaborate scenes played out among the djiné don of the Malian west. There are hardly more than ten or so gangi who possess precise personalities and histories.[7] Here again, rigorous local conditions do not permit the development of much refinement in the compositions' details. Perhaps the culture of possession was more complex and structured during more clement periods, in which followers had the leisure to develop their imaginary world out of simple pleasure. Now one attends to the most urgent things first, but the scenes are no less animated or lively, nor less eventful, as we will see further on.

The Gaw, Master of Ceremonies

The session is ordered around the possession of the gaw who has organized it or of an important person in the cult when the performance of the former is not possible. In any case, the gaw whose possession

6. I discovered the refinement and complexity surrounding the gods' coming among people in the fall of 1986 on my first trip through Salvador to Porto Alegre in Sao Luiz de Maranhao. These first impressions were very much confirmed at the end of a second stay in late 1987, when I was able to make the acquaintance of the Xango de Recife at the end of a long and wonderful ceremony in Yemanja's honor. As soon as material conditions permit, the cults of possession develop an ostentatiousness that in Brazil takes on distinctly baroque accents. And yet one could not say that the ordinary people of the Afro-Brazilian cults live in opulence! Daily existence across the Atlantic has nonetheless not crumbled to the point of dereliction reached by the people of the upper bend.

7. These are the great genii we already know and a few others, including Komaïga, Maïrama, Dia, Badji-Badji, and Kokota Djini mentioned in chapter 3 and appendix 3.

will be the height of the evening stays apart from the agitation at the beginning of the session. Although she or he masters the ceremony, it is directed discreetly by brief injunctions immediately repeated by assistants, one of whom is the griot. As the session progresses, the gaw sometimes sits down on a mat in the middle of the circle, facing the group of musicians and singers, isolating himself or herself, concentrating, the better to fill with the sacred airs and rhythms, and encouraging the descent of the gangi.

Once the priest is possessed, the choir strikes up or repeats the chants in honor of great gaw, while the griot and sometimes the gaw in a trance list those who are important to them.[8] Then the moment of the prophecies comes and the music stops. After this, the group returns fairly quickly to the opening ritual, always accomplished in an abrupt manner that makes the session seem to end with a fizzle. Without waiting, the public disperses in the night, avoiding crossing the dancing area, where it seems the genii tarry a moment before returning to their natural haunts.[9]

TRANSGRESSIONS AT DONDORO
The Impossibility of Neutrality

I have participated in many of these ceremonies, which I could categorize on a personal level: those in which people tried to extract money from me; those in which I was hardly accepted at all; those in which I benefited from an apparently benevolent neutrality, as in Tindirma; and finally those in which the participants tried to draw me out of my role of observer, as happened one evening in February 1986.

We had just arrived the night before in Dondoro, a little fishing spot on the north bank of Issa Ber in Sumpi district, between Sebi and Dabi. Moussa Founé, the local gaw, had long wanted me to attend a batou in his village. It was at his home the year before that I first witnessed an untimely possession, which was quickly stopped because it occurred outside any ceremony or ritual. No longer able to dance nor enter into trance safely because of chronic sciatica, the gaw had on the morning of our arrival summoned one of his closest follow-

---

8. This chant, called the gaw's chant, is one of the guarantors of the cult's continuity; see chapter 7.

9. This rapid translation of the knot of genii from the door to the batou to the center of the dancing area is perhaps a reassuring explanation because it circumscribes the genii to a precise point rather than allowing any nagging doubts about their possible dispersal. The brief concentration of genii at this point could also mean that the site is charged, magnetized by all that has been spoken and done. This sacred charge attracts its recipients, the genii, another emanation of the sacred.

ers, a fisherman and priest like himself, to take over his role in the ceremony.

This large and athletic man named Demba came to call at the end of the afternoon, koubour in hand. He spent the rest of the time playing it for us over repeated glasses of mint tea while the members of Moussa Founé's entourage busied themselves preparing for the event. Demba had suffered a serious mutilation of his nose in a fishing accident long ago. This anomaly broke the harmony of a classically handsome face and made him resemble the Mesopotamian scribe at the Louvre. The music kept on discreetly in a warm, friendly, contemplative atmosphere in which rest, relaxation, and the sense of waiting for what was to follow overcame the need to speak.

When the ceremony began, Demba crouched in the middle of the dance area, clothed in great white robes with a gaw cap on his head of a kind I had already seen worn by Bili Korongoy near Diré. He clasped the sombé in his hands facing the musicians. He waited thus until his genie wanted to invade him, surrounded by the rhythms and chants that had begun to vigorously. On the other side of the assembly, Moussa Founé was seated on a mat directing the ceremony's unfolding, his forehead held by a band, symbol of his priestly function. As always, supernumeraries entered into minor possessions—new initiates' performances designed to fill out the session. But the whole audience awaited the possession of the man with the broken nose.

The ceremony took place a scant ten meters or so from the gaw's yard, on a kind of small plaza bordered by some houses and two or three stocky trees with thick foliage, which obscured the already-dark night a little further. The relatively enclosed space contained the intensity of the rhythms, concentrating them, making them more vibrant, deeper, more suggestive. Several times Demba trembled, rose, tried to dance, then sat back down in his place, closed in on himself. The music and chanting became more intense. A griot came right up to him to sing the praises of his genie; he still did not come.

Finally the possession unleashed, violent, convulsive, frightening. After struggling confusedly on the ground, the possessed man stood up screaming and brandishing the sombé, which he made twirl before him. From this moment on the session began to exert a prodigious power of fascination despite the relatively modest audience and small musical ensemble, which were probably caused by the illness and isolation of Dondoro's gaw.

Perhaps my fascination sprung from the exemplary nature of this possession, which Demba brought unflinchingly to term once the initial disorder had passed, or perhaps it came from the force of the place, the soil. At certain points little clusters of sparks rose from this soil,

will-o'-the-wisps more crazed than usual, falling stars from earth that
leapt under the dancer's stomps and bounds. This fishing encampment
had developed on the remains of very old human settlements, like
most of the inhabited sites in the region. The grounds of these places
charged with history are veritable necropolises, which give off strong
emanations of phosphorus.[10] Was it this latter revelation, or the sustained rhythms of the musicians and choir, or the quality of Demba's
dancing?

I couldn't leave the show in spite of the late hour. No one was
paying attention to me, yet I felt I was much involved in this ceremony, overtaken by waves, vibrations, and shaking that had me par-
ticipating physically in a rite whose meaning partially escaped me.
Although no one appeared to be looking at me, I had the feeling of
a strange presence. The possessed, a great white bird, leapt, spun,
sometimes abruptly throwing his head backward. He still wore his
cap, held on tightly at the chin by a strap and ending at the top in a
fringed mass of pompons and a horsehair braid. At one point he struck
the ground so violently with his sombé that it flew into pieces.

The musicians stopped when it was time for consultations. The
possessed gave them in the most classic manner: in dialogue with the
audience. Then the music picked up again. Demba, bent in two, began
to dance very close to the band, against whom I stood upright to try
to discern some of the expressions coming from the white, wavy mass
with its persistent red mane. The silence that had fallen over the spectators (though they are normally so noisy that they must sometimes
be called to order) combined with the intensity of the dancer and his
determination to be one with the music and rhythms to establish a
ponderous atmosphere. I felt ill, but I stayed. The ceremony went on
a little longer in the thick night, more and more hellishly, it seemed
to me.

Finally, with a great cry, the possessed collapsed, his arms stretched
out sideways, his face turned toward the sky in a cataleptic state. The
genie had also fainted in his own way. Demba was helped to get up
and led off reeling to a resting place, looking haggard. Then the
bundle of sounds assembled through ceremonial order scattered into a
crowd of little noises dispersed around the periphery on the heels of
people going home.

I went back to the tent set up a few steps away near the houses,
unable to shake the feeling of a diffuse presence that had just come
back. Feeling it weighing on the thin walls of my canvas hut, I

---

10. I owe this observation to my friend Jean C., who accompanied me on my 1986
trip and made me notice the sparks flying under the dancers' feet that night.

couldn't sleep. I was in a state of great excitation mixed with fright. I ended up going out, despite strong apprehension, to walk around my house. Coughs scraped the throats of those sleeping in the neighboring houses; farther on, cocks spoke to each other in defiance of the cold night. This heroic walk seemed to break the spell, and I dozed off for a few hours.

In thinking back to that night, I can't help guessing that the followers and the gaw wanted to have me enter into trance or, more simply, tried to test me. But by what means? No word was said, nor any action taken, at least not in front of me. Yet what I experienced resembled, in much less terrible form, the assault by magic or sorcery that Paul Stoller experienced in Wanzerbé, as he has described in his book.[11] I am well aware that I can produce no tangible evidence of this. May I, however, consider as indicators the pregnant looks the two gaw threw me on the sly, the movements of the possessed toward me, and the final spell, that is, the feeling of a prolonged presence, the muffled bumps around the tent and on its walls?

The Bozo Hypnotist, the Radio-Cassette Machine, and the Untimely Trances

One year later, almost to the day, I find myself on the desolate beach of Dondoro. This afternoon, Moussa Founé Nabo comes up to the pirogue to converse with us far from indiscreet ears and glances. In the middle of the conversation, he turns brusquely toward the river and begins shouting at the genii, "This evening, you must all come so that Dian-Marri [myself, Jean-Marie] can tell his friends about a beautiful batou! Last night I went into the bush, all the way to the anthills, to the termite hills, to your trees; I went all the way to the river. I gave you food! The batou must succeed. If you sabotage the batou, I will no longer go up on the termite hills, on the *douhey,* into the *kobdié.*[12] I won't go down to the river at midnight! If for all my fatigue you don't come, you are not gangi any longer but shayṭāns![13] I'll give you no more milk, nor fogno, nor wakando, nor porridge. I'll make no more sacrifices of hens, bundi, and kobiri for you, because it's no use!"

The monologue lasts a long time, after which the gaw leaves us, though not without having requested the money needed to buy six batteries to power his huge radio-cassette machine. He has a tape on which he has recorded Démoudou, the leprous old singer of Ni-

---

11. See Paul Stoller and Cheryl Olkes, *In Sorcery's Shadow* (University of Chicago Press, 1987).
12. See appendix 4.
13. That is, demons and no longer genii.

afunké, whose inspired voice makes the genii's coming certain. The machine will be a precious adjunct to the village musicians and choir who, according to him, are not sufficiently endowed. I am even more willing to participate in this experiment because of my curiosity to know its results.

As it is already almost night, we meet up with the gaw in his yard in the company of Demba, who we met last year. At Moussa Founé's request, I have picked up Demba at his fishing place near Sibo, between Niafunké and Dondoro. He will again be the one to lead the ceremony because Moussa Founé, handicapped by his persistent sciatica, can no longer dance. While waiting, everyone listens to Démoudou's chants rising from the machine, which has been recharged with the new batteries. The leper is assisted by a person playing the djerkélé who has made enormous progress since the session I was able to record during my last trip. Stimulated by this effective assistance, old Démoudou surpasses himself—his voice rises, high, tense, then modulated, out of breath, dramatic. The great genii of the cult are each invoked in turn. We are suspended on the sacred music stretching into the new darkness.

Suddenly, as Démoudou sings Awa's praises, Demba stands up with a scream and brandishes the sombé, the sign of his priesthood that never leaves him. He gives himself two formidable blows on the head, fortunately with the less dangerous side, the double point turned skyward. Nonetheless, there is enough force in those blows to stun an ox. The immense gaw does not even shake, but the trance stops short. What has just taken place is the onset of an untimely possession by Awa, queen of the genii. Demba stopped it immediately by this shock treatment because only the place and time of the ceremony are right for such a manifestation of the sacred. His head bleeding, Demba goes away now from our circle, out of fear of being taken again. In fact someone quickly turns off the sound. After such an introduction to the evening, I wonder what will happen later on.

The ceremony begins two hours later under a full moon, which has just hit the eastern horizon. This pale, inverted double of sunset emits a bizarre, oblique light, which elongates shadows and creates a surreal effect even more pronounced than when the night star is at its zenith. The women of the choir stand on the side closer to the river, near the fairly modest group of musicians—two bomboutou and a gassou; the compact audience faces them. Between the audience and the musicians are the gaw, seated on a big mat on which I am also seated, near the machine, which is off for now.

I notice the presence of a healer-priest from the Djenné region who introduced himself to the encampment earlier this afternoon. I learned then that he was staying in a Bozo fishing ground near Dondoro, where he had been called to care for a patient attacked by water-genii. The fishers had sought a healer from their home area to escape the Ghimbala sphere. Although the locals also call him gaw, I have already noticed that he doesn't refer to the same pantheon, nor does he use the same curative rituals. He has just asked the local gaw for authorization to intervene in the ceremony. For this event, he has put on his performance attire, which closely resembles a Mandingo healer's outfit: hunter's tunic covered with talismans and bits of mirror, leather cap, small bells mounted on raffia ruffs attached around the ankles. His ornamentation and clothing, on the whole very fitting, contrast with the great floating veils of local followers.

The whole beginning of the session is marked by the confrontation of this priest, who is just the least bit provocative, with the two gaw he has come to defy on their own land. The Bozo, with the strength of age, sure of himself and very controlled, moves with ease in a milieu not in the least favorable to him. Approaching our group, he brandishes a short whip covered with leather and tufted with hairs at its end. When he gets to our level, he lays his instrument down in front of Demba, who does not flinch. Then he goes slowly to Moussa Founé and does the same thing, staring at him intensely. This time, it works. The gaw begins to tremble, he screams, and he tries to get up on his wobbly legs. His son and two other spectators run over to hold him down and keep him from further injuring his lower back. Demba frees him by rapidly placing his hands on Moussa Founé's head, and he falls back inert on the mat while the Bozo goes on to the next client.

When he sets his instrument before me, I perceive deep within his shadowed face an insistent, tough gaze that tries to catch mine. I am in a tight corner; I feel myself overtaken by a strange uneasiness and heaviness which certainly remind me of the pretrance states I have known before. I hold onto the mat so as not to fall into trance, and finally I resist. The Bozo quickly picks up his instrument and goes off. Later he returns for another try at the unfortunate Moussa Founé, diminished by his illness, and provokes a new trance in him, which Demba stops, this time very brutally, by giving his friend a furious blow with his own head. We hear the dull sound of the two skulls hitting each other.

The Bozo takes over the entire ceremonial space and executes some of his cult's athletic dance movements, totally out of time with the Songhay rhythms. The singers and musicians are all confused. At one point the Bozo tries to take onto the dance floor a woman who refuses to go. Then Demba stops him from continuing in his attempt, and a brief sequence follows in which I see the ensnarled hands of the two protagonists rapidly disentangling. Then the Bozo magician throws a series of predictions at the encampment chief and his brother that falls rather flat. He finally gives up trying to prove he is the strongest and chooses to retire, without ever having lost his aplomb. He reappears a few moments later, stripped of his Mandingo magician's outfit, clothed in a simple boubou.

Demba, who has met the challenge of these difficult minutes by resisting the Bozo's intimidation attempt, finally lets himself respond to the genii's calls. But the women are already tired, and the machine relieves them. It is turned up to its highest volume, and the voice of old Démoudou, raw as his leper's wounds, comes to the rescue of the village choir. Demba, who was moving around on the other side of the dancing area, returns and runs toward the machine. Facing it, he begins a supple, leaping dance, at the same time twirling his sombé around him. The electronic intrusion into this Ghimbala event boosts my interest in this ceremony, which has been so chaotic up to this point. Démoudou's surprising voice rises in the night while the women of Dondoro timidly try to keep his rhythm. Yet they can't follow the leprous virtuoso, and soon there is discordance between the rough choir and the fairly perfect performance rendered by the man on the recording, whose volume covers the village women's hesitant chanting. The women soon quiet and only the devilish voice of Démoudou remains, seeming particularly inspired tonight.

During this time, Demba surpasses himself, the focal point of all present. His impressive energy takes no time to make him enter into violent trance. He strikes the ground with his sombé with such unbridled force that the handle flies into pieces. The scene unfolds in almost the same place where he already broke the one inherited from his father a year ago. This mishap does not quiet him. Now he strides over the dancing area in a state of extreme excitation, frenetically shaking his head with its red bonnet and long plume, emblem of his function.[14] He asks for the possessed's whip to beat himself, and as it is not to be found, he takes up a fistful of long, dry, hard branches with which he ardently flagellates his legs. Then he leaps off, crossing the entire batou. He pulls Moussa Founé's cane out from under him and, before anyone can intervene, breaks it on his skull.

He quiets a bit and more fully controls his trance. His moving about becomes less abrupt, his movements less violent, and he begins to dance again in a harmonious way. This is the moment Moussa Founé chooses to enter into trance one last time, taken by Baana, the

14. This is the badji-foula, the cap mentioned in the preceding chapter.

unconquerable captive, the husband of Awa, Demba's genie. His possession is even stronger than the two preceding ones. He gesticulates and tries his hardest to get up. Three people fall on him to keep him on the ground but don't succeed; I give them a hand. We end up immobilizing him on the ground with great effort. Demba, who is still supposed to be in a state of trance, quickly puts the talisman ring that stops possessions into the gaw's mouth. Moussa's possession fades immediately and I see his body relax under our hands as he falls into a deep sleep.

But the session picks back up again: the young people responsible for the radio-cassette machine keep on playing Démoudou's tape, and Demba's possession, which he seemed to have mastered, starts up again even more intensely. The spellbinding music recharges the possessed in a perverse way and the trance takes a new tack, although it should normally be moving toward a close. Demba is on his knees facing the resounding machine, as he does normally with the musicians, and he continues to dance in this position. Then he takes off with huge steps across the batou. The voice never lets up; it penetrates him, saturates him, and plunges him into a state of irascibility and violence that I would have a hard time imagining if I weren't witnessing the strength of its enslavement over the giant gaw.

Demba suddenly leaves the batou circle; he appears to be looking for something. He stops, kneels, goes toward the village. His great, agitated body floats off in the distance in his washed-out blue clothes and finally disappears between the huts under a clear night sky. When he comes back among us, I ask one of my neighbors the meaning of all these tricks. "He's looking to see if there is a fetish buried in the village." Perhaps this is an allusion to the mistrust inspired by the Bozo, who by this time has returned home. Demba's long possession rises and falls to the rhythm of the cassette, rewound unceasingly to its beginning. Moussa Founé, in a comatose state, is incapable of interrupting his companion's trance himself.

It is clear that the gaw is becoming exhausted. Two experienced men—the encampment chief and his brother, the same ones who were confronted earlier by the Bozo—get up to hasten the departure ritual and ask the young people to turn off the tape. Demba finally drops. When he returns to himself a little while later, he gets up lurching, takes a few steps toward the village, and falls again on the ground, where he remains immobile for many long minutes as the spectators disperse. The next day he tells me that Awa was unhappy with the pale blue boubou he wore because he should have worn white, her color. He probably wants both to explain the violence of his attack and to reproach me for refusing to buy him the ecru cotton *ourki* he asked me for.

While waiting, I find myself alone in the tent to summarize the evening. It was not a model batou, in the sense that it was full of formal imperfections, both in its music and in its performances. Incidentally I did not observe, as I had the previous year, the little phosphorus flames leaping from under the dancers' feet, but the ceremony took place a little farther away, on the edge of the inhabited area. The session was thus chaotic and riddled with incidents, but nonetheless infinitely more lively and moving because of its dissonances and dramatic tensions than the beautiful, unsurprising, and cold choreographies of quasi-official, healthy cults, such as the candomblé of Bahia I had visited in Salvador in autumn of 1986.

This batou was completely fragmented by the disturbing presence of both the Bozo healer and Démoudou's recorded voice. In the ceremony, initially dominated by the confrontation between the Bozo and the two gaw, Moussa Founé, ravaged by his illness, succumbed. Demba, in full possession of his abilities, opposed the strength of the self-assured newcomer with his own. He resisted victoriously and only entered into trance when his rival had gone. On the other hand, he became entranced by the recording of Démoudou. If the Bozo's presence signified the intrusion of a different order into the Ghimbala field, Démoudou's voice represented the total incarnation of the aesthetics and universe of the cult. It threw the batou off center no less because, sustained and amplified by the machine with its six big batteries, it crushed the weak choir of the village women. In addition, the growing fatigue of the musicians and singers usually coincides with the progressive quieting of the possessed dancers. Nothing of the kind this time; Demba broke down well before the batteries wore out. The perverse continuation made possible by technology got the better of his fine energy, even though it was greatly increased by the trance.

Already in the preparatory phase of the batou Demba had been incongruously taken by Awa, which gave rise to that forceful ritual of self-exorcism, since genii and people must at all costs be separated outside of the places and times set aside for their meeting. The head-to-head contact with Moussa Founé and the brief placement of the ring in his mouth had the same effect during the ceremony. Thus, each time the genii make an undesired incursion into the world of people, they must be sent on their way more or less expeditiously.

For the moment, I find myself in the odd state I have already experienced several times before. I am almost as nervous as the possessed of this evening and can't get to sleep. To what is this due? During this time, the young people who have controlled the machine all evening long continue to play Démoudou at full blast in a little hut thirty meters away that overhangs the street leading to the Niger. I confusedly decide to transform my unease into aggression. I go out of the tent, walk toward them, and, when I am close enough, enjoin them politely but firmly to put a lid on that damned machine, whose batteries still work. Slightly calmed by this intervention, I end up falling into agitated sleep, during which I think I dream about gaw, especially about Kola Gaba, who is trying unsuccessfully to communicate with me.

The following night, on the beach at Sebi, I am convinced that wings flap around me in the thick darkness. Bats, birds, or gangi (now that I know they fly too)? I sometimes seem to tip over into a different reality.

THE PROXIMITY OF THE GENII

Prohibited Trances

I have witnessed other occasions of undesirable possessions that were stopped short in the same expeditious and sometimes violent way. Ghimbala followers are always about to receive their genii. Sometimes a trance crops up outside of a batou in response to an unforeseeable, disturbing event. The believer, shaken and frightened, responds with a "wild" possession. Then one of the entourage who knows the rule of the Ghimbala gets the ring the possessed always carries and puts it quickly into his or her mouth to stop the trance, as Demba did with Moussa Founé. Memories of these untimely possessions, demonstrating the fragile, unstable, emotive character of mediums, are so haunting that they are recorded in the most minute detail. This record is used in a ritual of protection and separation discussed further on.[15]

Yet the enumeration of these possessions does not yet consider the anthropologist's intervention as a traumatizing factor that may unleash an interviewee's trance. On several occasions, however, interviews were interrupted during recording because my interlocutor was taken by his or her gangi in the middle of a sentence. In Dabi at the end of 1984, Yero, an old, blind singer and genii-griot, was seized precisely while evoking the first attack of the gangi he had experienced in his youth. He held the sessey around his head very tightly and struck his forehead vigorously with the palm of his hand to make his distraction dissipate. At Tonka the following month, a gaw who was giving me names and characteristics of some of the gangi became uneasy, began

15. The kanji, the final type of Ghimbala curative ritual, is treated in the next chapter.

to lose his words, and then began to scream while striking his skull twice, hard, with the sombé, as Demba later did. Then he picked up the interview as if nothing had happened.

I cited three of these rather eventful recordings during a France-Culture radio broadcast in which I wanted to show the reality of trance, using these involuntary and sudden possessions as examples. The title of the show (used again for this chapter), "Live Devils," referred not only to hearing these recordings but also to the kind of immediate, immanent relationships the people of the Ghimbala establish with the sacred, as do followers of other territorial, polytheistic religions. The genii's descent into people makes sacred the ceremony's time and place. Followers have the feeling of participation in the mysteries of their masters' existence. The genii are there, right alongside people, which is clear for those who become possessed but mere hypothesis in relation to the others.

Gaw and griots thus turn toward the point in dark space, above the circle of spectators, where Baana, Awa, Moussa, and the others are apparently settled. Facing the night, they begin a dialogue with their invisible interlocutors to symbolically affirm their presence, hurling abuse at them, flattering them, taking the slightly confused audience as a witness ("He's there, look! Don't you see him?"), inciting those who permit themselves to laugh to further contemplation. Then they come up to the breech dividing the crowd to invite the genii to enter the dancing area through the passage set aside for them with the obsequious gestures of a majordomo standing at the walkway to a palace before an evening reception.

Between the Vulgar and the Sacred

Among the Ghimbala, as in any possession cult, a theatrical dimension exists, even if it is noticeably less developed than elsewhere.[16] The celebration of the meeting of genii and people, a veritable sacred drama, actualizes the fundamental links that unite them to each other. It expresses through each trance the widest possible range of feelings, and because of this it oscillates between the sublime and the ridiculous, even the extremely vulgar. This alternation between opposites, which

16. It is nothing like, for example, the behavior of those possessed by the *zars,* who take on a series of successive roles each corresponding to a different spirit. (See Michel Leiris, *La Possession et Ses Aspects Théâtraux chez les Ethiopiens de Gondar* [Le Sycomore, 1980].) In fact, among the Ghimbala, each possessed can only be taken by a single genie. The reason for this exclusivity, as stated by the people of the cult, has to do with the fact that the water-genii of the upper bend of the Niger are very demanding. Serving one alone is more than enough to occupy each follower.

are connected by their mutual transgression of the day-to-day, continues the whole time the genii occupy the area with their noisome presence. Thus exceptional choreographic performances inspired by the calabash drums and frenetic chanting give way to invectives and curses alarming the spectators, which in turn give way to contemplative moments that precede the delivery of messages by those possessed, which at last give way to those periods of rest in which the rather licentious pranks of the genii simply make the audience laugh. Once these different registers have been used and exhausted, the session suddenly stops with the brutal expulsion of the genii opposed by the single God of Islam.

Often the priest, already freed from his trance, mimes rather than undergoes the cataleptic state in which he must be plunged to close the ceremony, for one of the functions of a gaw is to be a good actor. Some abuse their talent, such as the different priests of Bambara origin I saw officiate near Niafunké; others remain in the background, such as Kola Gaba in Dabi, who is content to manifest his recognized position with a few authoritative supplemental gestures during a ceremony. The gaw, when their possession puts them in top form, become facetious and even openly vulgar with their followers, whom they heckle slightly in passing. Thus, one time when a spectator sneezed on a cold night, the gaw leading the session turned quickly toward him and cried out, "Put a rag in your ass or else you'll fart," unleashing the hilarity of the audience.

These sequences, during which religious ceremony changes into farce, occur when the gaw controls his or her own excesses and even when the possession state has not completely disappeared. The gaw seem to be aware that the comedic lines they deliver calm the often tense atmosphere sustained both by the vigor of the music and the violence of the trances.

The Violence of the Trance

This violence is a reflection of the relationships in a society in which the current crisis only reinforces the difficulty of individual existence. In the upper bend, power relations, more implacable than elsewhere, create a situation unimaginable to those who have not experienced it. I have never noticed in other cults, either in Africa or Brazil, violent manifestations comparable to those resulting from the Ghimbala's descent into their followers.[17]

---

17. Even the most violent possessions by the Hauka of the Niger that I observed at Bamako or Mopti, and even those by the *pombagiras,* the *exus,* and the *caboclos* that I

In the initial phase, the possessed roll on the ground with disorderly and confused gestures. They make inarticulate cries, groans, dreadful growls. They raise an impossible amount of dust when the batou organizers haven't taken the precaution of covering the ground with old mats, which protect the dancers in trance against possible wounds from stones or thorns remaining despite prior sweeping of the area.

When the possessed grow calm or show some signs of fatigue, the cult leaders and simple spectators recharge them by declaiming their genii's slogans, exhortations designed to start up their trances again. The possessed, as susceptible to such influences as mediums, respond to these inciting phrases with new excesses of energy. There is no kindness, no pity in these relationships—the nonpossessed sometimes push the possessed to dance to the point of complete exhaustion.

The high point of cruelty is reached in the flogging sequences, a specialty of the Ghimbala that I have encountered nowhere else.[18] When words are not enough, when the possessed staggers, stumbles, and falls, the gaw or one of his or her assistants takes up a whip with long leather cords, dipped beforehand in an extract of sacred plants, and begins to whip the unfortunate's legs. This evokes no cries of suffering from the person, since trance makes one insensible to pain. Often the possessed asks for the whip or whatever takes its place, as Demba did during the scene described previously. The local explanation of such procedures is that prolonged contact with a genie weakens the possessed by taking away energy. The gaw or his substitute gives the possessed strength again through this ferocious treatment, which "firms up" his or her legs.

FROM INTERPRETATION TO MATERIALITY OF POSSESSIVE TRANCE

Interpretation of Possession

The coming of the gods among people to which the phenomenon of possession corresponds constitutes a field of the immanence of the sacred. This direct contact of followers with their mystical masters

---

attended in Brazil (at Porto Alegre, Belem, Sao Luiz, and Salvador), were infinitely less convulsive than those of the Ghimbala.

18. The explanation for very violent possessions given to me by the actors in each cult in which they are practiced is as follows: God punishes a follower, takes revenge, or simply marks power over her or him by making the follower suffer. In these demonstrations of self-cruelty there are certainly masochistic impulses, the trials of the body going sometimes as far as attempts at self-mutilation. The whipping the Ghimbala inflict on themselves seems to go in the same direction.

represents a privileged moment in their relations with the genii and gives rise to a number of interpretations. The most commonly admitted one is that the possessed becomes, in the eyes of all, the living god. In Brazil and in Yoruba country, the gods—pure energy (*axê*)—need people in order to incarnate, to take body within their followers. In the Niger, the Tooru, noble genii of the classical Songhay cults, put themselves in the place of the follower's *bya,* that is, his or her double, or soul. The terms used to refer to the possessed corroborate this interpretation: they become "the horses of the gods," "the children of the gods." Each one of them, treated as an emissary of the sacred among people, relives the history of the god who incarnates in her or him. This idea, the most widespread by far, deserves a little more detail in the case of the Ghimbala, for whom I have noted at least three possible interpretations of possession.

The first is connected to the notions of being "straddled" or "overlapped" [chevauchement] and of being "incorporated." This is the most widely shared by followers. But a second and a third interpretation, proposed by the greatest connoisseurs of the gangi, are quite distant from common belief.

Mahaman Tindirma proposes that trance is produced by the simple, rapid contact of the follower with his or her genie, who throws himself or herself on the person, shakes him or her up, and then goes away. He describes this collision in the following way: "It's like electricity and poison at the same time." The violence of the blow recalls an electric charge; its effect within the body is lasting, like that of poison. In this idea, the genie, nestled at the edge of the dancing area near the opening, is content to bound over to the follower to strike and shake him or her up and then go back into place. The individual targeted and assaulted gives way screaming under the violence of the charge, and the beginning of a possession is always convulsive (the electricity metaphor). Then the possessed controls the energy that has been breathed into her or him a bit more and begins a more restrained performance, fed by the long-lasting effects of the initial shock (the poison metaphor). If the possessed gives signs of fatigue, the genie can recharge him or her by a new assault, and the trance continues to full term.

The third idea makes of the possessed a simple seer. The genii leave their places to flutter around the followers' heads. Each person recognizes her or his own genie. Sometimes the genie breathes into the face of the one she or he wants to go into trance, but most often it is enough to stare at the person. Then, as in the preceding direct-contact situation, the follower stands up, cries out, rolls on the ground, and begins to dance. From the genie, who can only be seen by the possessed, the follower receives injunctions and messages to be transmitted to the people assembled for the ceremony. She or he also displays the same physical characteristics and behaviors and enjoys the same capacities as seers in other regions of the planet.

For example, several adolescents in Medjurgorje, Bosnia-Herzegovina, see the Virgin Mary, talk with her, and communicate her messages to the gathered believers. It is a state of ecstasy that permits these adolescents to have their experience, and ecstasy, as it is minutely described by witnesses to the phenomenon, seems to be a category of trance.[19] In effect, the young seers of Medjugorje experience the same states of sensory deprivation and disconnection with the near environment and give the same signs of an intense interior experience as mediums throughout time. But instead of coming as a convulsive trance, as is often the case in possession, theirs is ecstatic. The nature of this phenomenon nonetheless remains the same, including the perception of an intense light before the vision itself.[20]

The experience of this luminous sensation has been reported to me several times by Brazilian possessed, who verbalize their practices more easily than the people of the upper bend of the Niger. In his or her experience of the trance, each projects the shapes of the social imaginary in which he or she participates. Thus, after this great light, the Brazilian followers see their orixa, their *exu,* or their *caboclo.* In the upper bend of the Niger, the gaw see Baana or Awa; the adolescents of Medjugorje see the Virgin.

Materiality of Trance

Several facts relating to the materiality of trance appeared during the session described earlier through the tear in the symbolic fabric that normally encloses cultural activity. The duel of the gaw was the first of these. Demba, in full possession of his abilities, resisted the efforts of the Bozo magician, who succeeded in making Moussa Founé—the gaw with declining strength—enter into trance with the help of his little flyswatter, the pretended receptacle of his power. But the massive presence of the Bozo, as well as his heavy, pressing gaze, resembled a hypnotist's practices. I therefore think I witnessed in this sequence a direct confrontation of strength and energy similar to the phenomenon of hypnosis.

The different, always expeditious, and sometimes violent procedures used to bring undesirable trances to an end constitute another

19. See Prof. H. Joyeux and Abbé Laurentin, *Etudes Médicales et Scientifiques sur les Apparitions de Medjugorje* (OEIL, 1985).

20. Ibid., 13.

curious group of facts. Demba gave himself an incredible blow with the sombé to stop short the trance that came on before the ceremony. During the batou, he delivered a violent head blow to Moussa Founé, who went into a deep sleep though he had been extremely agitated the minute before. I remember that I was also able to measure the effects on the old gaw's body of the brief and mysterious placing of the ring into his mouth. This brought on immediate end to his trance, although four of us had hardly been able to control him. What mobilization of energies, what physiological short circuits, could indeed have been induced by such actions?

Finally, the real influence of the music, voice, and sounds was sharply revealed in Demba's long possession, which kept renewing itself through the tape of Démoudou, the old leper with the inspired voice. The gaw came intensely under the spell of this shrill, raw voice, which would not let him go. The trance's variations followed the fluctuations in intensity reproduced on the tape. The dancer calmed down a bit when the singer was occasionally silent; he began his athletic performance even more strongly when the voice surged again—in particular, when it sang the praises of Awa, his own genie. This doesn't mean the poetic content of Démoudou's words was richer than that of most of the griots and singers of the upper bend. Some repertoires, such as Mahaman Tindirma's, have an evocative force greatly superior. It seemed indeed to be the rising and falling of the plaintive, nasal voice that played the key role in Demba's repetitive trance.

This last case recalls similar situations in which possessive trances provoke an eclipse in official order and dominant meaning, both of which usually weigh heavily on followers under the constraints of their society. These possessions "outside the norm" express the explosion of desires in the people dominated. The crumbling of the symbolic field permits the emergence of a linguistic beyond [*un au-delà du langage*] that echoes Artaud's vow "To break language in order to touch life . . . this sort of fragile moving source that forms do not reach."[21] Such events occur when the ceremonial flow upsets ritual order, as I tried to show some time ago.[22] Events recorded elsewhere in the west of Mali, in Côte d' Ivoire and just recently in Brazil repeat in their own way the ones pointed out here. They are often reduced to an explanation *a posteriori* given by those who are the privileged interlocutors of the gods, in this case the gaw. Demba, I remember, told

21. Antonin Artaud, *Le Théâtre et Son Double, Oeuvres Complètes,* vol. 4 (Gallimard, 1964), 18.

22. See Jean-Marie Gibbal, "Ordre Rituel et Flux Cérémoniel," in "La Cérémonie," *Traverses,* no. 21/22 (May 1981).

me the day after his interminable possession that Awa had wanted to punish him for wearing a light blue boubou instead of the white clothing she demanded.

This attempt to recover and confiscate a problematic meaning does not mask the presence in possessive trance of a reality that cannot be reduced to interpretation and to the categorizations typically proposed. There is an abstract and informal materiality in the phenomenon of trance: one could even say that trance is simply of the real, a vibration of the body that responds to sound, that other "vibration of the real."

6 / Separate in Order to Heal

THE GENII'S ATTACK

"The gangi attack someone in order to receive something from that person they don't have yet. They touch the person just to make them sick and so that they end up in the gaw's hands. That's the way the gangi have found to obtain satisfaction. The gangi don't have hatred and don't have favorites. Anyone can be attacked—it's destiny. They might not take someone who is in the water and take him or her in their sleep later;[1] they can just as easily take an angry man during a fight as someone who is very calm."

This is how Mahaman spoke in the waning light, the most beautiful time, as we crouched on the mat conversing. We faced the wide vista of river and beach as shapes and colors regained their sharpness for an instant after the crushing light of midday before lightly melting into the clear night. To temper destiny's heft, Mahaman added quickly, there are also dangerous times and places in the earthly world—certain trees the genii inhabit of whose shadow one must beware; the gourgoussou, hollowed-out hills, vestiges of past populations; summits of dunes, termite hills, anthills. As for the watery world—the usual great holes, confluences, stony passages, and great, isolated rocks. In the villages, some streets and alleys as well as all crossroads cannot be frequented at certain times when the genii walk about: at noon, when the sun is at its zenith; at twilight; and, finally, in the middle of the night. And certain families, especially gaw's families, are favorites of the genii, who have associated with them over time. Thus they will return to their hearths from generation to generation. Heredity and imprudence temper destiny a little—a concept inspired by Islam, of course.

What are the genii-illnesses? They are the different forms of madness, ranging from *hollo yeno*—cool, quiet madness—to *hollo foutou*—mean madness,—and many other torments. The genii can make their victim's body swell, give heart palpitations, and headaches, paralyze a bodily member, render a person insomniac or kleptomaniac,

---

1. Water is the genii's privileged element; watery places are particularly dangerous because the genii linger there.

and turn a man as well as a woman impotent (in the latter case, frigidity is perceived as impotence). They can stop the onset of menses or, on the contrary, provoke continual discharge of blood. The genie or genii responsible for the aggression have free range to make it slight or serious. They do not always choose a particular part of the body, but once an individual has been touched in a specific place, future contacts will always reiterate this initial blow. During ritualized trances, it is said, the possessed always endures the same suffering as during the first attack.

The genii-illnesses can be broken down into a series of oppositions: madness versus other illnesses; serious diseases versus slight ailments; patients who "scream" versus patients who do not. This last opposition alters the chain of curative rituals. But whether madness or simple illness, serious or slight attack, with or without possession, the gaw use the same plants and the same healing techniques—including smoke purification, daubing, washing, and special drinks—because the ailments concerned are all provoked by the genii. The illnesses caused by the Ghimbala do not noticeably differ from those described in Mali, especially those I have been able to observe among the djiné don. On the other hand, the gaw of the upper bend of the Niger have quite a complex arsenal of curative techniques and rituals, of which the following pages offer only a summary overview.

THE NOON DEMONS

Last evening in Attara, after the weekly market (to which this township on the Niger's northern bank owes its present importance, since the market draws people from all over), Issa Sogoba organized a batou.[2] This Friday morning, a sandy, disheartening wind blows, and we are having enormous difficulty folding the tent and putting our material away. There is no question of sailing under such conditions. I fill the time by furthering my historical research with an interview of a griot from the area. Toward noon, the wind drops as forecast. We are about to leave, but first I go to thank old Diallo, Almâmi's host. I am accompanied by a young police corporal who is passionately interested in the collection of traditions and has been following me all morning long, improvising as an interpreter. I also want to ask Diallo the name of a gaw from Akka, a village located where we exit Lake

2. Sogoba is the gaw of Sumpi, a big village of the Katawan, a small Tuareg kingdom begun in the last century in the Sumpi region to the northeast of Niafunké. This kingdom disappeared with the invasion of the French.

Débo. It seems this gaw has become famous for his ability to straddle hippopotamuses and ride them to the riverbank.

Our old host, whom we find in the company of his wife's twin sister, welcomes us in his courtyard, looking worried. We hear a beautiful melody welling up from a nearby room, soft, modulated, rising and falling plaintively but musically, capturing our attention. Diallo's wife has had a spell of the sickness that chronically keeps her flat on her back for long months. Two or three days ago I learned she was suffering from respiratory problems and nausea; no mention of a genie attack was ever made, though her present crisis certainly seems to suggest one.

I am at this point in my calculations when Issa Sogoba, gaw of the night before, arrives with a busy and concerned look. An adolescent follows him bearing some kind of old satchel, a doctor's bag and emergency kit at the same time. Luckily for me, Sogoba speaks French and we've already had several conversations. Today, after emptying his bag of tricks on the ground, he does not hesitate to describe the meaning of his intervention. It seems the aggressor has entered Diallo's wife's body through her right ear. She is lying on a high *tara*, which Sogoba approaches in order to breathe into the infiltrated auditory canal.[3] Then he spreads a little powdered baobab bark over the patient, puts several more pinches on three or four coals glowing in a ceramic holder, and makes her inhale the smoke that immediately rises from it.[4] Finally he prepares a drink with the same powder: he has her drink half and asks her sister, come from Goundam to help Diallo during his wife's illness, to wash her with the rest.

The gaw summarizes his whole treatment in these words: "This will stop the heart throbbings." He takes a swallow of the liquid before administering it, a common practice designed to prove to onlookers that the brew is not poisonous. Diallo's wife continues to emit her melodious complaint, sad and repetitive, while the gaw tells me a confused story of a fever blister, supposedly the result of a genie attack, that rose and fell from the bottom of her throat to the middle of her mouth. When he begins to blow on her, the woman feels pain in her right ear, and "she says she has fire on her heart and in her stomach." Because of what she has said, Sogoba makes her open her mouth and stick out her tongue; I see nothing. I ask the meaning of the plaintive

3. *Tara* is a term used throughout Mali to refer to the wooden daises on which people sleep.
4. The baobab (*kabé* in Songhay) is one of the trees whose leaves, bark, and roots are used in cures.

melody which has picked up again. The gaw answers me that the *djinarou* keep him from understanding. Then the sister comes in energetically. I learn that she does not want her twin to enter the Ghimbala society: she has had too many children and has grown old.

Up to this point the consultation has proceeded rather calmly; now there is a brutal change of tone. The wife, who was lying almost motionless on her bed, sits straight up after receiving the first treatment, her eyes startled, her body rigid, her arms stretched out in the air. At this, the priest-doctor is also taken by a violent trance, and he begins to speak feverishly, screaming, stamping. I seem to recognize some names of genii, curative plants, and cult sites in passing, but I can't grasp much because the corporal, who was expected somewhere for lunch, has taken advantage of my gossiping with the gaw to disappear within the first few minutes of the session.

During this time, Sogoba leaps about, gesticulates, and begins to blow in all the concerns of the house. Perhaps to chase the genii out? Since the gaw's possession, the wife's excitation has redoubled. Now she leans toward him pathetically, starting up her plaintive hum again. The two possessed go back and forth. With a violent start, Diallo's wife tries to throw herself on the priest, who runs to grab her as she nearly tips over. But he is not at all in control of his trance and nearly falls and drags her along as he goes—which then, of course, happens. We intervene to separate them and help them get up. A brief scuffle ensues, and then we manage to get the woman back onto her bed. A certain confusion reigns in the overheated room. We cough, sneeze, and cry under the effect of the tremendous dust raised by their fits. I'm a little lost. I notice I haven't even asked myself what I am doing in the middle of this unexpected drama. Meanwhile my situation is rather comical: I have no tape recorder and no interpreter, and I stopped writing quite a while ago.

Yet the wife calms down as Sogoba moves away a little, continuing his gesticulations. I take advantage of the lull to ask the sole child in the assembly, a little girl of about ten who has poliomyelitis, to go get Almâmi, who is awaiting my return a few hundred yards away. The girl goes off, dragging her leg. Diallo and his sister-in-law are standing side by side, immobile and resigned, looking exhausted, weighted down. Sogoba, still full of energy, continues his inspections, going back and forth from where we are to the back of a nearby room. It has another bed in it, on which he blows noisily several times. He never lets up his vociferous incantations, continues his leaping dance, and tears up his big toe quite seriously on a disjointed slat sticking out from the bed. Blood flows; in his trance, he pays absolutely no attention to it. Diallo bandages the toe hurriedly with an old bit of rather dirty plastic while I hold up the gaw and he hops on his good leg, his flow of words never stopping.

Now the excitation has moved from the patient to the gaw. She has pretty much dozed off while he kept up his frenetic performance. In the meantime, Almâmi has come, and I feel less lost when he begins to translate the words of the priest in trance, who is invoking the cult's great genii. "Moussa has come with a pretty belt; Moussa is here with his spear and his belt!" "Here is Baana, the unconquerable captive; here is Baana, the strongest!"

Then he begins to sing and mime Mama Kyria, the old, leprous captive of the Ghimbala whose name I hear carried along in the verbal flow while I recognize the gestures and attitudes of that genie. "The illness was given by Mama Kyria; each year you must offer him a new pot and a new sheep." Several times the gaw very evocatively imitates the genie, whose hands and feet are atrophied from his illness. "The woman is for Mama Kyria! You must put a red ring on her finger! The woman is for Mama Kyria!" he cries. So, still in a trance, he roots around in his apparatus for a ring of red copper and holds it out. Then he begins to dance again, imitating this terrible genie's walk, his curled fingers, his lurching steps. He emits groans, pulls back his lips, grinds his teeth. Finally he mimes combat with his invisible adversary that terminates in abrupt gestures of sending the genie on his way, accompanied by sharp exclamations. He puts the ring on the sleeping patient. "The woman is quieting down; the woman has quieted! Her devil is Mama Kyria."

He picks up his bag again, empties it onto the ground, and brandishes the little bag of *kabé*, the baobab bark powder he used earlier, which he now prescribes again as a smoke purification and a drink for three days. He begins declaiming again in a resounding voice, "Thanks to the karakorey, thanks to Baana, thanks to Awa, he is gone! May God leave Awa alone because it is Awa who showed me the way. Awa! We will treat the patient thanks to the kabé, the fogno, the karakorey. We will treat her!" And he invokes Nankulé and Awgoundou, important places in Ghimbala country where the genii reside, and adds, "When the devils leave their homes they bring back game." [5] Then he says, "If Kola Gaba's devils attack someone, Issa cannot heal them; if Issa's devils attack someone, Sina Kala cannot heal them." He finally cries out, "*La hilāha!* The devils are gone! There is only one God! The devils are gone!" as at the end of a public ceremony of the

5. That is, they find victims.

cult, when the genii are chased from the dancing area. The trance ends and he says again, now in French and more calmly, "The devils have gone," which confirms that they were indeed present the moment before.

While Sogoba regains his spirits and loses his genie, old Diallo reveals to me that this is the first time his wife's aggressor has manifested himself so clearly and the gaw designated him so explicitly. Sogoba begins giving me explanations again. I hadn't realized he was eating wakando seeds, so prized by the genii, the same as those distributed at each cult session. "Awa gave me the advice," he continues. "I understood that the woman had called Mama Kyria; she had even tried to sing his song, because it is this djinarou who was attacking her from the beginning."

To consecrate the protective ring, he continues, one must slit the throats of two cocks, one white, the other black. The copper ring is dipped in the blood of the sacrifices and washed several times, all this for three days. He explains to me that "the back room is all good." In trance, the gaw had reviewed all the talismans in the house; he had stopped before each one, in particular the one hung over the front door, and concluded there was no object that could upset the inhabitants of the house. I finally understand some of what he said when Almâmi was there. "I don't know if the one who did this put the thing under the first bed, or under the second, or elsewhere," he had said, taking the patient's hand and sending Diallo to inspect the second bed.

Sogoba has started to limp since the end of his trance. He seems very tired now. He led the session with great energy last night and was possessed for a long time. He did not fear entering into trance anew today and again expending considerable energy to demonstrate his skills. I invite him to come to the pirogue for disinfectant and a more effective protection of his wound. Before leaving the house, he gives Diallo a little powder needed to continue care in the coming days.

Going down the river I think about the violent scene to which I have just been witness and, in part, actor. I think again of the humble interior and the poor people I have just left. This drama, in which daily poverty is suddenly elevated to the dimensions of a sacred gesture, took place under a photograph of the twin sisters stuck right to the earthen wall. In it, I recognized both of them, beautiful and young, dressed in great ceremonial boubous with soft faces, virgin still to all suffering, crowned in a candid splendor. Now they are withered, used up by a too-hard existence, wearing clothing of no color, no age. The patient has lost six children of the seven she brought into the world; the only one left her is the little girl with poliomyelitis who went to find Almâmi earlier. The family's material destitution only accentuates this misfortune. How, then, can one not respond to this severity with violence of a liberatory cast? This person's trance thus appears a momentary refuge and the genie a possible alibi. The problems attributed to him (a knot in the throat, a blister that rises and falls, feelings of suffocation) remind one of behavior of a hysterical nature.

But the attack perpetrated by the old, leprous captive at high noon—the hour when the genii are indeed known to rise—as well as the gaw's untimely intervention, gave me more shadows and questions than clarity, starting with the issue of the day of the incident. It took place on a Friday, God's day above all others and the one on which, in theory, the genii vanish. Yet today . . .

It seems to me that Islam is also responsible for the sister's opposition to the patient's joining the Ghimbala. She of course cites her age, her fatigue, and the wear and tear resulting from repeated pregnancies, followed by the children's deaths, but I have learned since then that the twins are the daughters of an old Niafunké imam. Born in a highly Islamic milieu, they are loath to draw close to those who practice a faith their father certainly considered pagan. Furthermore, the One God was brought out to make the genii flee, as is often done at the end of sessions, underscoring again the ambiguous attitude of these gaw and their followers toward the revealed religion. These successive phases of submission and the transgression, and the manipulations they suggest, call for more information.

In the same way, the scene created by the gaw when he began to list, praise, and insult the main genii of the cult—especially Mama Kyria, the presumed aggressor—makes me wonder about the nature of his trance. As in the session of the night before, he stated all his knowledge; in addition, he mimed genuine combat with the aggressor-genie. Was he possessed by his own genie at that point? Or, taken with simple trance, was he not acting like an Indian or Siberian shaman, engaging in dialogue with the invisible forces he was confronting? How did he figure out the identity of the aggressor-genie? Was his trance, as it intervened during treatment, a frequent and recognized practice? The suddenness of the apparition, the confusion it engendered, the rapid changes of situation—what to make of these?

THE WELCOMING GIFT

Things look very different about fifty kilometers away in the order and clarity of the home of Kola Gaba, the great priest of the Ghimbala at Dabi near Niafunké. With him I became aware of the importance of the river-genii cult's therapeutic activity, at the start of my trips to the upper bend in January 1985. On his vast village compound, Kola Gaba continually hosts several patients, alone or accompanied by a family member. On several different occasions I have attended *yaré* rituals there.

The yaré is the welcoming gift the family of a victim offers to the genii during the first phase of the cure. The term includes the whole ritual that accompanies this gift. Each time it follows the same impeccable order, in a calm and contemplative atmosphere. Here is a summary description of one of the first I was able to observe.

The session takes place in a secluded room away from all indiscreet gazes except mine. The patient today, a Fula woman, presents herself clothed in her most beautiful finery: a mauve wrap-skirt of cotton damask with delicate veils, ears jeweled with the heavy, golden earrings the wives of well-to-do-animal breeders still wear. Her husband is here and helps the gaw's assistant to control a red billy goat.

The ritual takes place in four stages. Kola Gaba begins by making the patient kneel in front of the animal and asking her to bump her forehead three times against the emerging horns of the goat, while he moves a necklace composed of little bells, rings, and diverse talismans from the head of one to the head of the other. Then he has her sit on the side of the animal, which has already been turned over and is kept on the ground by the assistants. The magic necklace is passed three more times over the patient's body, in a movement going from head to feet. In the following phase, Kola Gaba asks her to get up again and orders her to step over the beast being held on the ground.

Finally, in the fourth stage, the assembly goes outside for the sacrifice. The animal's throat is cut while facing east, in the direction of Mecca; the woman sits on the goat's side, her back turned away from the scene, thus facing west. Under no circumstances can she now see the sacrificial blood flow as it is collected in a quite large pottery vessel and then poured into three smaller canaris. The whole ceremony lasts scarcely a half-hour, prior waiting and preparations included. The different acts have unfolded before a limited and completely silent audience. As for Kola Gaba, he has not stopped mumbling completely incomprehensible incantations against the clinks of the necklace and the tinkling of the bells, incantations he has never been willing to communicate to me following the ceremony.

The Fula shepherd had taken advantage of the annual transhumance toward the pastures of Lake Débo to bring his wife to Kola Gaba. He had been referred to this gaw after several unhappy attempts with other healers and even a dispensary doctor. The young woman was subject to successive phases of prostration and great excitation. Kola Gaba had diagnosed an attack of the genii as soon as he gave her the first treatments in the form of smoke purifications, for there had been an immediate improvement following them. The first purification allowed him to establish the diagnosis but was not sufficient to check the attack. The Fula man nonetheless asked permission to leave with his wife; two days later they were back, after the problems started again. They had both been in Dabi a month when Kola Gaba proposed carrying out the yaré to calm the genii and distance them from their victim.

The patient (whom we can call, as followers do, *malé bania,* literally "the master's slave") must next be integrated into the cult during a public session in which she reveals the name of the genie possessing her. For now, she is daubed with the blood of the sacrificed beast, mixed with a powder made from the genii's plants.

The Meaning of the Ritual

Simple observation of the gestures carried out during the ritual leads one to think they all combine to chase the evil—that is, the disturbing genie or genii—from the patient's body and make it enter the body of the goat given as a sacrifice. Without ever giving me the exact formula of the words he uttered during the yaré, the priest did explain in the yaré he exhorts the genii to leave their victim by mixing flatteries, polite threats, and promises, among them the gift of the beast whose blood they would very soon drink. In passing, the gaw draws his invisible interlocutors' attention to the animal's qualities; this is why the animal must not be puny or sick or unclean in any way for eating, for the furious genii will disdain the sacrifice and take vengeance. It also seemed to me that the intimate contact of the two bodies, the circulation of the cult objects from one to the other, and the patient's changes in position and stepping over the animal combine to sow a certain confusion in the aggressors designed to make them lose hold (as with exorcism). After a while, the genii should not know where they are nor where the victim is. The sacrifice that concludes this highly constructed ritual is destined to separate the genii from their human prey, at least temporarily.

The Importance of Smells

The confusion of the two bodies is accompanied by a confusion of smells likely to make the genii lose hold. As for the sacrificial blood, it keeps the one covered in it from being importuned by the genii riding around her or him. It protects the person from the genii's odor, which people are not supposed to be able to stand, just as the genii cannot tolerate theirs. It also constitutes long-term protection against renewed attack. "It's like an ID card," Mahaman tells me. The aggressor-genie who comes back to try again recognizes the odor of blood dedicated to him or her on the body of the desired prey. The genii remember, "even ten years later," that they have already consumed their share of the sacrifice and leave the gaw's client alone. Blood is considered a kind of indelible olfactory marker reminding the genii that things have been done in the right and proper ways.[6]

A RITUAL TO CONSOLIDATE
THE RELATIONSHIP

Six months at most after the yaré, the malé bania should again carry out a curative ritual to reinforce her or his relationship to the world of Ghimbala. This new episode bears the name *kaendi* (to stop behind) or *hangandi* (to cause to follow), depending on the gaw. Whatever its name, the ritual remains the same and greatly resembles the yaré ritual, with some important differences. The animal presented, a kid or a lamb, is not sacrificed but raised by the malé bania, who must care for it, not mistreat it, not slit its throat, and not sell it. If the animal dies, it must be replaced. At the end of three years, however, a new animal can be substituted for the old one, on the condition that the first be given to the patient's entourage.

As the animal is young, it is easily held at arm's length during the ritual by the gaw, who passes it over the client's body and wraps it around his or her waist by making the four hooves touch, if possible. In contrast to most yaré, the kaendi is not addressed to several genii

6. In principle, people and genii can't stand the smell of each other and try to avoid each other. But through the yaré sacrifice, it becomes possible for them to come closer together. On this occasion, the plants that the gangi like are mixed with the sacrificial blood. The effluvia from this mixture authorize promiscuity between the two worlds. Smeared with this preparation, the postulant can tolerate the odor of the gangi prowling around him or her; conversely, the genii forget people's odor, which is covered by the smell of the sacrificial blood mixed with the appropriate plants. In the same way, the preparatory offerings and sacrifices of batous are attempts to draw the genii down among people within a peaceful, codified, and controlled relationship. Marcel Détienne writes, "The sacrifice traditionally requires smoke purification of the odorific substances whose recognized virtue is to call the gods to the sacrifice meant for them" (Détienne, *Les Jardins d'Adonis* [Gallimard, 1972], 236). This olfactory aspect of relationship to the gods underscores the sensual, concrete nature of the polytheistic religions.

but only to the one who has become attached to the gaw's patient. Thus the animal must correspond to the genie through a precise composition of color and coat. There are seven combinations, as there are seven primary genii of the cult, the rest aligning themselves accordingly.

The two heads are bumped together only once in honor of the single genie concerned, whom the gaw addresses directly in these terms: "You have told us what we had to give you; we have given it you. You have demanded we bring it here alive in this yard [of the malé bania] so that you can leave the person and continue with the animal; we are doing so. Here is your animal!" After this the malé states all her or his hopes for healing, hand on the head of the animal, in whose mouth the patient spits three times in closing. The kaendi's manifest goal is to contain the genie by turning the illness he or she has provoked onto the animal for as long as the animal is in the courtyard of the follower.

A TRUE DIVORCE

Finally, there is an ultimate ritual, the kanji, also called *kangari* or *kangou* (to stick, drive into the soil), at the end of which relations between the genie and the person he or she is persecuting are put to an end. The Ghimbala followers do not necessarily do the kanji themselves. They call instead on old people exhausted by possessions, travelers going to distant and dangerous countries, and those who refuse to enter the cult for religious reasons. This is what the Fula emperor Sheikou Hamadou's daughter did since she could not devote herself to serving the genii because of her father. The methods of a kanji vary almost from one gaw to the next, except for the obligatory organizing of a batou during which the beneficiary of the operation is possessed, normally for the last time.

He or she thus submits, sometimes with blows, to a precise interrogation during which all the disturbing events that might unleash a trance are listed. The person must answer in the negative to a series of questions of this type: "Will you cry out [be possessed] if fire breaks out? If you find yourself on a capsizing pirogue? If lightning strikes not far from you? If a violent fight breaks out?" Then the gaw turns toward the members of the audience and asks them to complete his interrogation to avoid any possible omissions.[7] His concern for an

---

7. See appendix 5, which provides a description of a kanji ceremony.

exhaustive listing of circumstances favorable to the genii's intrusion among people (outside cult sessions) emphasizes the extremely emotive nature of mediums, who react to the suddenness of a dramatic event with trance.

Here, then, are the yaré, kaendi, and kanji, in order. They are high points of a process of continual care based on smoke purifications, washing, massage, offerings and small sacrifices of hens, and consultations of the genii through cowry shells or dreams. But containing ourselves to this simplified approach would somewhat efface the reality of Ghimbala therapeutic practices that the contradictory and confused session at Attara (discussed earlier in this chapter) allowed us to glimpse.

THE CONFUSION OF DIVERGENT PRACTICES

I had been seduced by Kola Gaba's sovereign attitude during the yaré session in January 1985. The gaw never once gave the impression of being overwhelmed by the forces he confronted, and he behaved with perfect mastery of his methods and their effects, to the end. Several days after the eventful performance at Attara, I was fortunate to attend another yaré at his place. It unfolded with the same economy of gesture, the same sobriety, the same contemplation as the one I have already described. I couldn't keep myself from asking the gaw for illumination on the excesses I had witnessed at Attara, though I was careful not to reveal the names of those involved.

Kola Gaba responded categorically: priests who allow themselves to be possessed during treatments are "little gaw," according to his own phrase. Nor is there any question of making the genii descend on Friday, God's day. "In any case, the genii don't come," he added. And yet Mama Kyria indeed manifested himself that day.[8] The essential elements of his statement have been confirmed by other gaw of great experience. For a cure to go well, the one leading it must converse with the genii as an equal and not allow himself or herself to be bested by them. If more essential information is necessary, the gaw can then organize a batou and enter into trance within the format of a ceremony without impairment of status. Yet younger gaw and a priestess told

8. After inquiring, I learned that Mama Kyria can manifest himself to people even on the day reserved for God because he is a Muslim genie. But he only does so in exceptional circumstances—to announce serious news, for example. Was this the case? Moreover, it seemed to me that the gaw also hurled insults at other genii, who apparently presided as well at this session.

me they frequently receive their own genii while healing a patient out-side the batou.

So here I am again confronted with the heterogeneity of practices and beliefs as well as of interpretations of the Ghimbala. I have at-tended other yarés in addition to Kola Gaba's. In one, organized in the Gombo encampment on the riverbank about three kilometers from his home, the instruments were not the same: a chain replaced the necklace, the bells were different and fewer, and a big spear was planted in the ground in place of the sombé. The actions were repeated on the basis of the number seven rather than three, and the whole ritual was more summary, the gestures more expeditious, not coin-ciding with Kola Gaba's. Each gaw thus appears to invent his or her ceremonial, instruments, and gestures. To each his or her own truth, almost.

That's not all: by going a little deeper into the subject, I realized that the rituals differ not only in the technical details of their unfolding but in the order of their appearance and even their principles. Thus the kaendi is not always a consolidation of the yaré. Quite often the gaw prescribes and executes it directly if the aggressor-genie is not very dangerous and the attack is light, or if the patient and his or her family lack the means to have a burdensome ritual done, especially in com-bination with organizing a public ceremony. In this latter case either the kaendi is enough, as long as the patient's problems disappear, or it precedes a yaré. Originally, everyone hopes to stop before this point, but as the aggressors return to their victims with great force, one must become resigned to doing the burdensome yaré ritual. With Kola Gaba and other great gaw, this ritual precedes the batou, which is felt to complete it, and in principle concludes the first phase of the therapeu-tic cycle. Yet I've met several priests who perform no yaré before gath-ering information about the identity of the aggressor-genie or -genii, as well as the nature of the sacrifices and offerings that could appease them. The information is delivered during one or several prior batous, of which there can be up to seven.

On these occasions, it is not necessary for the patient to be pos-sessed or for the gaw or other followers to be in trance and inspired by their genii, pronouncing what must be done. But so much the better if the genie descends on the patient along the way, because he or she can then be the one to indicate measures to take, as dictated by his or her own persecutor. Once the yaré is performed, it is not im-possible for the priest to feel some time later that he or she must per-form the same ritual again. Sometimes it is addressed to all the great genii, sometimes only to one among them. As for the kanji, while clearly the separation it establishes is definitive, this does not keep the gaw from giving the patient a protective object—ring, forehead band, or small cord of magic knots—in case the genie should have an insolent fantasy to remanifest.[9]

What to do with all this?

A SEPARATION PROCESS

Anthropologists generally attribute to themselves the right to elicit meaning from the lives of those on whom they plan to report. For the forest of contradictory meanings they thus substitute their own order, whose reductive serenity is superimposed on the complexity, conflicts, and obscure places in these lives passed through momentarily, all the while remaining external to them. In fact, I do not claim to do otherwise, but only to be conscious of the limits that each person's subjectivity imposes on any attempt at reconstructing a reality always perceived partially. With the present state of what I think I know of the Ghimbala, it seems to me possible to elicit some partial meanings.

All the slightly confused *bricolages* that have just been recounted combine to make the aggressor-genii lose their hold.[10] It is in this

---

9. These knotted cords are called *guli*.

10. Andras Zempléni speaks of a separation process of the same kind in talking about the Senegalese N'döp in a long article, "Des Etres Sacrificiels," in *Sous le Masque de l'Animal, Essais sur le Sacrifice en Afrique Noire*, ed. M. Cartry (Presses Universitaires de France, 1987), 267–317. It focuses on the interpretation of a group of possession phenomena: "The target of the ritual, I emphasize, is neither exorcism nor a simple 'symbolic alliance' with the *rab*, but *the transformation of an internal and inclusive relationship with an anonymous being into an external and exclusive relationship with a named rab*. A crucial point, 'healing' from the possession-illness takes place necessarily *by its conversion into ritual possession*" (author's emphasis).

I nonetheless think that symbolic alliance with the entity (god, genie, or spirit) is an essential aspect of possession, first for the priests, who are themselves very often possessed, but also for the mediums. See my *Tambours d'Eau*, in which I think I have demonstrated the benefits followers receive from a regular relationship with their genii, alongside the servitude these imply. Also, the sick person's healing does not necessarily take place by conversion of the "possession-illness" into "ritual possession." So the sacrifice or sacrifices do not always result in the patient's possession. I have observed this frequent disjunction of possession and sacrifice in Mali as well as in Brazil and even in Bahia, in a cult that claimed to be candomblé (the priestess was from Yansan; one of Shango's wives) while being open to *umbanda* and *macumba* influences.

I will specify, in addition, that there is no real initiatory moment among the Ghimbala (ritualized seclusion, symbolic death, etc.). The shortening of the initiatory period—its being stolen away or disappearing—can also be observed in numerous popular Brazilian cults derived from institutions closer to the African model, the candomblé of Bahia or the *batuques* of Porto Alegre, for example. It follows from this that the pos-

vein that the therapeutic batou is conceived, organized when the yaré and kaendi rituals are not enough. These ceremonies are veritable confrontations between good and sometimes bad dealings, held with the use of plenty of tricks. If the presumed aggressor does not want to talk, the ones officiating interrogate those close to, and particularly those above, him or her. Under the influence of the celebration, with its praises and sacrifices, the fulfilled, happy genii reveal the name of the one among them who has tormented the malé bania. "But the devils don't rush; they wait to be satisfied. When they feel you've made enough effort, they ask the one who's attacked to abandon the victim," says Mahaman. Yet the appropriate sacrifice and no other must still be made or the gangi will not leave. "The others say: if you don't do it [the right sacrifice] we can't intervene, but if you do it, we can."

Sometimes the genie responsible is absent or else is enjoying giving false information through the mouths of those possessed; these maneuvers must be thwarted. When several genii possess a victim, the gaw asks them to leave the person to just one of them. Then the gaw addresses that one, tries to identify it and make it leave, and, if unable to, organizes a batou. In principle, the gaw manipulates the invisible tormentors with respect for their superiority. Kola Gaba explains: "By seeking at the beginning [of the cure] I will understand if it is for one or several gangi. If the patient is attacked by several of them, I can do the yaré for all the gangi. Then I will do the batou if it's necessary for the one remaining. But I can't force the gangi; in fact, I'm too afraid to force them; I can only beg them to leave the patient to one of them. I consider the gangi as superiors: I give them presents when they visit me; I act in such a way that they are happy with me so they agree to do what I ask them."

On the other hand, when the kanji is staged, there is no more tricking the genii nor maintaining a dialogue, but simply hastening definitive separation. For this, any means are acceptable, even the most violent. The sacrificial sheep is mistreated with great kicks; the "devils" are threatened in the name of God with terrible torments and even destruction if they don't give in. The follower whom they are to leave

---

sessed of these cults embody more active roles and seem to be less submissive to the authority of the priest directing their *terreiro*. Among the Ghimbala, the priests' power remains strong but is exerted in another mode. The field of the possession is the point of confrontation between interpretations and local symbolic systems, which are contradictory to say the least and must be examined each time within their historical and social context. Thus I cannot share Zempléni's thesis because of its overly generalizing and systematic nature, despite its seductiveness.

undergoes the roughest treatment to make her or him, in a final trance, forswear belonging to the cult under the influence of real torture. The person is whipped hard or partially knocked out when the gaw or an assistant strikes the skin of a sacrificed animal set on the person's head during the entire time of the interrogation. The skin is held taut by three strapping men. Sometimes the person emerges from this with a swollen face, eyes darkly bloodshot (see appendix 5).

THE GENIE, THE PATIENT, AND THE GAW

The entire cure is a separation process conducted very differently according to the means at the disposal of the organizing gaw, the patient's personality, and the disposition of the principal aggressor-genie. All the efforts of the gaw and his or her acolytes aim to separate the genii from their victim, temporarily or definitively, so that the victim's torments cease. This is the meaning repeated from one cure to the next beyond all singularity of circumstances and diversity of procedures followed.

Everything starts with a declaration of skill by the gaw, who has noted an improvement in the patient's state following the initial smoke purification. These first treatments do not, however, permit the gaw to detect the aggressor's name unless the patient enters into trance and screams it out. In any case, separation is very momentary at this stage. In principle, the genie's identity must be clearly specified, the genie's wishes collected, and the distance between the genie and the patient ascertained. Then the gaw performs the yaré or the kaendi, or even both if need be, in the order set by the cure itself. Public sessions of the cult take place in the interim as a locus of information due to the transmitted messages. These sessions permit normalization of the relationship between people and genii through ritualized trances, which circumscribe the possible and accepted relations between these two worlds within the consecrated time and space of the ceremony. Finally, the kanji establishes definitive separation in answer to the family's wishes and makes the constraining service to the genii associated with possessions stop.

Great Genii and Supernumeraries

The complex commerce of gaw and genii reflects the idea that the former have of the world of the latter. Because this world is very hierarchical, it is enough to address the great genii, and the others who are subordinate to them comply as well. So the gaw only converse with Awa, Moussa, Baana, and Mayé, and sometimes with Mama Kyria and Samba Poulo. Thus the three steps over the animal in Kola

Gaba's courtyard corresponded to the invocations of each of the three primary genii, whose most striking slogans the gaw recited at the precise moment the malé bania arrived at the body of the prostrate animal.

In certain cases the gaw addresses only one of the great genii. Even if he or she is not the source of the problems, that genie, if satisfied with what is received, will intercede with the genie concerned because they are of the same family.[11] It is understandable, therefore, that if a patient is attacked by great Moussa's analogue, the gaw addresses Moussa. If Moussa agrees with the petitioner, "little Moussa" cannot refuse to abandon his victim. The great genii of the cult always win their case, according to Mahaman's formula, which is loaded with metaphors borrowed from contemporary society: "When you take a thief and bring him to the police station, it's no longer the policeman who arrested him who decides what happens to him; it's the police chief."

Unequal Therapeutic Powers

All gaw are not equally armed in their confrontations with the genii. Great and lesser gaw can be distinguished, and between them is an intermediate class of "middle gaw." The members of the first group have a wide spectrum of practices, techniques, and diverse prescriptions to make the genii give in. They use more plants than the others, among them always one secret weapon—the one that will provide the decisive purification to use in difficult cases. They can easily enter into contact with the genii through deliberate dreams, in which the path to take during the cure is revealed to them. (This practice of controlled dreaming, which emphasizes the shamanic-type power of the gaw, was introduced in chapter 4.) They can also organize therapeutic batous. The capacity for mobilization of these progressive means is such that the great gaw never have to go as far as the batou unless they want to obtain complementary information deemed essential, or unless the patient enters into trance during a preliminary phase of the cure. Kola Gaba tries as much as possible not to go to that point. In a period of one year (1986–87) he organized only seven batous but healed about seventy people.

The middle gaw have unequal access to shamanic dreaming. For them, this path is very complicated or even inaccessible. They prefer, after preliminary treatments, to proceed to therapeutic batous as their main sources of information. They organize these batous until they

---

11. For example, the gaw can address his or her personal genie, who becomes an auxiliary in the cure undertaken.

obtain the information permitting them to complete the two key rituals of the cure, yaré and kaendi.

Finally, the lesser gaw cannot establish close contact with the genii. They have at their disposal neither dreaming nor batous because they do not enter into trance.[12] Most of the time, they rather mechanically execute a certain number of acts that lead to the two rituals, which are accomplished in a rather summary fashion. These lay magicians, who do not have cult functions, are nonetheless considered gaw because they treat genii-illnesses that are not too serious; if an illness becomes serious, they send the patient to a more qualified gaw.

Mediums and Others

The patient's personality also orients the cure, in the sense that treatment unfolds differently depending on whether the patient "screams" or "doesn't scream," that is, whether the patient is or is not susceptible to trance. In the former case, the gaw can organize therapeutic batous to hasten the cure's unfolding. A patient "screams" during the initial smoke purifications and enters into trance. "Wild" possession is stopped immediately,[13] and the gaw abandons preliminary treatments to move straight into the public ceremony, during which the genii directly express their wishes through possessions. If the patient does not scream, the gaw has to take other routes to arrive at the hoped-for healing.

A Pact with the Genii

Unequal access to the genii, the foundation of the hierarchy among priests, rests on the principle described earlier: there are gaw merely chosen by people, and others elect of the genii, come to them without having been sought. These gaw make a kind of pact with the doubling world of the Ghimbala and remain in close relation to them. "I call them, they answer me," says one of these gaw. Another presents the relationship he and his assistant entertain with the genii in the following way: "We thank the gangi for sending us many patients, and when they don't send us enough, we make them presents so they will attack many men and women, who will come to us to be treated." If patients do not follow the gaw's recommendations to the letter and do not

---

12. They sometimes call on another gaw who has the power to organize therapeutic batous, and with the help of this gaw they treat difficult cases. I give the example of such a situation in the next chapter.

13. "Wild" possessions, as Roger Bastide uses the term, are unwanted possessions that happen outside of cult sessions, without protection of any kind. Generally, the genie provoking them are not identified.

satisfy his or her demands, the cure will not be complete and the genii will not fail to send their victims back to their ally.

Within the group of great gaw linked to the genii by this implicit pact, some are luckier than others and, according to their means, obtain better results than their competitors. It is said they are coddled by gangi who particularly like their qualities and who give them directly what they have refused others.

THE CURE: THE FUNDAMENTAL RELATIONSHIP

While it separates the world of people from the world of the genii, confounded for a moment during illness, the cure unites the patient with the therapist-priest. A strong connection of dependence is created in the former toward the latter during the long weeks, sometimes months, even years, that the treatment lasts. The patient becomes the malé bania, the master's slave. When cured, the patient continues to be called thus. The term accurately symbolizes the maintenance of the relationship created by the cure, during which the gaw transforms his or her patient into a veritable servant.

Thus, at the beginning of my inquiries, I encountered a gaw in Tonka who supposedly came from Nbétou, a large Bambara township to the south of Niafunké. He was accompanied in all his doings by a young man he was treating. The gaw wanted to demonstrate his powers to impress me. He took me through a labyrinth of alleyways into an ocher-walled compound that gave off the smell of old Africa and smoke, at the back of which his client was secluded. The boy was in a state of permanent subjection that resembled hypnosis. The master had him on a tight rein. He alternated between curing sessions—during which the patient-servant entered into trances that seemed to me in part provoked, sometimes falling on the ground and holding himself there, immobile—and requests for services, which the subordinate fulfilled without saying a word, like a sleepwalker.

A strange gaw, that Amirou Coulibaly, boastful and sensitive at the same time, violent and generous. It was he who had wanted to establish a relationship with me. As he didn't find me at an earlier point in the day, he left his sombé in a corner of the room where we took our meals to give himself a reason to come back and pick it up that same evening. Contact was established. I saw him assiduously for two days. He had a horse to use in the bush, and in town a moped on which he sometimes dragged me down the sandy streets. We left him at the port when we went toward Diré. Despite my efforts to find him again on later trips, I never heard from him again. He seemed to be unknown in Nbétou, where he claimed to be from. He vanished in the Sahel without a trace.

On the other hand, I did see the protagonists of Attara's eventful sequence again when I made another brief stop there on my way back to Mopti at the end of my 1986 trip. Diallo, who recognized the pirogue from a distance, was already awaiting us on the riverbank when we came up. Thus I learned that his wife had experienced no new aggression from her genie since the epic session unleashed by Issa Sogoba, the Sumpi gaw. Sogoba didn't show himself this time. Though I was soon to have dealings with him again, the old man seemed to be quiet for the moment.

☙

The gaw thus try to distance patients from their invisible aggressors out of the principle of separation between the worlds of people and genii, for their confusion is source of danger. It creates situations that cannot be mastered by ordinary means because it implies the intrusion of water, winds, storms, night—all the elements of genii incarnate—into the social universe. This separation principle is the basis for all combinations of individual treatments, rituals, and therapeutic batous to make the initial problems stop. Fear of direct contact between people and genii (beyond the cult sessions dedicated to it) is expressed with particular clarity in the diverse rituals and techniques used to make possession occurring outside ceremonies cease, as well as in the meticulous enumeration of events likely to unleash this kind of trance made during the kanji. The gaw thus hold a central place because they are the guarantors of the shifting equilibrium ruling relationships between the two worlds.

The diversity of cures also illuminates differences in power and notoriety among these different priests of the genii. The great gaw are clearly those chosen and cherished by the genii. They obtain the best results in the cures they undertake. There is no doubt that this therapeutic efficacy is the basis of a large part of their reputations. They also recognize willingly that their treatment is ineffective for certain attacks of madness. "Patients who are drooling are attacked by shaytáns and not by the gangi; I can do nothing for them," says Kola Gaba. Less insightful gaw try hard to treat children incapable of speaking—without results. Each case I have encountered concerns a child who has survived cerebro-spinal meningitis while probably still a victim of incurable brain lesions. He or she is in perfect health but has lost the ability to talk and emits only inarticulate sounds.

The clearly expressed hierarchy among gaw, echoed by the hierarchy ordering relations between great and lesser genii, does not keep the diversity of curative practices—fruit of the cult's decentralization—from creating a strong sense of dispersion. The Ghimbala cult seems to become diffuse like the river along the multiple branches, ponds, and lakes of the region. But a deep cohesion among the possessed of these places does in fact exist. What links the patient to his or her gaw during the cure sets the tone as the fundamental relationship of belonging to the Ghimbala community.

7 / The Genii Club

In February 1987, I stop over again in Attara to greet old Diallo and get news of his wife. It seems she is doing much better and has not needed to visit Sogoba again. Today she goes tranquilly about her housework. In fact, Diallo does not even know where the gaw might be right now. It is impossible to learn anything further; since it is late, I decide to spend the night on the beach. While the two young crew members set up the tent, I climb the nearby dune that covers the local gourgoussou with the cemetery at its foot. I have just enough time to bathe under the final rays of an exemplary sunset and lose an oh-so-precious nib pen. Once I notice, I go back onto the dune looking for my work-tool in the company of dear Almâmi. He does not fail to murmur some protective formulas before we cross the field of the dead with its occasional outcroppings of skeletons and crania, dislodged at the mercy of the rainy season's showers, which gully the soil, and of the wind, which constantly reshapes this unstable relief.

We are protected, but the pen is no less eternally lost, absorbed by the sand. We do not tarry, for it is dangerous to stay around the peaks of the dunes, especially at twilight. Below, one of the gaw's relatives has been told of our arrival and waits for me near the fire of our encampment. He informs me that Sogoba has been staying for some time on the other side of the river to treat a difficult case. He is in Kormou, a village on the Ambéri branch, scarcely six kilometers from here overland. By pirogue it takes several hours because one has to go around the isthmus that separates the two branches. So we will go there tomorrow.

AN ASSEMBLY OF GAW

We arrive in Kormou, which looks just like all the other towns. On the bank, women wash their dishes and take advantage of the opportunity to bathe between the pirogues drawn partly onto the sand. The middle ground is taken up with children, who stop playing and dash over to the foreign craft. Above, sheltered from floods, the somber gray mass of the village cuts into the light sand.

For those who go by river, everything always comes together and falls apart on the bank. The announcement of our arrival, disseminated by the children, spreads quickly indeed. Here is Awa Koulikoro, the local priestess, who comes to greet us even before I manage to come up to her. She is followed shortly by Issa Sogoba, who is flanked by Séry, another gaw from the village of Sumpi, an enormous, wiry, athletic man with an angular face. On the other hand, Santché, elder and master of both of them, has not come down. I hasten to mention that I am going to visit him as soon as I have heard all the news, which turns out to be abundant and fascinating; Issa Sogoba tells it to me in French.

He moved here three months ago to live with a family that had already dealt with gaw from his village for one of their daughters four years ago. First had come the fruitless attempts by the marabouts and Awa Koulikoro. Then Santché's sister, head gaw of Sumpi, had been delegated with her cowries to diagnose by divination. She concluded that the young woman was being attacked by the most famous genii-couple of the Ghimbala, Awa and Baana. Early treatments resulted in improvement, but then the sacrifice of a white sheep to Awa and a black billy goat to Baana was neglected. The family waited until the problems returned before calling back the Sumpi gaw. Issa Sogoba was sent to scout. In the interim, two other cases of illness attributable to the genii were declared in the village. Overwhelmed by these events, the gaw called his elders to the rescue.

At this point, the initial family has just decided to make the promised sacrifices. The kobiri will be sacrificed in a yaré for Awa; the bundi will not have its throat slit but be kept in kaendi for Baana. First, however, all necessary information about the cure must be obtained from the genii at the public ceremonies, during which the possessed will deliver the awaited messages.

The three priests have introduced themselves to Awa Koulikoro and brought her into their therapeutic cycle "because we cannot work without the agreement of the local gaw," as Sogoba told me. Earlier she had declared in trance that she was not able to treat the three cases, which were then given to the nonlocal priests. She had also taken advantage of this opportunity to merge the cure of one of her patients with those now belonging to the three visitors. There have already been two public sessions. During one, a young man went into a trance and declared that the gaw who had to heal him was not present at the batou. So Séry, in another possession, revealed in response that they should send the young man to Bili Korongoy, the Gaïrama gaw who lives about one hundred kilometers away, near Diré. That leaves only three people to treat, among them one who is dying. She has already dealt with two other gaw, but her family has not followed the prescriptions. There will be a batou this evening if she is not dead by then.

Before we part from each other, Sogoba gives me his version of the case of Diallo's wife: "It's very serious, because the illness will return." The sacrifices have indeed been made, but there has been no public session during which the patient could be ritually possessed because she has refused. Her sister has encouraged her in her resolution: an imam's daughter cannot dance with the Ghambala. So the cure is incomplete.

An epidemic of eye illness rages in Kormou. Everyone is struck by it, especially the old people and the children. I spend part of a day distributing little bottles of eyewash. As my modest stock starts to diminish disturbingly, I begin dispensing the drops myself, promising to put them in again before my departure. It is a temporary relief of the suffering of these children, most of them very young and painful to see, their swollen eyes so full of pus they can barely even open them. It remains a laughable intervention, however, given the vast sanitary needs of this completely undersupplied population.

After a long wait, I am finally told around eleven o'clock at night that the third batou will in fact take place as planned. Awa Koulikoro, whose old, sick husband had needed her, began calling together the obligatory participants—singers, calabash players, dancers, griots—in the proper way very late. A little frustrated by this delay, the three visiting gaw are in a hurry to get to the essential part: if the seriously ill client dies, the session will become impossible. Once the ritual closing of the calabashes is done (after a polite exchange between Awa and her colleagues to determine who will do it), the session begins vigorously. We are on a small plaza within the village, sheltered from the wind. Séry, Sogoba, and Awa are quickly possessed. Santché, leading the ceremony, restrains himself. He does not enter into trance but instead listens to the mediums, whom he encourages with his voice and whose messages he incites by shaking his cattle bells between two fits of dry coughing that bow him a little further.

Sogoba, in a possession more spectacular than violent, plays the fool as is his wont: he leaps, yaps, clowns around. Awa, on the other hand, is having a rather discreet possession. The host but not really the initiator of the operation, she keeps to a restrained role, and her trance is an extension of this role. Séry is violently taken by the djini Badji-Badji, but he calms down fairly quickly and delivers the most important message of the evening: the dying woman is under attack by both genii and sorcerors. The sorcerors must be eliminated to treat the genii's attack. The patient's family has neglected to sacrifice two red roosters, which is why their child is so seriously stricken. Séry turns toward his petrified clients and cries out his verdict several times: "You had to kill the red roosters to chase the sorcerers away—then we could have tackled the genii!" He concludes by delineating his own responsibility faced with the sadly predictable result: "If the gangi can't chase the sorcerors out, she will die!"

The dust rises in the cold night. Santché coughs more and more; the gaw, the musicians, the choir, and the griots are no longer able to provoke possession in the two frightened candidates turned loose in the batou. It's not for lack of united and redoubled efforts on the part of all the participants: they plunge the two patients into a bath of sound, chanting, and rhythm, while the possessed take them by the hand and try to pull them into the dance. This attempt to provoke contagious trance fails. The patients do not enter into direct contact with their genii and dictate the path to take in their cure. Ultimately, on the therapeutic level, this proves to be a useless ceremony.

The mediums become exhausted. Santché, more and more fragile, decides to break the session at around two in the morning by freeing his collaborators from their genii. But the women of the choir and the musicians do not agree and want to continue the event. One final confusion ensues, caused by their attempt to keep the genii among people while the gaw tries on the other hand to hasten their departure. He must then perform a more hurried ritual, placing hands on heads and rings in mouths with the usual incantations while the chanting and music continue. When everything finally stops, I go back to the bank of the river, exhausted by three hours of uncomfortable observation, imagining in what state the evening's actors, who have expended themselves without restraint, must now be.

This long day in Kormou affords a glimpse of how the gaw collaborate, how they sometimes come up against the patients' families, and how the network of belonging and subordination uniting the cult's followers is woven.

FROM COLLABORATION TO DEPENDENCE

Episodic Collaboration between Gaw

The assembly of priests I had just observed corresponded to a way of working together which is episodic but still frequent. Thus, one or several gaw called to consult in a village not their own establish with their local colleague a relationship that is fairly precisely codified.

They introduce themselves to the local gaw and ask him or her to participate with them in the cure to be undertaken, even if they are the ones actually responsible for it. They leave it to the local gaw to organize the sessions. She or he not only participates but often takes advantage of the opportunity—as did Awa Koulikoro—to have one of his or her own patients participate in them. The family of this patient thus has only to share the costs of the cure with the families of the other patients, rather than to assume all of it.

As part of her role, Awa Koulikoro also assembled the followers, a function indispensable to carrying out a therapeutic batou properly. She was then asked to carry out the ritual closing of the calabashes; after a polite exchange with Santché, she refused to do it. In other cases, the local gaw ends by allowing herself or himself to be convinced. This same courteous and rather formal ballet is repeated to determine who will perform the sacrifices at each point during the cure. Finally, if the cure is successful, the visitors share their earnings with their local colleague—no mere formal detail.

Regular Collaboration

In possession there are also forms of regular collaboration between priests—for example, those established on an egalitarian basis between two great gaw living in neighboring villages. Thus Hamadou Fofana in Tindirma and Bili Korongoy in Gaïrama meet when they need each other, support each other in difficult cases, and ask each other for advice. All the elements of their situations combine to favor their working together. They come from similar social backgrounds: the first, in Tindirma, is a Songhay blacksmith; the second is a Fula captive (dimadio) of distant Bambara origin. Both are aged and thus of the same generation. In addition, one is a priest of Baana, the other of Moussa; their genii are complementary.

In the same way, Sina Kala, the gaw of Sokoura, and Oussou Kondjorou, Waada Samba's descendant in Doundé, near Ngouma, have rather close relations even though their villages are much farther apart. They met during a tour the latter made in the Sah region to see one of his old patients; they became friends during cures they undertook in common. Quite recently, a patient of Oussou Kondjorou's had a relapse. Approached by the family to try a new cure, Sina Kala gave treatment only after receiving his friend's authorization. He of course expects to be treated in the same fashion, although normally it is competition that dominates between gaw.

Gougouré and Samba Alley, two gaw from the banks of the Bara Issa near Koumaïra, have another kind of association founded on their complementarity. The first does not do therapeutic batous. When the cure requires a session of possession, Gougouré asks his neighbor to do one at his home. He also goes to him for sacrifices: "I spit my incantations onto the knife; I pass it to Samba; he slits the animal's throat." Then they share the earnings from the cure. On the other hand, sometimes Alley sends his colleague patients he has not been able to cure. The superior age of the first gaw compensates for the disadvantage of not being able to organize ceremonies and balances relations between the two friends.

Hegemonic Position

In principle, the need to call on a priest with greater skill creates a dependent relationship on him or her, ensuring the greater gaw a position of hegemony.

For example, Kola Gaba of Dabi sits at the center of a constellation of lesser gaw, including those in Mangourou, the village next to Niafunké in the east, and those in Sumpi, to the west. They come to consult him, but he does not go to them unless he must treat a case for which he has been requested. He never leaves his place of residence, in fact, except on the express demand of a family whose patient cannot be transported and after his name has been invoked during divinatory sessions (or at least suggested to the family of the genii's victim). The priests dependent on Kola Gaba come to ask his advice, discuss their cures with him, show him the plants they use, and try to obtain other plants as well as new secrets.

A whole little world gravitates around the great gaw: singers, calabash, n'jarka, koubour, and djerkélé players; and genii-griots (*djiné garassa*), not to be confused with people-griots. Privileged relations develop between the gaw and the griot, especially when the griot is in service to a single priest. Mahaman mostly works with Hamadoun, the Tindirma gaw. The two men complement each other. Mahaman humorously defines their collaboration in this way: "Hamadoun needs me like the President of the Republic needs his journalists."[1] Griots know the genii's history better than the priest. They know how to sing their slogans and their praises at the right time. It is because of their talent that the genii descend in droves during cult sessions. On the other hand, the gaw knows the plants, the sacrifices, and the curative rituals and establishes direct contact with the genii through trance if need be. Mahaman works with Hamadoun and refuses to play

1. He is referring to situations in which journalists are the public-relations agents of governments.

regularly for other priests. At most he will collaborate with Bili Korongoy, because he is Hamadoun's ally.

Yet there are more and more "freelance" griots and singers who
form no alliance with any one priest and rent their services as needed
for ceremonies. Farka and Démoudou, both from Niafunké, are good
examples. The latter is an exceptional singer, so he can only be had
for nearly his weight in gold. We witnessed the impact of his voice on
the followers at Dondoro in chapter 5. Other actors in cult ceremonies
are less well endowed. Thus players and singers, occasional musicians
who perform only when the gaw organizes a session in their village,
are very poorly paid.

THE ENDURING RELATIONSHIP BETWEEN GAW AND FOLLOWER

We know that a strong and personalized relationship between therapist
and patient develops during the cure, justifying the name given the
patient when the cure is terminated: malé bania, or "follower of the
gaw." This relationship endures, for the former patient is held to a
certain number of obligations to his or her master, as a member of the
master's order.

These obligations are more or less restrictive according to the kind
of cure the malé bania underwent and the future relationship he or she
establishes in relation to the cult. But whatever their status, all the
cured are required to give the gaw a minimum tribute in the form of
an obligatory annual contribution. I will speak about this before dis-
cussing the obligations that vary according to each follower's position.

The obligatory annual contribution

The annual contribution is called the *taba yessi,* or "taste next year,"
because in principle the follower brings it to the annual feast that takes
place the evening the annual fast is broken, called *djiribéré:* New Year's
feast. The gift the gaw receives will thus be consumed during the year
beginning the next day.

The fee varies in content, but it is imperative that the malé bania
pay it once a year, preferably the night of the djiribéré or, failing that,
shortly afterward. It is paid either in kind or in money; in the latter
case, it is a small amount varying from one to two thousand CFA
francs.[2] In-kind assistance depends on the follower's activity. A fisher

2. That is, twenty to forty French francs. [This is approximately four to eight U.S.
dollars. CFA originally stood for *Colonies Françaises d'Afrique,* and now stands for *Com-*

gives dried or smoked fish; a farmer, a sheaf of millet or rice or even tobacco, sometimes the fruits of harvest. A woman may offer a mat she has woven herself, or spun cotton. Nothing is determined in advance; it is enough to give taba yessi when the time comes.

The person unable to bring a gift the night of the djiribéré does not come to the ceremony, held back by the shame of coming empty-handed. The malé bania behind in her or his obligation indeed tries to pay up as quickly as possible. In 1985, Sina Kala received just twenty followers for his cult's annual feast. But in the days following, another fifteen came. Each new arrival brought his or her taba yessi. The late-comers begged the gaw to organize a new session for them, and he felt obligated to comply.

The taba yessi symbolizes the malé bania's respect for her or his gaw. The gift renews their link of allegiance each year. Followers think that the person who fails to fulfill this duty over two or three years risks becoming the gangi's prey once again. In this case, the gangi appear as the real allies of the gaw, whose interests they defend. The malé bania whose negligence is penalized by a new genii attack has to be much pardoned by his or her malé before the healer deigns to resume treatment.

Formal, obligatory assistance to a gaw is reinforced by more spontaneous gifts made by the malé bania out of simple appreciation. Thus it is fairly common to meet followers who come to stay in the courtyards of their masters, to whom they offer assistance in the form of work. Men go into the field for several days; women assist the wives with their housework. These occasional housemaids sometimes remain several weeks.

However, recent years of crisis and famine have greatly disturbed the whole system. On the followers' side, much lower fees are paid. At the same time, gaw have a tendency to make the rounds of their followers ahead of the annual feast day with the goal of collecting support due at a later date, though not without having warned them of their visit, as tradition requires. Twice I have met great gaw returning from these expeditions. In early 1985, Bili Korongoy returned quite discouraged after seeing several followers who live southwest of Gaïrama. Famine was threatening, and he was able to bring back only the most minimal subsidies. In 1986, Oussou Kondjorou, Waada Samba's descendant, turned to the same practice among his clients in Bara

---

munauté Francophone Africaine as of 12 May 1962. It is the acronym for the African economic community of countries both French-speaking and formerly under French domination. Zaïre, for example, is not a part of the CFA zone.]

Issa, northwest of Ngouma. He, too, made only a meager collection. Yet both enjoy an excellent reputation. Their wretched results are a measure of the crisis people of the upper bend are enduring.

Different obligations also weigh on the followers according to the nature of their connection with the gaw. The malé bania who have been treated without going through possessive trance have minimal obligations. They have to give the taba yessi on the evening of the annual feast, which they attend in their master's village. Beyond that, they have only to participate in batous their gaw organize in the area in which they live. Past patients whose cures occurred through possessive trance must give supplementary fees. It is said that they were mounted by a stronger genii than the others. But this distinction has its inconveniences: because they dance and are possessed in the ceremonies, the gaw calls on them more often. From among them the gaw chooses the supernumeraries whose possessions animate batous before the gaw's own possession.

Finally, there are the "apprentices," those destined for careers as gaw. These people follow the malé wherever he or she goes and often spend more time with her or him than with their own family, in their own village. They are held to a daily collaboration.

THE DIFFICULTY OF BEING TOGETHER

Tensions between Priests and Followers

The malé bania the gaw drag along from batou to batou are often poor souls that a priest is manipulating. Their often-violent possessions, provoked at the beginning of each ceremony, exhaust them very quickly. When they can no longer haul themselves around, the choir, griots, and musicians recharge them with completely indifferent cruelty using chanting, praise singing, and appropriate rhythms. Then everyone's attention turns to the gaw as soon as she or he is possessed by her or his own genii. The gaw's possession is the high point of the ceremony, while the supernumeraries are left to finish their trances in the corner, unless they still have the strength to stagger about, deprived of inspiration, to general indifference. These more or less obligatory assistants find service to the genii very constraining: too much time lost, too much fatigue. They complain in private conversation but don't dare or can't publicly refuse to accompany the gaw in ceremonies.

As happened in Kormou, they often violently bring to the surface tensions occurring between the healing priest and the patients' families. Many families do not have the means to or do not want to take on the expense of treatments, especially sacrifices. So the gaw threaten them, as seen during the session described at the beginning of this chapter. Many relapses are attributed to the fact that the cure was not followed with care. The deep social crisis in which local society is currently plunged stirs up these sources of conflict. The families do not acquit themselves of what they owe the gaw; the gaw then see their revenue moving toward zero. In consequence, the priests pay the appointed singers, musicians, griots, and official mediums less and less. These people then complain about not being sufficiently recompensed for their efforts, their participation, their faithfulness.

Tensions between Priests

Crisis also does not improve relations between gaw, in any case usually suspicious, even competitive. But the gaw know each other well. They know how to appraise the relationships of domination and subordination connecting them. The networks of alliances, the lines of opposition that join and divide them, mean that some hesitate before intervening in the fief of a reputed colleague unless they have good prior relations with him or her. A fairly strict hierarchy orders the Ghimbala world de facto. The great gaw are those who obtain the best results. Their successes are perceived as signs of their positions as the genii's elect. They are the focus of the whole population, not just cult followers. They do not express unfavorable opinions about each other in public, unless one of them has been the object of attack or provocation prejudicial to her or his reputation.

The one to whom such disagreeable things happen can in turn reveal the weaknesses and boasting of his or her adversary. Yet the rule remains discretion, though in private each gives in to affirmations of being stronger than his or her neighbor. Beyond their colleagues, the gaw are severe in their criticism of those new-style singers who, without being genii-griots, flatter and praise the genii successfully throughout the region with their musical talents. "But they barely know the genii's names, nothing more—they have never seen them! It's not enough to know the name of the gangi to work with them. We know them intimately because of our heritage, because of our dreams, because of the meetings we have with them."

Appearances are nonetheless preserved; the protagonists in these complex situations officially respect each other, know they are condemned to live together, and prefer to safeguard communal peace as much as possible. Thus tensions between gaw are less obvious than those that periodically oppose priests and patients' families or cult followers. Yet on the whole, the Ghimbala world is a tough milieu, in which people are highly critical of each other. The strongest tensions emerge between gaw who live in the same area and have not managed to establish a collaborative relationship or at least a state of neutrality that defuses conflict. But to the person who is shocked and critical of this, one could respond that all fairly closed and self-governing environments in the world are this way. The Ghimbala are no worse in their intrigues than many others (the French scientific community, for example) who endure a far easier historical situation and whose craving pettiness, intrigues for power within the group, and annealed passions and hatreds easily equal those of the priests of the upper bend. At least the gaw live out theirs with the panache inherited of an epic tradition.

THE GHIMBALA COMMUNITY

In sum, one must not believe that frequent antagonism—despite its potential violence—and difficult relations between followers and their priests manage to sunder the Ghimbala community. All are caught in a weave of intense relationships uniting them through cures, ceremonies, and annual celebrations. This is the true cement of their membership in the genii cult, beyond its dilution within the diversity of local pantheons' rituals and each gaw's innovations.

The connection between gaw and follower extends beyond the village framework because ways of recruiting the latter mean they are often dispersed in locales far distant from those of their masters, as we have seen. A great gaw's order can thus affect a whole region. This traffic is two-way, its pattern superimposed on the space of the upper bend. The gaw go to the villages where they are called to consult when a patient is not transportable, and they return when they want to collect the followers' fees before the agreed-upon date. Conversely, other patients are brought directly by their families to the therapist-priests. Also, at least once a year and sometimes more often, followers converge in the homes of gaw for the djiribéré.

The traffic of each group occurs along literal paths of communication—water and land. In the first case, it follows the course of the river and its principal arms longitudinally in a noticeably southwest-northeast direction. In the second, the itinerary taken is rather crosswise, in either a north-south direction or the reverse. The path of water is preferred by travelers because it is less burdensome and faster. Otherwise, most travelers are condemned to walk under the sun along dusty trails, without the money needed to pay for a place on one of the rare motorized vehicles handling local traffic. The little pirogues that used to ferry people all year long from one end of the country to another (except during great drought) are now usable in this way only seven months out of twelve. Starting in mid-February, the overland

path is more commonly used. But in many cases, both kinds of loco-
motion are combined: part of the trip in a pirogue, pedestrian crossing
of a band of earth separating two branches, then river travel again.

Messages, information, and even rumors concerning Ghimbala life
circulate by means of people all along the river. News is passed from
Timbuktu to Mopti during trips and at markets. I remember the
crossing Demba made in my pirogue in February 1987. An old patient
of his father's whom we passed greeted him. Demba answered him,
as he had other members of the cult encountered earlier, that he was
going to Dondoro to honor and assist Moussa Founé in the batou to
take place at that gaw's home. The river, artery of life, cements the
unity of the Ghimbala, who also derive from the river their cult's
origin.

The Birth of a Gaw

Now here is Douré's tale. He is the gaw from Sadjilambou, a large
village downstream from Diré, and the story tells how he became a
gaw. What he says is a nearly exhaustive illustration of the sometimes-
tense, sometimes-harmonious relationships among the Ghimbala possessed and of the movement of people and news along the watery
pathways of the genii lands.

FROM MOUSSA'S FIRST ATTACK TO THE FIRST TREATMENT'S FAILURE
From his adolescence, Douré maintains a close relationship with
Moussa, one of the great Ghimbala genii. Moussa first turns him crazy
after Douré destroys a termite hill where this genie resides and tries to
make away with the gold hidden there. Afterward Douré spends his
time in the bush, clambering up the dunes, climbing in the genii trees,
and going to the edges of the great water holes. He takes off from the
village every night at Moussa's call, which he follows, screaming,
from termite hill to termite hill. He continues in this way for some
time, wandering in the bush and at the Niger's bank until his family
tries to have him treated. But the first attempt fails. The gaw gathered
are not able to make him enter into trance during the batou they
organized.

ENTER BILI KORONGOY, WHO TAKES THE TREATMENT IN HAND Then
Douré's elder brother and mother decide to call on Bili Korongoy, the
great gaw living in the neighboring village of Gaïrama on the other
side of Diré, upstream. He succeeds in calming Douré: "As soon as
he put his hand on my head, the devils disappeared." But the precautions taken to strengthen this initial result do not keep the problem

from recurring. The young boy again begins to "flee into the bush," and his brother, helped by several villagers, captures him again near a termite hill. So Bili Korongoy brings him to his village. Douré is to reside five years with the gaw, who treats him, makes him dance, and makes him enter trance "until my spirit became whole again." Treatments and apprenticeships alternate; the master's and student's genie is the same: Da-Moussa. The latter is of course in a position of complete dependence on the former, who makes him enter into trance at the outset of each ceremony and asks him to serve him beyond sessions.

FLIGHT TO MOPTI AND CONFLICT WITH LOCAL FOLLOWERS One fine day, Douré, who can no longer stand the life of a serf, decides to escape to Mopti without telling either his gaw or his mother. Naturally he ends up in the compound of Bakaïna, a retired policeman who comes from the upper bend of the Niger, at whose home the Ghimbala commonly gather and organize ceremonies. [In fact, it was while attending some in this place that I made contact anew with water-genii followers during 1981.] Very soon, the young traveler enters into rivalry with the local gaw and followers, who are jealous of his inspired possessions. A series of incidents ensues that almost ends tragically during a cult session. Douré's rivals take advantage of his trances to nearly kill him, under pretext of making him undergo the trials proving the sacred basis of his prowess as one of the possessed. "They hit me until the blood spurted. Then each one took a mortar and struck it on my head. They wanted to break open my skull but they couldn't!" Bakaïna interrupts the massacre and asks that a new session be organized. "Because there are quarrels, we must do a batou to find a way to get along and to designate the gaw of all Mopti."

In the meantime, Bili Korongoy has been told the news of the plot thickening around his student. He sends him a package that probably contains protective charms and, more important, puts him in contact with a gaw from the area who is his "close friend" and who from that point onward is to take care of Douré and advise him. Finally the decisive evening arrives, for which the following probatory trial has been prepared: a sum of money belonging to Bakaïna has been buried in great secrecy at the edge of Mopti, at the foot of the breakwater over which the road to Sévaré runs. The various possessed have to find this sum of money. Several gaw enter into trance and give erroneous information. So Douré, inspired by Moussa, asks that the batou stop and the assembly follow him. He leads everyone onto the breakwater, right to the spot where the money is buried. He hesitates a bit, but his genie is watching. "I went slightly beyond where the money was. So Moussa pulled me backward by my clothing and said to me, 'You mustn't get lost, you mustn't blind yourself, because I am not blind and I have taken you just to open your eyes.'"

"I turned toward Moussa, I looked on the shoulder, and I saw the money buried under the ground." At the possessed's request, a worker digs a hole, and a sum enveloped in a piece of paper is unearthed. Douré brings it back into the batou yard, where it is triumphantly counted: thirty thousand Malian francs.[3] Bakaïna then makes the following speech: "He who found the money is only a malé bania; his master has not yet finished the work of initiation. You hit him hard yesterday, and today he performs a miracle. Now the Mopti gaw must leave him alone. If they hurt him again, their mothers' homes will be destroyed!"[4] After this memorable evening, Douré leaves Mopti for Djenné, then Ouagadougou, where he stays for three years in service to an official.

INITIATION RESUMED, LAST TENSIONS, AND THE STUDENT'S FINAL CONSECRATION Douré finally goes back to Mopti, where his brother awaits to protect him during the return trip to the heart of the upper bend "because they had made me return by magic, and traveling on water became dangerous." He finds Bili Korongoy, who reproaches the malé bania for his overly long absence. The gaw knows everything his student has done over the past few years, thanks to the Ghimbala of Mopti, to travelers on the river, and to his spells.

Douré and his family now prepare themselves for the final rituals. The gaw sacrifices the required animal and cuts it up, explaining the different operations to his student, giving him the appropriate incantations, indicating which pieces go to which genie. Then Douré begins to serve Bili again for a time, while the gaw completes his apprenticeship by telling him about the plants and how to gather them and by designating him a place on the river. But he still lacks an important attribute of the role of a gaw to which he is destined: the badji-foula, the bark cap his master wears, bearer of the magical strength of each gaw. "I can't meet other gaw or make someone dance without the cap and Moussa's tunic."

Bili Korongoy takes a lot of coaxing and is in no hurry to emancipate his student. So Douré decides to make his cap himself. When he completes it, he soaks it in a bath in which are steeping the plants his

3. At that time, Mali had not reentered the CFA zone. Thirty thousand Malian francs were worth three hundred French francs [about sixty U.S. dollars].

4. A popular means of vindication involves cursing those close to the person one wishes to punish.

master has taught him about. One Thursday, genii day, he meets Da-Moussa, who tells him about yet other plants as well as new sacrifices: four animals—a kobiri, a karakorey, a *dionieri,* and a bundi. He saturates his cap with blood from the sacrificed animals. In returning to Bili he draws his testing to a close: "He thought my cap more beautiful than his own; he looks at it, feels it, and tells me it is very, very good. I answer him: "I can't put it on my head before you authorize me to."

Bili Korongoy finally decides to hold a great ceremony for Douré's consecration. In the middle of it, the gaw asks his student to get out his badji-foula and congratulates him in front of all the followers gathered on the quality of the headdress, which he blesses. As Douré puts it, his blessing is literal: "He spits incantations on the cap." Then he thrusts it on the student's head after asking God's and the genii's protection. Beforehand, the gaw has tied around his student's forehead the sessey, that band which is also a sign of protection and power. Now he predicts a fine gaw's career for him, from the east to the west of Ghimbala country ("from Haoussa to Gourma"). Then everyone dances until dawn. Before they separate, Bili Korongoy takes the followers still present as witnesses to declare that Douré holds all the knowledge and instruments that make a good gaw.

In the following days the master sends his student on his way to a village where he is to treat a case of paralysis provoked by genii. The situation is not an easy one: the person came back from Abidjan in a critical state. Marabouts and gaw have failed up until now, but Douré succeeds in obtaining healing. Thus begins his existence as a therapist-priest, during which he treats people using techniques ranging from consultations to batous. Though he is emancipated from Bili, Douré does not forget to bring him the taba yessi every year. "After the harvest, I bring Bili's share on my head and add clothing and money."

The Gaw's Chant

Douré's biography shows us how the Ghimbala followers experience the genii culture that underlies their whole existence. The continuity of their world is indeed clearly affirmed by a chant struck up in every public ceremony: the gaw's chant. Here is how Sina Kala declaimed it in trance one night in Sokoura, on the Bara Issa:

Waada Samba is dead, but other gaw have come!
Housseini Gankoy is dead, but other gaw have come!
Mahaman Alfa is dead, but other gaw have come!
Hadia Malado is dead, but other gaw have come!

> Issa Soumaïla is dead, but other gaw have come!
> Bokar Hamma Sylla is dead, but other gaw have come!
> Kunandi Samba is dead, but other gaw have come!
> Hamadou Ousmani is dead, but other gaw have come!
> Sidi Mahaman is dead, but other gaw have come!
> Boukari Diara is dead, but other gaw have come!
> Logbo Tissi is dead . . .

And he enumerated a good thirty names in this way before going off through the crowd screaming.

Issa Sogoba expounds the gaw's chant in this way:

> Waada Samba was the emperor[5] of all gaw
> but now Kola Gaba is the emperor of the gaw!
> Housseini Gankoy was the emperor of all gaw
> but now Santché is the emperor of the gaw!
> Logbo Tissi was the empress of all gaw
> but now Sina Kala is the emperor of the gaw!
> Bokar Hamadoun died before I, Issa Sogoba, became gaw.
> One gaw dies, another comes; God is great!

Thus the gaw's chant takes one of two alternative forms: either an enumeration of all the great gaw of the past, starting with the founding gaw, Waada Samba, or the invocation of each of the great gaw who has died, to whose name a living gaw's name is linked. It is a chant of prestige wherein the same great gaw from the past are almost always named. On the other hand, the choice of the living gaw depends in part on the chanter's strategies and alliances. The names of the half-dozen greatest gaw of the upper band recur each time, however, because it would be dangerous to leave them out.

The chant simultaneously affirms the cult's continuity. The great gaw of the present are associated in words with those who ensured Ghimbala renown in the past. This chant contributes to constituting the Ghimbala as a popular religion across time and space, a truly living community despite the tensions, jealousies, and tragedies they endure. These are caused by the surrounding poverty of the country in which their actions take place.[6]

♣
ⵗ

In trance, in the middle of a ceremony, a candidate to be cured of the genii cries out the name of the gaw who should heal him or her but

---

5. The chanters say "sheikou" in reference in Sheikou Hamadou.
6. In February 1988, the popular foundations of the Ghimbala cult appeared clearly

who lives at the other end of Ghimbala country. At each djiribéré, followers converge from the far corners of the upper bend on the one who treated them and remains their master. The gaw's chant, struck up at each batou, causes the names of the great priests, dead or alive, to be heard. These latter know each other sometimes without ever having met, simply because they have heard of each other during batous. A passing traveler talks of gaw encountered upstream or downstream. The river reinforces this movement of people, ideas, information, and legends, weaving a web of complicity and faithfulness within the membership of the genii world that is common to all. This vast system of relationships and exchanges thus becomes the surest guarantee of Ghimbala continuity. But it is threatened both by social crisis and by the thrust of Islamic fundamentalism.

---

during a ceremony organized in the little village of Mékorey, which is on a branch of the river between Sumpi and the Niger itself. The local gaw was heir to an old lineage of genii-priests whose founder, according to local tradition, went to Hambdalaye with Waada Samba. The entire village community was gathered for the batou. The good relationship between those officiating and the spectators was forcefully demonstrated. All the women present joined the soloists' chanting in chorus; there were numerous verbal exchanges between the possessed and the spectators; the spectator's contributions recharged the dancers. The whole population of this village is saturated in the genii culture.

8 / The Solitude of the Gaw

THE MALEDICTION

Going around a bend in the Bara Issa, we discover the little village of Sokoura, haloed in five o'clock sun. This is where Sina Kala lives, the last great gaw I've been told to talk to before we return to Lake Débo. Rumors of my research trip through Ghimbala country have already reached him, and he is half-awaiting my visit. He immediately suggests that we organize a batou. I tell him we are leaving the next morning. He asserts that the session can take place that evening. I hesitate.

After amply documenting the numerous priests who live on the banks of this branch and spending several days tacking from ford to ford between the sandbanks, we are in a hurry to get back to Lake Débo. I fear we won't make it, for the river is already so shallow in this beginning of 1985. Moreover, the pirogue's rice reserves are almost exhausted, and of course there is no question of allowing the followers of Sokoura to expend themselves on a empty stomach or close to it. As of February, the country is in famine. We also have to get back to Mopti without restocking because our finances are at their lowest. On the gaw's side, he really wants me to attend a ceremony he has organized and in fact makes any interview contingent on it. He knows all the other priests of the cult who have already worked with me and he would consider it a dishonor if I merely passed through. Besides, it is certain the genii will make interesting declarations, as he gave me to understand.

The experience of the past weeks spent on the river has taught me that much information difficult to obtain "cold" around a tape recorder emerges spontaneously during public sessions. It is repugnant to the priests, and rightly so, to reveal their genii's history and slogans and, even more so, their incantations on command, whereas they accept me perfectly well as a discreet but attentive spectator to the sacred gestures revealed at the proper time. It is my job to know how to listen, record, and retain. So I end up accepting and sharing the last sack of rice, already more than half-empty. I add three thousand CFA francs to share in the costs of the batou (probable sacrifice of poultry;

remuneration of the musicians, singers, and genii-griot). I let them know I can do no more.

Nothing is left to do but wait for the ceremony at nightfall. At twilight, the river's edge resonates with the bursts of laughter and hand claps of two little girls dancing near the tent. They have come from the village to fill the two vessels that will hold the orchestra's bomboutou. They shout with joy, a fruit of the coming event, which is a break from the ordinary rigors of village life.

At the beginning of the batou there are one or two possessions of supernumeraries, as violent as they are brief, while concentrated, immobile Sina Kala, seated on a mat at the back of the dancing area, awaits his genie's coming, sombé planted in the ground at his feet. Suddenly his possession takes hold, convulsive as they often are in the beginning. The gaw rolls on the ground, moving in all directions and raising a cloud of dust. Then he gains control of himself a bit, gets up, and begins a long, athletic, graceful dance, armed with his sombé, which he twirls in the nocturnal emptiness. Still in a trance, he strikes up the gaw's chant, calling out the names of his great predecessors who are no longer among the living. He leaps off again to the rhythms of the musicians, who have picked up after his long, exhausting tirade. He stops again for a brief declaration: "The *toubabs* should soon do something to make the country rich again.[1] To work this area, they must take the names Djini Ouloussou, Djini Younsi, Djini Ouyoussi, Djini Ayoussi. . . ." And another ten or so names are invoked of genii whom I do not know, probably his private band. The music and dancing pick up again. This time when they stop, Sina Kala tosses out astounding predictions that impose silence on the suddenly attentive audience.

"If people are unhappy, it is because they have abandoned their heritage. They have said the genii did not exist, that the shaytāns did not exist, that slitting the throats of chickens and sheep should not be done because it is pagan.[2] It is because of this neglect that the country is unhappy. If we take up our tradition right away, the country will be rich again." And he adds, "When Sheikou Hamadou made Waada Samba come with Seïni Gankoy, with Moudou Beïri, with Mahaman Alfa, to Hambdalaye, there were many saints, there were many sheiks. At that time the peasants listened to the marabouts and also to the gaw! The marabouts said that what the gaw do is false. Yet these are

1. The toubabs are the Europeans.
2. If the genii and shaytāns do not exist, it means that those who affirm the opposite are liars.

not lies: if they were, Sheikou Hamadou would have had all their throats slit!"

Once his speech is ended, Sina Kala, his features lunatic, goes off across the batou, frenetically shaking a fistful of bells and emitting a long moan that rises from the depth of his chest toward the sky. The end of the session is less dramatic: the spectators go back to laughing. The batou can also fulfill its role as entertainment.

I have noted this kind of message on other occasions, shouted like a curse. "The genii are punishing you for having abandoned them. Return to them if you want the water to return!" a gaw shouted one day. Another solemnly proclaimed, "God has said that every person should do his or her work! God has said you must not criticize others! God has said you must despise no one! The marabouts are not doing what God has said!" Public statements made by the possessed are like the less excessive but often disillusioned declarations made in private. Thus Kola Gaba, most aware that the therapeutic utility of the cult gives it the right to exist, says, "We do not want any problems with the marabouts, who continue to despise the Ghimbala. But when the marabouts have a patient they can't cure, they entrust it to the gaw."

Bili Korongoy favors mutual noninterference in other gaw's affairs. "When black has left its path to go toward white, it's no good. But if white goes toward black, it's no good either. White must work on its own side and black the same on its own."[3] In other words, marabouts and gaw should stay on their own sides and not mix their practices. The old gaw diplomatically adds, "I don't begin treating a patient when I know the marabout has not yet removed his hands." Another gaw exclaims that ultimately, beyond any excitation provoked by overly intense nighttime sessions, "The marabouts have sabotaged the Ghimbala, so everyone has given up. Those who have given up will regret it. The genii take vengeance by causing drought."

AN AMBIGUOUS AND CONFLICTUAL ALLEGIANCE TO ISLAM

In private as in public the gaw show their exasperation toward a less and less accommodating Islam. Over their long coexistence with it, the Ghimbala have taken a position of diplomatic withdrawal. They have recognized the monotheistic religion's hegemony and ratified the superiority they conferred on it by offering numerous testimonies of their dependence. To begin with, the genii do not descend into people

---

3. Recall that black incarnates paganism and white is the color of Islam.

on Friday—mosque day, God's day—nor during Ramadan. During this period, it is said, the Islamic genii go to Mecca to pray. As for the others, the pagan ones who do not make the pilgrimage, God keeps them chained in the depths of their watery homes. Only Mayé, the warrior genie who holds the sombé, goes from place to place to feed those in seclusion.

People also begin every cult ceremony with the *bi-ism Allāh* (in the name of God) to place the ceremony under divine protection. Only afterward do they ask the genii to descend. At the end of the session, they dismiss them again under the name of God: *"Lā ilāh illā Allāh(ou)! Lā ilāh illā Allāh(ou)!"* the gaw and all the audience intone—"You must simply rise and disappear! There is only one God!" Another sign of obedience to Islam is that the animals sacrificed at different points during cult activities are turned toward the east, in the direction of Mecca.

The infiltration of Arabic into ritual words pronounced by the cult's actors during different ceremonial activities seems to me a much more eloquent testimony. These phrases—bits of *sūrahs*—are merely words sown throughout the religious discourse and are learned orally by the upper bend's peasants, who know neither how to read nor how to write. Thus the Arabic used is often distorted because those using it don't always understand the meaning of the words they utter. Some gaw develop a real inferiority complex toward the religion of the Book. One of them carries a thick book of prayers with him everywhere, incantations and diverse texts written in the language of the Prophet. He inherited these spells from his ancestors, but he is illiterate. (Sheikou Hamadou impressed the popular imagination of his time merely by writing to the different provinces of the empire to demand that the gaw be exterminated. Some tellers of the legend emphasize this detail.) Other, less-bereft priests transform their ignorance of writing into a positive position: "The marabouts write. We do not write, but we have everything in our head and our heart," they say.

The long cohabitation of the two religions has favored their rapprochement. When great Kola Gaba's assistant, old Yero of Dabi, died in February 1987, the separation rituals set in motion by his death took a syncretistic turn. Islam came first—a sheep had its throat slit after one week and was shared with the neighborhood, as all the Muslims of Dabi do so that God pardons the dead person for his or her sins. After twenty-one days came the Ghimbala's turn. Kola Gaba consecrated an offering of wakando mixed with milk, fogno, and bastard mahogany bark. He then entrusted the preparation to his and Yero's sons. The two young men went to place a part of the genii's food in each of the pools of the village territory and announced the news to their inhabitants: "Yero is dead; here is your part of the offering." Then an inventory was done of all the deceased man had used in his cult activities: bunches of plants, knives, spears, bells. These different objects were not destroyed but transformed, in the kind of change that precedes putting things in order so as to start using them anew: the bunches of plants were undone and done up again; knives, spears, and bells were melted down and reforged.

Finally, the syncretistic character of the distorted Koranic quotations of which Ghimbala ritual language is full is accentuated by numerous references to esoteric Islamic tradition—to the Holy Places, for example, especially to Medina, whence many genii apparently come; and also to King Solomon, who is supposed to have had a privileged relationship with the genii. The three therapeutic rituals begin by quoting this prophet: "May God give peace to the prophet Souleymani"; "I am making this prayer in the name of Souleymani"; "I beg the prophet Souleymani to help me in God's sight that this patient heal." Then the gaw passes on to invoking the genii.

In reality, the Ghimbala cult continues to draw the substance of its daily practices from polytheistic principles that are always being reinvented, despite the signs of obedience to Islam it tries to give outside observers. This syncretism leans in favor of the genii. Here is the deep nature of the Ghimbala, challenged by those lately contemptuous of them. Their attitude of apparent submission is no longer enough to protect them from the mounting intolerance of some Malian Muslims, especially those who appeal to Wahabism, which has been increasing these past years in the upper bend of the Niger as elsewhere in Mali, impelled by the wave of fundamentalism running through contemporary Islam. For that matter, the same phenomenon occurs in Niger on the other side of Songhay country, where Islamic fundamentalists and Tooru followers have already entered into open conflict several times.[4]

Thus criticisms expressed by the gaw in private now burst out during the batou. In public the gaw reassert the cult's founding epic. The example of Sheikou Hamadou, whose faith can hardly be questioned, is contrasted with that of the present Islamic detractors of the Ghimbala. He at least accepted the cult in the form in which it has come to us, a therapeutic cult whose members contest neither the existence nor the primacy of the one God.

In a sense, the current fundamentalist outbreak, which accentuates

4. Paul Stoller, in a lecture given in January 1987 at the Ecole Pratique des Hautes Etudes, reported on a recent conflict that had erupted in the Tillaberi region. The flooding was late, and the Muslims had the upper hand.

the basic antagonism between Islam and local religions already inscribed in the cult's symbology and history, only accelerates the slow
disintegration of the Ghimbala's position. The genii cult's field of activity is narrowing; public ceremonies are fewer and less varied than
before. Long ago there were six different types of batous. Even
twenty years ago each gaw still organized two types that have mostly
fallen into disuse now: one for his or her personal genie, the other to
ask all the Ghimbala, and especially Baana, for a good rainy season.
Each was conceived around the sacrifice of a sheep or a goat. The third
batou was for the genii's leave taking of humans just before Ramadan.
Next came the great ceremony of fast breaking, just after the fast; then
the ordinary therapeutic batous. Finally, in the case of an unforeseen
catastrophe that befell the village—an epidemic, for example—the
gaw could organize an exceptional session at the request of the population to obtain the genii's protection.

Most of these ceremonies have disappeared, and besides the therapeutic batous, the gaw now organize only the djiribéré, justified because the genii are forbidden during the Islamic fast. Followers often
take advantage of the annual feast to make a general sacrifice to the
river-genii. The two ceremonies, once separate, now coincide, except
that the pagan sacrifice is a bit shortchanged in favor of celebration of
the Islamic new year. In some rare cases, the sacrifice before the rainy
season is maintained as well as the one to the gaw's personal genii.
Oussou Kondjorou, Waada Samba's descendant and Baana's priest,
merges the two ceremonies into one since his genie is also the one who
commands the rains. The sacrifice propitiating the river-genii to favor
the floods is generally condemned by the Islamic authorities. "Only
God commands the rains!" they say. The gaw abstain, intimidated,
and the ceremony becomes forgotten.

Sometimes the imams go even further and actually take over the
ceremony to their own advantage, which does not particularly correspond to a fundamentalist interpretation of the Koran. Thus in Sumpi,
northwest of Niafunké, the imam sacrificed a young black bull and
asked God for a good rainy season. The animal was led through the
village and then on a tour of the mosque, next to which he was finally
sacrificed. It is not surprising that control of the sacrifice intended to
make rain should be the object of competition between imams and
gaw. The obsessive desire for good flooding is central to the local
peasantry's concerns; they are similar in this to other Sahelian populations. The priest who performs this sacrifice becomes the holder of
religious power in the villagers' eyes, though this does present some
risk of rapid loss of credibility in these years of repeated drought.

Finally, haughty Islam, which currently takes the lead in criticizing the Ghimbala, condemns the possession phenomenon itself, stigmatizing it as diabolical in nature. So certain gaw, especially but not exclusively among the young, are beginning to give up organizing public sessions of dancing, even those with a solely therapeutic purpose. Thus I met several gaw who no longer organize batous although their parents, whose powers they inherited, held them frequently. They now prefer to turn away from procedures too readily termed pagan and to fall back on more discreet rituals that do not require possession, contenting themselves with the simple activities of healers. Such an evolution in contact with enterprising Islam has been noted elsewhere in West Africa.[5]

The victorious pressure of Islam also constrains the Ghimbala's spatial influence. Gaw are deserting the small cities and medium-sized townships, abandoning terrain to the Koran's zealots. Cities in the region have always been centers of power and thus of Islam, associated with power since the Songhay emperors' conversion at the end of the fifteenth century. In these areas today reside most wealthy and pious merchants, the main doctors of the faith, descendants of the dominant families, and Islamicized civil servants. Conversely, the great gaw officiating in these urban areas, more open to the external world, have gradually disappeared and not been replaced. One can still meet cult followers here, but the gaw prefer to withdraw to the smaller villages or simple encampments, where they pursue their activities away from indiscreet gazes and critical words, far from the embryonic modernism concentrated in the little cities, closer to their protective genii. Akka, Sebi, and Owa are large villages that no longer have priests settled within their walls, although sessions are held there from time to time, just as in the region's small towns. But the gaw have withdrawn to the areas surrounding the towns, to Gaïrama and Sadjilambou, near Diré; to Dabi, Sumpi, and Mangourou, near Niafunké; and around Lake Oro, in the environs of Tonka.

A CRUMBLING SOCIETY

Islam, despite its virulent contemporary forms, does not suffice to explain the current regression of the genii cult. The terrible crisis of the society of the upper bend must be included in the picture. During the past few years of repeated drought and famine, the different sec-

---

5. Andras Zempléni already noted it twenty years ago in Senegal. Public sessions of the N'Döp tended to give way to private rituals, culminating in the construction of home altars and avoiding possessions. See Zempléni, "La Dimension Thérapeutique du Culte des Rab," in *Revue de Psychopathologie Africaine* (1966).

tors of the upper bend's economy have crumbled, starting with agriculture. Irregular, insufficient rains no longer foster the millet's normal growth, even the early varieties. The Niger's too-weak flooding and too-rapid subsiding have seriously compromised rice production. In Sokoura, for example, there has been no cereal harvest worth speaking of for seven years despite the increased flooding of 1985, which made famine's ugly head drop slightly. At the start of 1987 the situation was again critical, and all the villages in the district were to receive direct food aid.

A little higher up in Dabi, grasshoppers and small rodents took over during the drought. When I stopped there, the villagers were suffering from an invasion of mice. Just in the time it took us to unpack, there were three in our tent and bags. They were devouring everything: seed grain, puny food reserves, meager growth in kitchen gardens. The presence of mice, like that of the invading jerboas a little farther on, is perhaps attributable to the encroaching desert, which chases the animals ahead of it.

Livestock is also severely hurt by pasture reduction, the evaporation of watering holes, and, just as seriously, the disappearance of bourgou. This richly nutritious plant traditionally grew in moist, marshy hollows. The drying out of these hollows over time caused the demise of bourgou. Attempts at reseeding promoted by the Malian authorities and nongovernmental organizations intervening in the area have produced good results but have not yet compensated for the reduction in the traditional areas once covered by this plant. Bourgou is essential to the regional economic balance, for it allows people to go from an extensive form of livestock raising during the rainy season to a relatively intensive form during the hottest months at the end of the dry season. At this point, the herds are concentrated at the center of the delta in the bourgou fields.

On the livestock market at Tonka in January 1985, the animals offered were still well fed, but herders were in a hurry to sell. Buyers kept lowering the prices; everyone knew that in a few months most animals who had not found takers would be dead of hunger. When I came back through the Lake Débo region just before the rainy season, the same year, the approach to the road from Youvarou to Dogo was strewn for miles with zebu carcasses. One can imagine the bankruptcy of small and medium-sized herders, condemned to pursue their seasonal transhumance within the region. These herders contrast greatly with the new type of herder: big-city businesspeople or senior executives who have invested in building large herds, which their appointed shepherds drive toward the moist southern edges of the country.

Fishing, the third pillar of the regional economy, is also seriously affected by drought, though not reduced to zero as are the other two types of production in many cases. Dried fish once constituted the basis of Mopti's prosperity. It was sent there to be exported to neighboring countries by merchants. Its production has now collapsed. Many of the Niger's species spawn in shallow waters in the rainy season, when the river emerges from its bed. Yet flooding in recent years has been too little to permit the cycle to take place normally, and the resulting deficit in reproduction has been aggravated by increased fishing. In consequence, the quality of life for fishers continues to drop.

The Diou-Diou encampment provides an example of this situation. Located a few kilometers downstream of Youvarou at the mouth of the Issa Ber, the main branch of the river, this hamlet was prosperous twenty years ago. It is partly deserted now, and numerous houses are in ruins. The few remaining inhabitants are not only consigned to paltry catches but also condemned to overwork. Now everyone drags the heavy nets, including women and sometimes very young children. I remember seeing children and little girls barely ten years old harnessed to enormous dragnets, which they were pulling around at midnight, nearly sleeping standing up. The same small community had tried, during the last famine of 1985, to do a little gardening, an unusual activity for these fisherpeople, who were hardly at ease with it. Yet they had to survive by any means. When I returned at the end of February, I found gardens that had completely dried out although they had been green two months earlier. I learned that the makeshift gardeners had not even had the strength to water their parcels, although they were near the river, because they were so undernourished. That same evening, some young people returning from an unfruitful journey came to ask for a little rice for dinner.

Things have been worse in the region of the upper bend during this period; there is no point in going on and on about it. Suffice it to say that the region is always close to famine, while on the whole Mali has regained its balance with regard to food. The facts of such a situation lead one to turn explanations of the cult's present regression upside down. Social crisis makes effective the virulent criticisms of Islamic fundamentalist believers—merchants, some administrative and political employees, certain religious leaders—who are among the haves, somewhat sheltered from the present rural crisis.

Conversely, the gaw and their followers are caught in the great torment of the herders, fishers, and local growers, who plunge deeper and deeper into poverty unless they resign themselves to emigrating. Once there were more gaw, more followers, more cult sessions. It is easy to understand how these people with no energy left—having long lacked the minimum to survive, to clothe themselves, and to eat—cannot find the additional personal energy and material resources to nourish the life of their cults. The astounding thing in all this is that the Ghimbala still exist despite the terrible difficulties overwhelming them.

But priests and followers take these conditions of extreme penury into account in order to perpetuate their religious and therapeutic practices. Thus Awa Koulikoro, the Kormou gaw, inherited a familial cult devoted to two big, black stones stuck in a Sebi street, on which one of her ancestors saw Baana appear. She used to sacrifice a black goat there, but today she is content to offer two black hens to the genie of the site, awaiting better days. A gaw from the Bara Issa remembers that his father sometimes slaughtered three sheep for the annual feast there, while today, with great difficulty, he sacrifices only one.

For the same reasons, it is harder and harder to carry out the therapeutic rituals. So the gaw often accept their clients' substitution of two hens for the quadruped demanded by the genii. They feel this will do if the animals are slaughtered together, because they have four legs between them. Despite this testimony to the flexibility of the gaw, even the alterations offered cannot always be paid, since it is impossible to ask anything of people who have nothing. Yet even in normal times, remuneration for cures undertaken by the gaw and supplementary expenses represent significant sums of money for people whose level of revenue has always been very low.

As an example, for a case that is easy to treat and requires only one batou, Bili Korongoy (who is renowned, it is true, as a gaw) asks ten to fifteen thousand CFA francs, plus sacrificial grains and animals. Contributions in kind are meant to be consumed by the participants once the genii's part has been taken out. If the case turns out to be difficult and to require a longer treatment, the sum of money demanded can go as high as fifty thousand CFA francs, of which part can be paid in advance, with the balance paid only if the patient heals. As the patients' families can no longer afford such expenditures, many cures stop short. The situation described at the beginning of the previous chapter echoes the conflicts engendered by this environment of poverty.

Thus the diminishing number of public sessions is caused by general impoverishment, which paves the way for the reductionist schemes of those agitating against the survival of paganism. In this context, the gaw and their clients and followers also have a tendency to adopt treatment procedures that are easier to put into effect because they are more discreet, require fewer people, and are thus less expensive. These include the small rituals that call together only the patient's family and, even better, treatment administered within the restricted relationship of a gaw and his or her patient.

AGING AND ISOLATION OF THE GAW

The general situation makes the gaws' condition more and more fragile. It is this evolution that creates "gaw's solitude," born of the very way those who become gaw fulfill their role. Their power is never guaranteed except by talent, inspiration, and the capacities public opinion ascribes to them. Though there is a minimal continuity ensuring hereditary transmission of functions, it must be remembered that this does not happen automatically. The genii's choice often jumps a generation, and new elect can also emerge from the ranks of the followers.[6] In any case, the reputation of the child will often be measured by the reputation of the parent. And how many times have I heard it said: "His father was a great gaw, but he is worthless!"

In the final analysis, the characteristics of performances build reputations, and first and foremost is the power to heal. Success with cures ensures the healer's renown, but this is still not quite sufficient. A strong constitution and robust health are required to accomplish the multiple tasks of the cult that require greater-than-normal physical capacities—to play the exhausting register of possession, from which individuals emerge completely spent; to confront mad, sometimes violent, people who must be mastered and subdued. Each ceremony also demands of its director a renewed performance, because normally it is centered around the gaw's possession. The performance, the beauty of the dancing, and the energy the gaw expresses will be appreciated and noted by the spectators. When strength declines, the gaw has himself or herself replaced by someone younger and is content to control the ceremony from a distance. But this delegation of power is not always done in the best of conditions; some of the gaw's esteem can be lost, as in Moussa Founé's case in Dondoro. The gaw

---

6. The fragile transmission of knowledge can be disquieting to a person worried about the continuation of the Ghimbala. Heredity and predestination are both necessary to make a "complete gaw." I met a very old priest on the Bara Issa, at Tissi facing Saraféré, who was resigned to die without having transmitted his heritage because the only student he had judged worthy of receiving it had passed on before him. The cult is thus put on hold in every place where no postulant of quality presents herself or himself to relay it. This does not keep Oussou Kondjourou, Waada Samba's descendant, from affirming that his knowledge "will pass 'like that' to someone else, thanks to the genii." Will this devolving knowledge survive the torment that has fallen on Ghimbala country?

also has to know the genii's histories, the places they inhabit, and the plants they like better than others. Renowned priests are able to name in order the holes in the river and the pools where the Ghimbala live, from Koriomé to Lake Débo, while giving each site's identifying detail—a certain tree growing on its banks, a fabled animal spotted in its proximity.

Many gaw I have met must have possessed exceptional strength in their youth. They are big and athletic, sometimes giants like Bili Korongoy or Demba, or else stocky, broad-backed, and possessing a concentrated strength, like Sina Kala and Douré, the gaw from Sadjilambou. Bili Korongoy still deployed an impressive strength when Moussa rode astride him on the one occasion on which I saw him dance during a cult session. But when the old man returned to his normal state, it was painful to see his great, emaciated carcass staggering about.

Those who are aware they are aging usually tend to reduce the number of occasions on which they enter into trance. Thus Kola Gaba completely controls his faculties as a medium. I have never seen him allow a trance to go to term during the many cult sessions organized in my presence, despite the maleficent intentions of the spectators, who did everything possible so that he would become possessed. This gaw has transformed his former physical capacities into a moral ascendancy, a spiritual authority that continues to impose his leadership without his having to prove anything at all with his body. He has surrounded himself with people and ensured that there is someone to relieve him.

For many others, cult activities and renown diminish along with physical strength, especially when their unstable position frequently incites them to show off skills and knowledge that push the limits of their capacity. When they have not known how to or have not been able to surround themselves with dependents or to choose a successor, they experience a precariousness that only worsens with time. Bili Korongoy, older than Sina Kala, less well organized than Kola Gaba, is experiencing a progressive isolation and destitution despite the renown that continues to spread his name throughout Ghimbala country when those reciting strike up the gaw's chant. The gaw himself, on his somewhat-destroyed compound at the edge of the village of Gaïrama, feels sick, defeated, exhausted.

Thus, the uneven fortune of each order is closely tied to its leader's history. The gaw's physical decline causes an inexorable decline in the cult's activity. Sina Kala has been seriously ill lately, probably hit by a bout of cholera. This disease has recently reappeared at different points around the upper bend, periodically and lethally insofar as it strikes peoples weakened by long years of malnutrition and scarcity. The gaw's strong constitution permitted him to escape it, though there were several deaths in his village of Sokoura. But he was never able to recover his prior vigor completely, and now he refuses certain ceremonies. "Before, when I was strong, I did a batou just before Ramadan to say good-bye to the genii. Now I only do the djiribéré after the fast."

If the possessed enjoy an endurance decupled by their trances and do not feel the fatigue as long as the trance lasts, they leave their performances in a comatose state and are paradoxically still so excited that some of them suffer from insomnia the rest of the night. In addition, it is not surprising that they need several days to return to normal activity. Undernourishment does not help matters. Over the longer term, repeated possessions create irreparable lesions in overworked bodies. I have hardly ever met gaw over fifty who did not complain about great pains in the lumbar region or, even worse, drag themselves about, sadly half-paralyzed by a terrible sciatica.

In old times, priests went through their initiations, took their freedom, grew, and then declined and disappeared. But other initiates replaced them and ensured the cult's continuity. It was this way forever, as the gaw's chant forcefully signifies. But today a relay is not ensured with any certainty. Gaw die who have not found students worthy to replace them, and the cult disappears in the dead person's area for a time, at least, if not forever. Those who recite the genii's legend can shout themselves as hoarse as they wish, making the names of all the great ancestors resound in the night. But their pathetic calls will not stop the inexorable withdrawal of a kind of religious expression closely tied to the balanced presence of humans in their natural environment, as well as a certain social if not physical distance from those who dominate them, unless the climatic trend reverses and the evolution of local society creates new possibilities of existence for the Ghimbala.

THE DESIRE TO ENDURE

The great gaw, who are at one and the same time priest-therapists and heads of orders, are walled up in the growing solitude of their aging. To this is added the crisis of the period, which makes competition more bitter and the cult's daily survival more uncertain. Physically weakened, the gaw are threatened still more by the rise of fundamentalist Islam, so unlike the Islam cultivated by the mystics of an earlier age—the pure fruit, as are the gaw, of the local soil and history, who lived familiarly if not easily with the genii of the area.

The terrible survival conditions of the region's inhabitants—so rigorous that they are hard to conceive for one who has not directly confronted them—are not the cause of the Ghimbala's disappearance. Nonetheless, they spur the transformation of the cult's normal activities. There are still many gaw and followers from Timbuktu to Lake Débo, even if there are fewer than before. There are even more congregations of the possessed in the region than there are groups of *djiné don* (their analogs in Soninké areas, whom I studied in 1979) in northwestern Mali. Although in a rural environment, this cult is not in a crisis comparable to that the Ghimbala endure.[7] The Ghimbala keep on, thanks to their role as gatherers-in of the popular religion.

The extraordinary tenacity of these people, hanging on to their dunes, their gourgoussou, and their dried-up river shallows like all the world's peasants do, prevents the cult from crumbling along with the economic and cultural sectors of Ghimbala country. Until just recently there were communities of weavers along the Bara Issa, in the Koumaïra and Saraféré regions. These artisans, keepers of a high tradition, created cotton cloth in bright colors and extremely sophisticated geometric designs. These masterpieces were some of the most difficult to make, as their illiterate creators had to learn the different patterns by heart. Then famine caused a drop in orders and forced the weavers, deprived of material support from the great, ruined families, to emigrate toward Mopti or even farther. They have rented their services to other buyers, learned other weaves, and created other designs, at the cost of forgetting their cultural heritage. Now their ancient knowledge is lost forever.

The genii cult constitutes one component of the local peasantry's personality. These people could not abandon it without additional disruption. This is all to the good of the gaw, who of course never miss the chance to remind people how closely linked they are to the Ghimbala and especially how dangerous it is to detach from them. Nor should the adaptive capacity of priests and followers be scorned. Like all adherents to popular polytheistic and decentralized religions, they often respond flexibly to changes imposed from without. The gaw learned long ago to use cunning with Islam, and they continue to do so. The general impoverishment of society also forces them to lighten the cult's functioning. Thus they simplify rituals, lower the cost of cures, come up with substitutions for sacrifices. Perhaps the present growing scarcity of public sessions is a sign of the cult's evolution toward types of activities closer to lay magic—turned more toward

7. The opposite is true in urban milieus, notably in Bamako, where the cult of the djiné don is in full regression.

the immediate satisfaction of individual needs than toward the religious preoccupations that engage a whole society—in its search for a balance between genii and people.

❦

In the final analysis, let us note that the weak institutional power of the gaw unceasingly forces them to prove their strength. The competitive atmosphere that characterizes part of their relations tends to foster a defiant attitude at the heart of their behavior. The general crisis striking the inhabitants of the upper bend of the Niger isolates and weakens the genii-priests. The conditions in which they exercise their cult functions dramatize their vision of the world a little more. This vision is far from serene, since they are already heir to the idea of generalized antagonism in relationships between individuals. I have often heard it said in the region, "For us the end of the world has begun." It remains to be asked whether such despair will be overcome by the ingenuity and vitality of those experiencing it.

9 / From Experience to Fiction

GHIMBALA IN CHIAROSCURO

At the end of this trip through the world of the river-genii, I can sketch the following portrait of the Ghimbala: Numerically in the minority but not marginal, they express the singularity of the country that gave them birth, and they do this in two ways. First, they appear as a cult of the water-genii who people the interior delta, in a region where people live by the rhythm of the flooding and subsiding of the Niger. Second, the followers distinctly remember the trauma of Fula expansion at the beginning of the last century, which precipitated the appearance of the cult in its present form: a popular religion under the domination of Islam, which tolerates it insofar as it fulfills its therapeutic function. On the other hand, the Ghimbala have forgotten all of their distant but nonetheless certain Soninké origins, specifically their relatedness to the djiné don of the Malian west, with whom they have no interaction.

In this cult, celebrating the meeting of people and genii during ritual possession shapes the social imaginary, in which the worlds of the genii and people on the one hand, and collective interpretations and individual imagining on the other, mirror each other. Thus the classical integrative function of possession is fulfilled. Moreover, the Ghimbala offer the possibility of decoding history. Priests and followers interpret certain events from the colonial period, as well as the recent ups and downs of their struggles with Islam, through the actions of their genii. Some symbol creation operates similarly—the appearance of new aspects among the main cult genii, for example.

At the same time, we must recall that the process of shaping the social imaginary and playing out latent or overt conflicts does not explain everything. Observation sometimes abuts against a reality irreducible to shapes, when trances deconstruct all possible symbolic systems. The phenomenon of possessive trance is part of the profound

A first sketch of this chapter was published under the same title in the *Cahiers de Sociologie Economique et Culturelle,* Institut Havrais de Sociologie, 7 June 1987.

hallucinatory capacity of all humanity, and as such it escapes our total comprehension. This text must also remain part of the nonrealization of thought while remaining faithful to the initial movement of the journey toward the unknown. Thus the end of this river chronicle will only be reached by traveling over all that exceeds the anthropological project, that is, telling about my first approach to the Ghimbala, although it is true that an experience cannot be broken down into details. What indeed of the reality of such an experience could be expressed in writing?

I will thus assemble some scattered bits and, to begin, say a few words about my fluctuating relations with the gaw, because they are an integral part of the idea I have of their world and are thus part of the light bathing my travels along the river.

FLUCTUATING GAW

Introducing myself into the Ghimbala milieu was not easy: mistrust. Very legitimate mistrust because, in this land, everything coming from outside is more often a source of disturbance than of improvement. Mistrust also because the Ghimbala milieu is closed, as are all possession cults in the world. Part of the knowledge is acquired esoterically. I was ably supported in moving ahead by Almâmi, assistant and friend, and Alkaya, guide. Both come from the region; they know its ways and customs and have maintained numerous friendships there. The 1984–85 research, which I did in an extensive way by attempting to meet the greatest number of potential informants, ended satisfactorily, despite some barred claims I will speak of soon.

When I returned in 1986, I discovered a complete reversal of the situation. A year earlier, I had had to beg the gaw for interviews, and they had tried to extort the most advantages possible from me, all the while biding their time before interviewing. This year they practically paid me to accept meetings. Several gaw living farther from the river came to the banks to meet me on my passage. Three of them changed prearranged dates of ceremonies so I could attend them—without my asking. To keep me more securely at the Gombo encampment, they even went so far as to have Démoudou, the leprous singer whom I had asked after casually, come from Niafunké.

From this phase, in which I was overwhelmed by the sudden and often embarrassing ease of my relations with the gaw, I will recount the edifying anecdote of Hamadoun Boureïma, the Mékorey gaw descended from a companion of Waada Samba. I had missed

him the first time at the end of 1985, when I met his sister Aïssata
Boureïma in Sebi.

❧

In 1986, when I stop in Dondoro at Moussa Founé's, Hamadoun Boureïma lays siege to my tent until I agree to interview him. He then
offers to organize a batou in his village on my return to Timbuktu.
One month later, I meet him again at the Gombo encampment near
Dabi, where he had come to wait for me. He insists that I come to his
village by reminding me that I had agreed in principle. I hesitate. I
have felt sick for several days, and I want to return to Mopti to leave
on the road to Ngouma, where I have to meet Oussou, Waada Samba's
descendant. I end up canceling the batou Hamadoun wanted to organize for me.

I am going to spend the next night at Sebi's bank on the other side
of the river, however, so I offer to drop him off not far from his
village, just to spare him a few kilometers on foot. We halt for lunch
before the stopover at Dondoro, where I plan to see him off. He disappears into the bush, leaving me the following message: "Tonight I
will come back to you in Sebi." I am slightly nonplussed. Why not at
Dondoro, a stone's throw from where he lives? When I reach that
hamlet I learn that Moussa Founé, the local gaw, had become angry
with his colleague and forbidden him access to his territory. I think to
myself that in his message earlier, Hamadoun probably wanted to save
face. I doubt that he will come to Sebi, which we soon reach.

Yet well after nightfall, when we have already dined and each has
gone to his quarters for the night, he surprises me while I am spread
out on my mat in front of the tent, my gaze vaguely lost in the starry
sky. I stand up. He is accompanied by three other people, who have
not come empty-handed. One holds a gallon of liquid butter in each
hand, the second three hens. The third escort pulls a pretty, castrated
goat along by a cord. For a brief moment, I stare hard at the four men,
staggering with fatigue. They have just walked several tens of kilometers, quickly. The gaw, whose travels began long ago this morning,
his face hollow from the effort, looks especially exhausted. This does
not stop him from offering me all the wealth, presented with a noble
and encompassing gesture. Embarrassed, surprised, I stall, wanting to
think before accepting, and ask him to return in a moment. He retires,
but not without leaving his presents beside me.

I immediately ask Ali to assemble the crew members so we can
consider the situation together. My companions are unanimous: "It is

an affront if you refuse!" "But I don't like goat meat!" I say, laughing. "We like it fine," retorts Alkaya. Almâmi ups the ante: "Castrated goat meat is like mutton." In fact, the animal in question is a house-goat that has been coddled and well fed.[1] "It's very fat," Ali adds, testing its back. "And cow butter is very good for your health," Almâmi concludes.

On the unanimous advice of the crew, I thus accept the presents. But the gaw still looks disturbed. His face finally lights up when I announce that I will also interview him the next day. And with a large smile of satisfaction he sits down in the pirogue the next morning. I have nothing much to ask him, but I nonetheless converse with him for a good hour out of courtesy.

♣

Hamadoun Boureïma is a gaw in dispute. Although he is descended from one of the most prestigious families of genii-priests, he has been reproached for taking up the tradition too late and for not making the most of the rich heritage that has been given to him. Not surprisingly, he is trying to consolidate this insecure reputation in every way possible. And apparently, during my stay, interviewing with me was included in the race for prestige all gaw pursue.[2]

Why be offended by the means used to build a gaw's renown? They remind one of the means employed by Western doctors in quite another context. During the phase in which a doctor's honor is determined and clientele constituted, she or he well knows that reputation is not measured strictly by successful therapeutic action and that in fact the reverse is true—credibility depends on authority. In any case, in 1986, I had become an element in the strategems for power and honor of the Ghimbala gaw. That year, we returned to Mopti in a pirogue that had become a minor Noah's ark. Hens cackled in every corner, and Hamadoun Boureïma's goat was joined by a splendid white ram, a gift from Awa Koulikoro.

This privileged situation only lasted one trip. When I came back in 1987, times had already greatly changed. The gaw were more and

1. The house-goat [*bouc de case*] plays the same role as the house-sheep. These animals live close to people in the middle of their courtyards. They are particularly well treated, washed regularly, combed, and sometimes bejeweled.

2. This gaw disputed by his colleagues later turned out to be a very good chief of his order, as demonstrated during a ceremony organized in his village, Mékorey, in February 1988. See chapter 7, note 6.

more demanding with me after Dabi, where Kola Gaba's welcome was quite openly cool when he asked me what I was going to do for him this year. The height of it all came when I met up again with Bili Korongoy around Diré. The gaw had just given a first treatment to a patient. We passed each other on the river, but he barely responded to my greetings and maintained an absent, scowling look throughout the exchange. Pretending he needed to rest, he refused to stop for long and added, "I thought that after all I had done for you and all I had told you, I would have no more problems with taxes." This literally meant that I had never helped him to the point at which he would become rich enough not to have to worry about finding his contribution money every year. It was a floating interview, rapidly concluded. I preferred to leave it at that for that year.

What indeed could have happened? I asked myself about our past relations. I had been perhaps a little expeditious with him when it was time to go back to Mopti last year, but that detail seemed insufficient to me to explain such hostility. So I did some checking and learned a barely believable story that nonetheless turned out to be true. During the past year, an unknown white man had landed by plane at Goundam, a city thirty kilometers to the north of Diré, to meet the gaw D. H. This gaw had accompanied the visitor to France, according to the developing legend. After several months of absence, he returned to Goundam, his pockets apparently filled with gold. Following this episode, he spent his time bragging and proclaiming himself the best in the region. The news of this enriching trip spread throughout the Ghimbala milieu, and the gaw I was used to meeting were upset: "What? And what about us? With all that we've done!"

I don't know this newly prominent gaw, who lives too far from the river for me to reach, and who was also never called to my attention. But he had heard of my research, from what I learned later in Bamako through Almâmi, who met up with the person who usually lodges this personage. On his most recent visit, however, the gaw had had to be content with a few visitors because his mysterious interlocutor—an American, it seems—secreted him in a villa, where the priest gave him his knowledge. We learned that the European trip had never actually taken place and that at the end of some weeks, the person in question had returned to Goundam. I know nothing further, but the whole incident as I experienced it is revelation enough about the rivalry for prestige among priests, beyond what it teaches me about my relationship to them.

Here is how, chronologically, this relationship seems to have evolved. The first year, I arrived an unknown, external to the system, and I incited reserve on the part of the gaw. All the same, I interviewed a good forty of them. The information was hard to obtain, and most often I had to pay for it.[3] But this was nothing to be upset about. First of all, the transmission of knowledge has never been free in Africa, and the Ghimbala are no exception to the rule. Second, there was no reason for the stranger I still was to them to call on their services for hours on end without compensation. While most of the gaw agreed to talk with me, my enterprise nonetheless produced the strangest episodes.

For example, I had chosen to do some interviews in the township of Tonka with priests who had come from all over the area on market day. I set myself up in a room in the administrative encampment. As there was no chair, I had the visitors sit on my trunk, and I sat on the edge of the bed facing them. As the day went on, my interlocutors became less and less talkative; the last one, looking frightened, barely answered me. Finally, rumor spread that I had captured and enclosed a genie in the trunk so that he would spy on everything said in the room. Those who revealed their knowledge to me would supposedly lose all their powers.[4]

Before I found myself on the river again in 1986, several things occurred. Just after my first trip, administrative directives from Bamako finally reached the local authorities. These directives enjoined them, at least as a matter of form, to facilitate my work, and made my presence official, for better and for worse. After that, the fact that during the famine of May–June 1985 I came to the aid of the ten or so villages and encampments I knew the best gave rise to unforeseen effects. Public rumor probably exaggerated the volume of my distributions. This delicate operation, to me morally necessary, was nonetheless to be a source of complications. Perhaps people imagined that I was going to do the same in 1986. I certainly noticed that such intervention had caused a nascent discontent among those who had been closest to me, for reasons which were to be articulated in the following stage.

In this earlier stage, I also realized that a certain number of priests I had met prided themselves on being the best. The people's opinion followed suit. They said to themselves, "Only the great gaw have worked with the white man, who came to find them on the strength

3. The price was never set in advance and depended on the length of the interview. It varied between 20 and 120 French francs [4 to 24 U.S. dollars].

4. An interpretation to compare with the modern legend told in chapter 3, and one that indeed began in the Tonka region.

of their renown." In fact, on my first trip, I had met with all those who accepted an interview. Only after that did I choose some special informants, among whom of course were great gaw. Nonetheless, during this stage, a meeting with the anthropologist authenticated a gaw as a member of the highest rank in his or her world.

Then came the event that was to encumber the third trip: the American's impromptu apparition and departure with the man from Goundam for an unknown destination (perhaps Paris, it was said). This new rumor precipitated a debate that had not surfaced during the preceding trip. Some of my informants had not liked the method of my distribution of emergency aid two years earlier. Sacks of grain had been designated for village communities, not for individuals, and given to representatives of these communities—village chiefs and counselors. When a gaw lived in the place concerned, I had thought it enough to ask him or her to participate on the committee charged with distribution. However, this measure was judged insufficient, given the renown of the priests concerned, and I now found myself reproached by several of them for not having given them all the food aid, which they would then have distributed themselves. "These people would not have known you if I had not been here," they all told me.

Thus I have become an extension of local society's internal stratagems. What will it be like during my next trip?

♣

One evening on my journey I was asked to "close the calabashes" before a ceremony. Another time, poor Sogoba wanted me to intervene to stop the little game a group of young people was playing that involved sweeping the space of the batou with their flashlights, something the genii detest; this was disturbing the dancers. And I didn't do it. In retrospect, I regret that a little. I could have said to the village assembly, "You want the patients to be healed? OK. For that, the gangi must be made favorable, and they do not like light. Light bothers them. They won't come, or, even worse, they will get angry! You will not get what you want if you do not tell those playing with their flashlights to stop sabotaging the ceremony!" Moved by an obscure duty to be reserved, I did not give this minimal speech, which would have argued using the conditions that guarantee ritual efficacy.

These incidents illustrate the way an anthropologist's presence disturbs the lives of her or his hosts, and how they respond to the anthropologist by implicating her or him in their own affairs. Conversely, immersing oneself in different means of relating to the real can cause substantial perceptual modifications for the person giving himself or herself over to such experiences.

FROM BEING OPEN TO THE OTHER TO HAVING ONE'S OWN SUBJECTIVITY UPSET

I spend my time, when I am there, listening attentively to what my hosts tell me, and if they tell me nothing, I incite them to talk. I have my ears open to the least word; I note everything I can. I imagine my colleagues do the same. From this relation to others, we draw the primary matter of our meditations. There is a sure pleasure in being around these people that makes of anthropologists—focused idlers—pillars of conversation, just as there are pillars of bistros (among whom there are surely good anthropologists who don't recognize themselves). But as part of this faintly professional interest in others, distant, exotic relationships must not be privileged over those with the neighboring suburbs or even the next block. Like Georges Perros, I'm convinced that people everywhere are equally interesting once fraternal communication has been established and all differences abolished. Thus, to set apart a group, an institution (the Ghimbala), a certain kind of individuals (the possessed), is only valid if I make this choice with regard to the questions I ask myself and the task I set before myself. I will return to this point shortly.

Until then let us note that continuing to be open to the other and, in a broader sense, to what happens outside can be a pretext for hiding oneself, losing oneself, forgetting oneself, unless there is a healthy return to oneself. This last permits us to become conscious of the place from which we think, and it allows our own vision of the world to be transformed freely when outside figures meet those we all carry within us. Thus the subject sinks deeply and melts into an experience redoubled, far different from those gratuitous games of wit that force themselves on the subject and overshoot it. Yet the person who just goes along with the movements of beings and things—a condition for going beyond one's usual way of looking, which is itself created from the cultural determinism and multiple components of each person's life—runs the risk, most particularly in Africa, of being confronted with a perception of the real that is very different from his or her own and profoundly disturbing. It is useful to find the form that makes the transmission of such an experience possible.

Thus, when confronted with things inexplicable in terms of common understanding, Paul Stoller, an American anthropologist who has spent long periods of time in Niger,[5] initially proposes to model his anthropological approach on that of the painter, in the sense that Merleau-Ponty understands it. The painter allows herself or himself to be penetrated by the surrounding world and then expresses in her or his own style the relationship of presence established with it.[6] The great painters, those who renew human sight, have managed to filter the real, to establish a system of synesthetic correspondences, to concentrate their whole lives in their passion for seeing, ultimately "giving back to the object what [it] provokes in us," as Cézanne has said. The work of art is not reality and does not represent it, but rather refers to certain of its constitutive elements, amalgamated in the reflection of the person who made the work—a reflection of his or her interpretation of the world.

So with the anthropological text. "Just as painters, according to Cézanne and Klee, should allow the universe to penetrate them, anthropological writers should allow the events of the field—be they extraordinary or mundane—to penetrate them."[7] The work of art also has privileges of immediacy and materiality superior to those of any anthropological reflection, which has to pass through the written word and its ordering. This detour causes a reconstruction of the real that is further from the primary experience than are the creative arts.

Stoller also reports in a narrative mode the different phases of an initiation into Songhay magic that caused him to slip into another reality.[8] In this fascinating tale, not at all removed from the sometimes-terrifying trials he underwent, he explains how he had to discover the hidden meanings of the words, attitudes, and gestures of his partners in magic little by little or else find himself in danger. His participation in the magic's occult relations of domination and submission forced him to change his anchoring in reality, which is hardly easy to endure.

---

5. Stoller reports an act of magic of which he was a victim in Songhay country. He was awakened in the middle of the night by the feeling of a bizarre presence. He found he could not move his legs. He ended up conquering this paralysis by reciting the protective formulas his master had given him before he began the trip to Wanzerbé. The next day, he returned to the magician who had received him in a hostile way the day before, and who was perhaps responsible for the problem overcome. He took a resolute and provocative attitude; his interlocutor's attitude changed completely, and that day she appeared very welcoming and ready to help him. See Stoller, "Eye, Mind, and Word in Anthropology," *L'Homme* 24 (July–December 1984).

6. Maurice Merleau-Ponty, *L'Oeil et l'Esprit* (Gallimard, 1964).

7. Paul Stoller, *The Taste of Ethnographic Things* (University of Pennsylvania Press, 1989), 54.

8. See Stoller and Olkes, *In Sorcery's Shadow*.

This book leaves in the reader's mind a revelation of events as incomprehensible as they seem to have been to the author.

In his work, Kabire Fidaali too gives himself over to a veritable deconstruction of his own personality in order to assimilate the teaching of a healer from Ouagadougou, who chose him as a student.[9] He experiences different forms of somatic and psychic disturbances, among them states of aware dreaming during which his master appears to him, although he is supposedly at that moment in Côte d'Ivoire, more than a thousand kilometers to the south.

When he tries to reconstruct the content of his experience discursively, the concepts of anthropology, physics, and psychology are of no use to him. He nonetheless establishes a field of coherence for the ideas transmitted through an epistemological detour, which allows him to bring out the implicit foundations of his master's knowledge. He then gives an explanation of the phenomena observed, whence it emerges that the healer's practices seem to rely on an archaic, coalescent perception of the world that is anterior to language. This perception is made possible by mobilizing all the senses and working at a level of attention sensitive to the body's internal messages. This approach focuses on the acquisition of unprecedented physical faculties that will be used in the cures undertaken.

FROM THE SEBI CONCERTO TO THE POETRY OF OTHERS

Human thought and behavior are traditionally measured by laws regulating social relations and individuals' psychic organization. In the same way, a certain number of physical phenomena escape classical anthropology and psychology because they are external to the construction of the formal universe these two disciplines propose. The researchers I have just described initiated exploration of the flows of roving energy and of uncommon means of communication, and they have reached an experience/knowledge located partially beyond language, in a relationship to the world in which the gulf between subject and object is erased. Each has gone deeply into and internalized the visions of his interlocutors, sharing their perception of the real and acting on it in a certain way just as they do.

Possession, which has to do with the phenomenon of trance and with hypnosis, participates in this same kind of reality, incomprehensible through conventional instruments of knowledge. For my part, I

9. See Kabire Fidaali, *Le Pouvoir du Bangré* (Presses de la Renaissance, 1987).

did not go nearly as far into the experience of possession as did Stoller into Songhay magic and Fidaali into his acquisition of *bangré,* the knowledge of the healer from Ouagadougou. Nonetheless, it is the same search for substantiality beyond the perception of a purely formal universe that guides me. So, too, does the desire to express the whole of my experience lived in Ghimbala country as broadly as possible, including the aspects that appear farthest from anthropological observation in its restrictive sense.

⚜

I have always been attentive to the polyphonic presence of the insects peopling the African night. Each evening, even after a long stay, I wait for the concert to begin. The musical volume varies according to the period and the time of day. It is at its fullest during the hot season after several hours of darkness. But the instrumentalists tire as the night wears on, and the points of sound are more scattered as the darkness relaxes, little by little, around the sleeper, who is quieted by immersion in this space vibrating to infinity.

Since I began riding along the upper bend of the Niger, I have often taken refuge under the roof of the long, black pirogue when resting at a sandbank awaiting a meal or later, before going to my tent, sitting on dry land a few steps from the bank. These are moments of calm, spent reading by the glow of a gas lamp or dreaming at the water's edge. I realized one evening that the outflows from the invisible concert, seemingly heard mostly on terra firma, were invading the area around the craft in swarms and mixing with the claps of the river against the hull. I was greatly intrigued by their variations in intensity and distance. The sounds splashed up from all around, sometimes very near, within arm's reach above the water; then retreated; then came back. Some remained a small distance away. Then the great sound wave would pick up its recurrent, immutable rhythm again. I did not understand these variations in intensity and distance, which, after a few attempts, would resolve into a new balance. I finally discovered that large insects with pale wings came to nest in the spaces of the mats of which the pirogue's roof was made, attracted by the light. Then they started their score again, interrupted for a mere instant, while others humming just as loudly were content to fly around us in the night.

This discovery, as minimal as it was, never ceased to enchant me for the rest of the journey. It happened in Sebi, the old township planted on the southern bank of Issa Ber. The site has been inhabited since the beginning of time, as an imposing tumulus still dominating the poor earthen houses bears witness. In the fifteenth century, Askia Mohammed, great emperor of Gao, built a mosque there that still stands in massive and untamed splendor. From its roof, one can see the river glinting like a mirror, nearly impassive unless the wind causes it to shiver suddenly. After the fall of the Songhay empire, the village became an outpost of the pashalik of Timbuktu. A small garrison surveyed the river traffic from there. Now Sebi, crumbling under its history, poverty, and sand, has fallen into lethargy like most of the little towns of the upper bend.

It was in this worn-out place that I made the acquaintance of Aïssata Brahima, the first genii-cult personality to accept an interview with me. We had entered the area of Ghimbala influence two days ago after crossing Lake Débo. I had noticed then that all the gaw in the villages where we landed had gone on trips or had died and had not yet been replaced. But Aïssata maintained the continuity of the genii cult during the absence of her brother, who was the gaw of their order. She received us toward the end of the morning on Christmas Day 1984. Before beginning the interview, she did a protective smoke purification and consulted the cowries to know whether she was authorized to talk with us. Then she settled in on a mat, facing the door open to the outside. She threw kernels of shells, worn from long use, right onto the sand, in the ray of light that struck across the ground all the way to where she was. She made the warm tones of the earthen walls, coated with ocher and red, sing. She expressed herself in laconic, calm sentences.

Suddenly, she turned toward B. and made an insistent revelation to him, translated immediately: "Your heart is sad; you aren't laughing as you usually do. Is that true?" "Oh! I'm fine," he grumbled, without answering the question. Aïssata went on imperturbably: "You should make an offering of milk to a beggar to regain your peace." The consultation concerning the genii began, and we spoke only of their world. Later in the day, however, B. came back to the incident himself and said to me, "Aïssata was right this morning. I was down in the dumps last night, and I still am." It was the first holiday season he had spent away from his family since the birth of his two children.

Aïssata had introduced us to the universe of Ghimbala followers to whose parade of disturbing events I was to grow close throughout my stays: unforeseen, untimely, violent possessions unlike anything that has been said or written on the phenomenon, arising suddenly outside cult sessions when people carelessly provoke the genii with unconsidered words or attitudes; evocations, exalted and contemplative, of meetings with these genii at dangerous times—in deepest night or at midday, when the sun smashes the world; disturbing relationships of therapist-priests with their patients, who obey their least injunction, their least snap of fingers, like sleepwalkers.

When I returned to the Ghimbala region the following June at the end of the dry season to convey the emergency aid, the river was nearly nonexistent. Along certain branches—such as the Bara Issa, which was almost completely dried up—I sometimes drove right in the river bed. Some months before I had traveled freely over these waterways, and now I wondered if I were indeed in the same world. The melting sky crushed this corner of the earth, which seemed as though it would always be desert pressed by sandy winds. My intervention—made necessary by the famine burdening my hosts of the previous winter and possible through some friendly support and the help of two nongovernmental organizations—unexpectedly revealed certain information.[10]

Much more than when I held to my discreet observer's stance, I became aware through taking action of the total lack of autonomy of the peasants in the upper bend, an area dominated by a feudalism being reborn. Operations at which I was present gave rise on many occasions to confrontations between the villagers and the old and modern authorities, and sometimes even provoked their arrival on the scene, although the preceding months' interviews had left them indifferent. Local relations of domination and submission were brusquely brought to the surface: on one side, standing fast for a brief moment, enjoying a power that seemed to me exorbitant and limitless through behavior and speech, the representatives of the old ruling families, administrators, and new political authorities; on the other, members of the peasant community, who each time relived their tight allegiance to their leaders with an attitude of humble, fearful submission.

The rapture caused by immersion in the vibrant night of insects, the horrendous relations of people with their gods, the revelations about tough peasant conditions—all were integral parts of my experience of the Ghimbala cult: the rhythm of nighttime ceremonies in unison with the surrounding world, the violence of the gods both echoing and responding to that of people toward each other. And do not the gods sometimes help their followers when there is no more hope for the pity of the human powers that be?

To those who object that the process of going more deeply into personal experience and the questioning it causes in the author risk dependence on an approach too subjective to produce anything more than better understanding of oneself, I clarify that the choice of re-

10. The organizations involved were Médecins du Monde and Terre des Hommes.

search and the place it is accomplished depend on the fictions and myths each of us forges and on the path each tries to clear in life. I have tried to express this necessity in the first part of my book *Tambours d'Eau*. Earlier in this chapter I wanted to show that Stoller's and Fidaali's approaches likewise go beyond simple autobiographical reflections.

Michel Leiris clearly talks of this kind of concern in *L'Afrique Fantôme*. Thus his interest increases when he begins to frequent adepts of the cult of the zars in Gondar. His previous poetic practice fits his hosts' sensibility, and he is enraged not to be able to let himself be more penetrated by the world he is discovering.[11] The work in which he reports these premises is no more work of fiction than the one in which an author places himself or herself behind a theorization of the origin of social play, whether we are talking about general laws of exchange (or words, individuals, goods), about an agonistic conception of human relationships, or, on the other hand, about the dream of a primary harmony that history allegedly disturbed. In each of these cases, too, the point of view proceeds from a typically European, ethnocentric myth of the possible objectification of the real, which allows the other's truth to be attained while remaining removed from that other.

The sciences of nature renounced their claims to absolute objectivity long ago. When people are the object of science, the multiplicity of possible viewpoints accentuates even more the subjectivity of choices involved in interpretations. In recent interviews, Claude Lévi-Strauss thus states that for him the social sciences are only an approximation of science: "I don't feel I am doing science in the strictest sense of the word, and I don't think that what we call human or social "sciences" are sciences. To claim that they are would be an imposture. That is why scientific reflection, as it manifests in all its greatness . . . serves me as a guiding light. I look at it . . . and I tell myself I must go toward it as much as one can, while being certain that one will never reach it."[12]

The anthropological vision becomes no less interesting as it comes under the effects of resonance or correspondence that, according to

---

11. "Dreaming of the incessant lightning of the day before, of the strange charm emanating from his daughter, weighing the enormous price I attach to setting down their words, I can no longer stand methodical research. I need to soak in their drama, touch their ways of being, bathe in living flesh. To the devil with ethnography!" (Michel Leiris, *L'Afrique Fantôme* [Gallimard, 1968], 352).

12. Special issue of the *Magazine Littéraire* devoted to Claude Lévi-Strauss and his work, October 1985.

Deleuze, are woven between different intellectual disciplines during the same era.[13] Anthropology, at the outset, is the art of relating. The experience of others, whether they be from over there or over here, requires an effort at understanding, an openness of consciousness that allows itself to be penetrated by the world to the point of a certain forgetting, or at least a relativization, of oneself. In no case can social acts—and even less the actors—be treated as things. Moreover, the observed observes the observer and will change her or his discourse with successive interlocutors according to the affects and desire that circulate in each relationship.

If Colette Petonnet's works among the subproletariat of the Paris outskirts speak so well, so movingly, it is because their author has made that trip toward the other that is indeed more than a recipe for participatory observation.[14] As she recently told me, "To absolutely exclude the emotions is dehumanizing, but to let them filter through the weave of events one must master them, or else be submerged and deliver only one's own *affects*. Not all intellectuals excel at this controlled act of accounting for oneself and erase or suppress what risks disturbing rational order." One must thus hear the network of crisscrossing messages sputtering throughout the research and, even if the project's aim is to account for only one precise aspect of the real, not ignore the other components of the situation observed, nor the diverse circumstances that compete with the establishment of interpretations. Interpretations are reconstructions of past experience, and it is good for them to keep the trail of the events that gave birth to them by drawing the subjectivities present close together, which allows one to go the farthest possible distance toward coming to consciousness of phenomena.

This attempt to share the other's vision is welcome in situations in which it concerns perceiving religious events relative to possession. The followers in trance express a concept of immanence that institutes the sacred, melded from their mouths and their movements. This is what Roger Bastide suggests in *Le Candomblé de Bahia* when he criticizes the attitude of Clouzot, who admits his disappointment after having trespassed in the sanctuary of the Eguns.[15] "We found nothing, nothing but a terrible moldy smell," Clouzot says. After reproaching him for his action, Bastide adds, "Indeed, a lot of effort for nothing. . . . As for the secret, it exists only when the priests of the Eguns

13. Claire Parnet, "Entretien avec Gilles Deleuze," *L'Autre Journal* (October 1985).
14. Colette Petonnet, *On Est Tous dans le Brouillard* (Galilée, 1979) and *Espaces Habités* (Galilée, 1983).
15. Roger Bastide, *Le Candomblé de Bahia* (Mouton, 1958), 62, n. 26.

make their invocations." Secrets and mystery are integral parts of human presence, of the sacred game that unfolds in the gods' honor, and they disappear outside the circumstances that give rise to them.

Lacking a perspective from inside the physical reality of the phenomenon of trance, of which possessions are the expression, I have at least tried to translate the vision of the Ghimbala priests, a vision poetic because it is strong, archaic, primordial, fracturing the real. The gaw draw from their experiences as visionaries all they say of the genii, of their watery homes, and of the multiple places they inhabit. I think the great European poets, who for the past two centuries have been rediscovering and utilizing their capacities for clairvoyance, are exploring the same zones of the real as the priests of the upper bend of the Niger, even if they are not swimming in the same waters. For me, the underwater travels of the gaw and Nerval's precise hallucinatory wanderings in *Aurélia* offer points of similarity.

Little by little, I became aware that at the heart of my exchanges with the djiné don of the region of Kayes and Bamako was a yearning for trance and clairvoyance, which led me to become fascinated with the phenomenon of possession in contemporary Malian society. It seems to me that trance, whether or not it is possessive, has something to do with poetic experience as it is expressed at its highest. Such expressions are found in the works of those who, since the German romantics and Nerval, have left the illustrative and celebrative to experience and go beyond the illuminations of being—from Rimbaud to Perros, from Desnos to Artaud, Michaux, and certain others, to cite only poets writing in French.

The poetry of experience is born of contact with the outer states of consciousness.[16] Marking its trail means passing from a place qualifi-

16. This is the only kind of poetry in question, as far as trance is concerned. Hubert Fichte favored a poetic approach in acceding to others' reality. I note in a collection of texts published in Portuguese under the title *Etnopoesia: Antropologia Poética das Religioes Afro-Americanas* (Editora Brasiliense, 1987): "Science may not only be developed through poetic categories, poetics may also be set in place through an empirical and logical process of diverse types." (38). But perhaps he is restricting poetic expression too much to mean the construction of "verbal correspondences" that are due to linguistic research: "Anthropological research should transform itself into a dialectical process, a correspondence of the linguistic kind." This aim restrains the field of poetic experience to and within language. His own poetic experience is itself confronted by the African diaspora cults in the Americas, the special domain of possessive trance, which should have merited a less conventional poetic treatment.

Yet Fichte's tale exerts a successful effect of seduction thanks to the detailed reconstruction of interviews and situations in a style whose fluidity derives from the apparent absence of connection. The characters, evoked in suspension, experience their destiny in a baroque way that still constitutes one of the dimensions of South American reality.

able in terms of the unformulable, of solitude, of loss—the fall between a bottomless consciousness and a limitless outer world—to
another in which the poem recreates what has happened. The person who remains in the place of breakdown and explores it, often in
spite of herself or himself, risks losing the return ticket and being
plunged—once, unfortunately, and for all—into silence and madness.
Putting both the absolute and the void (nothingness) to the test at the
same time, awakening at the end of a coma seems to me comparable
to the experience of shamans, seers, possessed—to what they do and
say during trance. But they, once they return, remember nothing.

Philippe Lacoue-Labarthe devotes himself to a tense climb back up
to the source of the poetic text in his inspired reading of the two
poems by Paul Celan. Although in agreement on numerous points
with the author, I disagree when he says, "There is no poetic experience in the sense of a 'lived' poetic or poetic 'state.'"[17] One could retort
that there is a manner of being grafted onto the world that is favorable
to a poem's apparition. Georges Perros's entire work bears witness in
this way, it seems to me.[18] But that type of poetic experience is not
reducible to poems. A person can live poetically in this world without
feeling need of the poem, or even without finding the means, the time.
And the poem is a residual result, as Lacoue-Labarthe himself has
written, citing Celan, who speaks of a "singable residue." "I am writing in the margin; the text is elsewhere," says Perros.

It seems to me possible, starting from these several intuitions, to
make a number of connections between the poets and the possessed.[19]
At a certain point of paroxysm, trance, like poetic writing, escapes
social control and fractures institutional reality. There are also untimely possessions, in which the person in crisis utters words that
disturb the ceremony's order: a meaning is being sought; being wants
to arrive at existence. In the same way, the poet of experience faces
the unnameable, which she or he tries to bring over to the side of
the speakable, thus enlarging our perception of the real through a
founding word. But while the possessed—activated by the language
running through them, for which they become a kind of receiver-
transmitter—forget everything they have said on returning to them-

---

But the author's words nonetheless remain within the field of the usual representation
of society and the individual.

17. Philippe Lacoue-Labarthe, *La Poésie comme Expérience* (Christian Bourgois,
1986), 33.

18. See for example, his spiraled reflection on what poetry is, which gives nerve to
the different volumes of *Papiers Collés*.

19. J. M. Gibbal, "L'Ecriture et la Transe," *Térature* 5/6, (Autumn 1982).

selves, the poet holds the position of a medium who remembers through writing. Writing allows deformation of the language to one's own advantage in order to create one's own language and deepen one's experience of the world.

I plan to prolong these preliminary reflections, on one hand by the most precise possible observation of trance states, in connection with the messages transmitted by the mediums, and on the other by study of the great poetic texts of the world that take this direction, and perhaps by interviews with certain living poets who practice the search for outer states. Then it may be possible for me to advance some response to the enigma of the reciprocal revealing and covering of the real and of the word. But the state of the body in trance, traversed by variable intensities, will probably seem to me a black hole in knowledge for a long time. Meanwhile, I must note that the movements and the words of the possessed irradiate the real with unusual meanings and confront us at the same time with perceptions that escape any institutional knowledge, in the same way that founding poetic revelations are affirmed beyond any mastery of the world.

APPLIED AND LIVING FICTION

Once the field of lived experience has been exhausted or at least momentarily abandoned, the fiction takes shape, as the anthropologist, a writer among other things, attempts to account for the first phase of his or her activity. Thus, when I emerge from the bath of intense communication and distance myself from the strong perceptual impressions that accompany it before, during, and after the genii come among people, I reconstruct the world of the Ghimbala possessed with words arranged within the double perspective of my mother tongue and my personal history. Yet these possessed do well without even the most embryonic discourse on the multiple occasions on which they express the vibrations of their being above and beyond language—through their trance, their movements that arise from it, the modulated and not articulated sounds they sometimes make. They are no less accepted, accompanied, and taken under wing by the community of followers assembled, participants in their experience. It is as distant from a solitary, pathological manifestation as is a condomblé ceremony in Bahia from a rock concert, as Bastide has shown in *Le Sacré Sauvage*.[20]

I will thus try to account in writing for an experience that leaks out

20. See Roger Bastide, *Le Sacré Sauvage* (Payot, 1975).

all over. I know that I am more sensitive to certain aspects of the real than to others and that I will speak more easily of the first, perhaps in this way slighting certain sections of the past in constructing my own fiction. Still, this is a fiction in some sense applied. In no case can I elicit from the gaw the opposite of what appears to be the core reality of the Ghimbala: that it is a therapeutic cult submissive to the presence of a dominant Islam, which puts its existence in danger, particularly at the present time. To affirm, for example, that the rise of Islamic fundamentalism and the current economic crisis favor the maintenance, even the expansion, of the Ghimbala would be on the order of an insane interpretation and an atrocious farce.

Each book of anthropology renews in its own way the fiction of being a person among people. And if Roland Barthes has written that anthropology is "the social science closest to fiction,"[21] it is perhaps indeed because questioning the way we are together should start again with each new confrontation with the other, on pain of being replaced by the deathly certitudes of those who believe they have understood the meaning of this adventure once and for all.

21. Conversely, isn't poetry, of all literary forms of expression, the fiction closest to the experience of the real?

Thoughts from the Between

Every time I return across Lake Débo, I manage to spend a long evening on the river, knowing I will reach Mopti a day late. This year, we stop over at Bouna. I decide to pitch the tent on a grassy mound set out over the water on the other side of the township, whose shapes I see melting into one another, their contours blackening. The air darkens while gasps of a faintly audible hubbub cross the stretch, a few cries rising from it at times, borne on the quick, light wind. I savor the final moments of voluntary banishment in this lost land that I ready myself to leave until my next stay. I wait a long while at the bank of the Niger, which quivers at my feet. In the distance, a few poor fishing lamps slip and tremble on the waves. I can scan the black space all I wish—no genie comes to visit me, not even Adjirata, apparent tormenter of my nights, who Kola Gaba says is responsible for my insomnia attacks. But no matter! From one year to the next, the Ghimbala keep on, in the extreme rigor of their situation. Neither intrigues and quarrels nor threatening poverty manage to strip them of their poetic charge.

And I think that the Ghimbala live poetically in an innate way, as Hölderlin meant it when he wrote that "man is poet in this world," and not through some kind of specialization in their use of language. They draw strong language from deep within the visions the genii procure for them. They go back and forth between a merging kind of thought—nocturnal, rising from the deepest places in their dreaming—and an attempt at discernment that generates precise actions. In the face of possession, my fascination remains; I am always as astonished as when I first encountered it. The core of the phenomenon moves away as I draw nearer. Will I one day have a clearer idea of what this state of intimate union of spirit and body is made of, other than through the usual words used to designate it—to which I, for that matter, add my own? It is said to be a relative of hypnotic states, but what, then, is hypnosis?

At this point, anthropological observation gives way to the emergence of the poetic word of the other. Leiris comes to the assistance of this drawing together of anthropology and poetry, of which he is a living example. Recently he declared, "Anthropology is useless, it changes nothing. . . . [I]t doesn't change things, no more than art does. . . . Anthropology certainly contributes something, even if it is only in showing that the sacred is one of the most important factors in the life of societies. . . ."[1] Clearly this is promotion of an activity that thus joins the ranks of valueless, useless, gratuitous things such as the air we breathe, of which poetry is also a member. This latter, an essential component of the freedom to be, can borrow its revelatory force from the anthropologist in search of living and gradual incertitudes. Frequenting the Ghimbala is a good example.

During a recent debate in which the scientific status of the social sciences was at issue, one of the participants very pertinently emphasized that in psychoanalysis the passion to know transforms the other into an object of knowledge and thus distorts the relationship during the cure.[2] In the same way, by transforming others into objects of research, the anthropologist's will to know has often provoked their revolt. My tribulations with the gaw, described at the beginning of the last chapter, also illustrate such a situation. My hosts' reactions and my responses complicated the relationship. Dialogue continued nonetheless, though not without an ever-renascent misunderstanding, because they and I were not asking ourselves the same questions.

The anthropologist's paradox sometimes has to do with knowing how to translate into her or his own language, with a certain exactitude, the principles of life, the organization, and even the emotions of people for whom she or he feels only indifference, even repulsion. Malinowski's *Journal,* recently published in French, illustrates this position. I prefer by far the loving attitude of Jacques Dournes, who gives a most accurate account of the imaginary life of the Joraï people

1. Jean Jamin and Sally Price, Interview of Michel Leiris, *La Quinzaine Littéraire,* no. 491 (August 1987).

2. This debate took place during the seminar Psychanalyse et Sciences Humaines at the Noesis de Calaceite Center, Spain, 24–30 August, 1987. François Roustang spoke there about this giving-off of energy, this strength that appears in the relationship between the analyst and the patient. This strength, not included in precisely psychic forms, has to do with the pursuit of liberation, which grows out of the patient's analytic experience. But it deviates into transference love insofar as the patient's will to be collides with the analyst's own desire to confine the other within the restrictive status of object of knowledge. Thus this "object" responds to the therapist's attitude by transforming itself into a loving subject. Transferential love, characteristic of this phase of the cure, is apparently the means chosen by the patient to escape the situation just described, and to make the analyst get out of the position of observer by implicating him or her in the relationship.

of the high Indochinese plateau because he knew how to let himself share his hosts' dreams.[3]

It is, moreover, not necessary to idealize people, nor to pretend to understand them totally, in order to love them. One must also know how to accept them in their obscure and incomprehensible difference. Yet among those faced with the task of revealing the real, a widespread attitude consists of ignoring or contesting the existence of that which is not comprehensible in terms of established knowledge.

In speaking of possession, for example, a trance could be understood as mere simulation, discourse between the possessed and seer priests, an occurrence comparable only to—and thereby reduced to—a social event produced by the environment. Such events we can, however, no longer consider simply as things. In the Ghimbala cult, certain words, attitudes, and events escape my comprehension. I content myself with reporting them, without effacing their effect of astonishment (tales of travels underwater, meetings with the genii) or their disturbance of my intellect (such as the ring being introduced into the gaw's mouth, causing his possession to stop immediately).

Besides, why would one want to say everything, and especially to explain everything? There are those holes in knowledge through which thought breathes, freed from theories so compact and complete that there is no longer even the least void, the least air circulation, in their articulations.

In an earlier time, people assimilated the inexplicable, the incomprehensible, to the sacred, immediately confiscated by the gods, thus making the real sacred insofar as it escaped them. The death of the gods, who were once upon a time considered holders of absolute mastery over the world, made people infinitely pretentious. Yet to accept this share of unknown, of mystery, not in an attitude of passive adoration but in an awakened state, allows the possibility of a progressive unveiling of the world, which one must have the modesty and lucidity to never consider definitive.

From these long hours, spent going deeper between sky and water in a moving void before returning over there, remains the grace of a

---

3. "Now that I find myself twelve thousand kilometers away from them—without hope of seeing them again—and that their presence, violent and tender, continues to invade my dreams imperiously, wherein I once again feel their vulnerability and their jealousy (which I share with them), I cannot satisfy myself with serious analyses and classical theses. I can no longer love elsewhere, unless it is otherwise. It is perhaps in the imaginary that we are brought together" (Jacques Dournes, *Forêt, Femme, Folie* (*Une Traversée de l'Imaginaire Jorai*) [Aubier, 1978] 11–12).

memory in which the weightless light fades the surrounding landscape and mixes with the wind, the claps of the waves against the hull, the cries of some birds, nomads like us. And the path is simplified for a brief instant while, alone, I contemplate the Sahel in the sun, slowly consuming its loss.

Postscript
Trance, Possession, and Possession Cults

Authors usually approach possession through the more general phenomenon of trance. The phenomenon of trance is expressed by bodily
states and behaviors that escape the usual state and behaviors of an
individual seated with trance, and these correspond to unusual faculties in the individual.

The manifestations of this state span a wide register of neurophys-
iological disturbances. The person in trance is prey to great agitation.
He or she trembles, shivers, pants, and is taken with convulsions. In
the other extreme, the person can appear paralyzed, features distorted,
fainting. Halfway between these two states, the person can experience
ecstasy—a beatific smile on the lips, gaze lost in the distance, rhyth-
mic movements. In a simplified way, I would say that trance appears
an expansion of the body's usual economy, with convulsive states on
one end and cataleptic states on the other. A continuous process may
ensue, with the person in crisis (*criseur,* to use Bastide's term) going
through these different stages—convulsive, ecstatic, cataleptic—during the same session.

These states are accompanied by phenomena said to be of "altered
consciousness" such as loss of immediate perception of the environment and desensitization to stimuli coming from it (that is, a state of
sensory deprivation); loss of reflexive faculties; the experience of immediate, merging connection with the world; and amnesia once the
trance is ended. They are also accompanied by the appearance of
exceptional faculties lasting only for the duration of the trance: divinatory gifts; gifts of languages not usually spoken (glossolalia); therapeutic gifts. Among great trance figures, let us note diviners, seers,
shamans, and spiritualists.

Possession is a category of trance. The bodily states of the possessed
are similar to those of people in simple trance, and their faculties comparable. But the phenomenon of identification distinguishes possession from shamanic or prophetic trance: the possessed identifies with
the mythical personality of a god, a genie, or a spirit. The possessed
abdicates his or her own personality and becomes the god or the genie
in question in the eyes of the spectators to the trance. The possessed
behaves like the entity supposed to have invested her or him, adopting

character traits and replaying certain details of the mythical figure's biography. The possessed becomes, in the eyes of followers, the god living and incarnate.

The possession cults are religious institutions whose adepts are seated with identificational trances. In order to use the term *cult,* there must be a consistent set of collective religious practices that imply a body of shared beliefs, an organization of clergy and followers, a religious calendar, and places where the rituals and ceremonies recur. The Ghimbala meet precisely these conditions.

APPENDIX 1
The Meeting of Sheikou Hamadou and Waada Samba

Waada Samba was already seventy-six years old when the Dina began. When Sheikou Hamadou called Waada to Hambdalaye, Waada delayed his answer. His brothers counseled him not even to go because Sheikou Hamadou had announced he would slit the throats of all those who held batous. Waada told his brothers that if Sheikou Hamadou sought the truth, he would not slit his throat. But the brothers didn't want him to go.

He stayed in Doundé a whole year. Sheikou sent him messages all the time so that he would come to him. He did not move. When he was ready to go, he ordered his brothers to go, one to Gao, another to Tindirma, the third to Almina, and the last to Kikara. When someone wanted to make war, the brothers were to find allies. Once his brothers were dispersed, he himself left with Kondjorou. At that time, Kondjorou was a very strong, very vigorous man.

When they arrived in Hambdalaye, they met Démo Kossi, who had slandered them to Sheikou Hamadou. They greeted Sheikou Hamadou, and Sheikou Hamadou answered them. They waited a fairly long time. It was during this period that Waada Samba one day said to Démo Kossi, "If you don't greet me, I will strike you." Sheikou Hamadou asked him, "To whom do you address these words?" Waada Samba answered, "To your genie who is near you on the right side, and whom you call Ali Soutouraré."[1] "Ah! You know him?" "We were together for twenty-six years in a pond, near Djenné, before you settled here." Sheikou smiled and wanted to say nothing more. They remained that way several more days.

After some days, Sheikou called Waada and said to him, "I found out you did batous; you gathered men and women together." Waada responded, "That is true." Sheikou asked him, "Why do you strike

---

1. According to the Macina Fula tradition brought back by Hampaté Ba, Ali Soutouraré is the warrior genie who accompanied Sheikou Hamadou into combat and ensured his victory.

people and say bad things to them?" Waada answered, "I know that you have a daughter, Aïssata, and that she has been in irons for four years now." [Turning toward Almâmi and me, Oussou Kondjorou clarifies, "Like the boy you saw in my courtyard."]

Waada said, "I know that if I had not come, it would not have been easy to treat your daughter." Sheikou Hamadou answered him, "It is true: I saw you in a dream; we tried everything to treat my daughter and we found nothing. And you, how are you going to treat her?" Waada answered, "I must organize a batou in Hambdalaye." Sheikou Hamadou exclaimed, "May God protect me from that! As long as I reign here, there will be no batous in Hambdalaye!" Waada said, "If I don't hold a batou, I cannot treat your daughter."

They were not able to agree. Sheikou called his people to explain to them what was happening. An educated marabout said to Sheikou, "Is it not better that your daughter heal, that we marry her and she have children who will increase the Islamic people, than to leave her in her madness until her death?"

Sheikou said, "It is true; if she heals, she will have a husband and children, but how can we accept a batou here?" The marabouts answered him, "You brought the people from Binga, Diaptobé, and Aïré here. They knew nothing of Islam, not even reading, not even prayer—they were animals. Some scrabbled in the garbage, others begged, still others gleaned a few kernels when the grain was beaten. You are in the process of purifying them, teaching them to pray. You can order these people to gather behind the city to have the batou with Waada. As they are not yet in the religion, you can use these people in this way before they become Muslims." Sheikou said, "Is that your way of thinking?" "Yes, it is thus." Sheikou said, "So we must ask Waada." Waada said, "I have to be shown the site. If it is good, I will agree."

Sheikou, accompanied by one of his entourage, found a place between Séghé and Hambdalaye. Waada accepted the choice: Hambdalaye could be seen in the distance. He asked that branches be cut, and with the help of ropes the chosen site was closed off. He made three entry doors into the batou, just as there are three doors to a mosque. (Where I come from, too, one enters the place of the batou by three doors.) Waada sang and danced, hopping on one foot. He said to Sheikou Hamadou, "I want to hold the batou here either Thursday night or Sunday night." Sheikou Hamadou said, "It's up to you." Waada said, "Then it will be Sunday night." (That way he could continue the batou for three days to have a better chance of healing the patient.)

At that time there were only strips of cotton fabric with which to clothe oneself. Waada had a little boubou made (a turki) and a pair of pants with a rope-belt, and had the daughter dressed in it. Then he made the people scheduled to participate in the batou come out of the city, as well as those who had accompanied him to Hambdalaye. There was Moussa Gakoy (his descendants are finished), Kola Lagara from Jiba, and Balla Mama from Sassi. There was Bantassi Hidié who played in the batou (his descendants live near our village), and also a man, Hamadou D. Baba, who was a singer.

Before the batou began, Sheikou Hamadou asked two men who were going into the bush to gather dry wood to bring back all the animals they could catch, without killing them and without anyone seeing them. The first man was named Ali Fullani, from Macina, the second Saïdou Mossi. They arrived in the bush at the end of the afternoon. Ali Fullani made his bundle and bound it. He called Saïdou Mossi, who said to him, "I'm going to try to cut some strips of bark so I can also bind my bundle."

At sunset, he found a hare crouched in a corner and captured this hare. The man from Macina asked him, "What are you going to do with it?" "But you know perfectly well that Sheikou Hamadou asked us to bring a harmless animal back alive?" "Ah yes! That's true! But you didn't understand what he said. You are black; you will stoop to anything. Leave it alone." "I won't let go of it unless Sheikou Hamadou tells me that is not what he wants. He said 'an animal we can bring to town.' There is hardly anything but this hare we could bring back without difficulty. I captured him, and I'm not letting him go." He covered the hare in his old clothing, and he took it in his arms. The Fula wanted to take it from him, and he did not let him.

They returned to Hambdalaye and passed by the Koranic schools at the hour when the lamps were starting to be lit. The Fula met Sheikou Hamadou and said to him, "What you asked us to find we have brought you." He wanted to hurry and take the hare from Mossi's arms, but Mossi did not give in. Sheikou Hamadou criticized him: "Let him do it; don't resist, or people will understand what is happening." Then he added, "How can we keep this animal so that he doesn't die before the end of the batou?" Mossi said, "When will the batou be?" Sheikou answered, "This evening." Mossi said, "I can keep him."

Sheikou answered, "This evening." Mossi said, "I can keep him."

He gave the hare to the Fula and to Sheikou for a moment and ran away into the bush to cut a few sticks. He made a kind of basket, into which he set the hare. He dug earth out from all around it to set the basket in the ground, so it didn't move despite the hare's leaping. He gathered a quantity of leaves and set them before the hare with a little holder full of water. With his companion and Sheikou, he stepped away to observe the hare, who was agitated and made the basket move until it was tired. Then it went to pick up the leaves laying there.

Sheikou said to [Mossi], "You are right; you can keep him, you take good care of him. Waada is a magician; he will hold the batou this evening." Then Sheikou Hamadou called all the marabouts and asked them to designate fourteen people who could be taken into confidence, who know *istikhārah* well, so that they could consult their true dreams in such a way that they could guess the name of the animal he had captive: "I have an animal; I don't know its species. All that God has shown you you have only to tell me."[2]

When the hour for the ceremony approached, Waada made a stop near Sheikou Hamadou to greet him and to say he was going to the batou. Sheikou said to him, "Come and see—I caught an animal I want to tame. I don't know its name; you look and you will try to tell me what it is." Sheikou added, "I don't know if it is a bird, a snake, or some other animal. It is just hidden nearby—you look; I don't know what it is. I would like you to tell me what it is."

Waada acquiesced and went to the batou. When all the malé bania began to sing his praises, he stood up and began to dance.[3] At the same time, he made Sheikou Hamadou's daughter dance and struck her with the whip.[4] All this lasted almost until dawn. He ordered the girl to be brought to his house and to be given water to wash. Then Waada stood up again to cry out loud, "What the marabout is keeping at his home is called *tabay* in Songhay."[5] He repeated this three times and continued to affirm it in his batou: "That's what they are keeping there! Two men, a black man and a white man, took the animal at sunset."

The people who were present exclaimed, "We don't understand at all!" So he began again to dance, and to repeat the same things: "It is an animal from the bush that has four paws, with long ears and very silky hair. I don't know its name in Fula, but this animal is called tabay in Songhay."

Shiekou Hamadou ordered Alfa Issa Sira Gatou, who could speak Songhay in addition to Fula, to go to the batou and to write what

2. Istikhārah is divination by dreams in the Islamic magic tradition; "true" dreams are distinct from those that are only illusions—sent, for example, by the demons.

3. That is, he was possessed.

4. One of the Ghimbala practices described in chapter 5.

5. Waada was again possessed. The marabout he refers to is Sheikou Hamadou.

Waada was saying in Songhay. Alfa Issa came from Koyïba; he understood Songhay and needed only to listen and to write.[6] He wrote everything Waada declared. People asked him to translate for them. He answered, "I say nothing."

When daylight came, everyone left to go to sleep. After Waada had taken his first meal of the morning, Sheikou Hamadou called the two groups. In the meantime he had asked Mossi at dawn, just before prayer, to take the animal, without anyone seeing it, and hide it under the shelter where he taught. He asked Mossi, "Can you set it there without anyone seeing it?" Mossi went to find a pot to turn over the hare. He made holes in it as big as his finger so the air would get in without anyone being able to see the animal through it, unless a person were right next to it.

Sheikou Hamadou left the people who were there where they had gathered and went to the mosque to make his prayers. When he came out, he ate and called everyone together with the Other.[7] He first asked the marabouts, "What did you see last evening?" "Of course, we saw it is a bird." But then the marabouts began to contradict each other. Some affirmed that it was a guinea fowl, others that it was a partridge. They continued their dispute for a good while until Sheikou Hamadou said to them, "Shut up!" Then, addressing Waada, "I heard it said last night that my daughter sang for you and at that time exclaimed, 'Waada Samba is the Sheikou of the devils.'"

Waada answered him, "You heard well; that is what God did." Sheikou asked him, "And you, Waada, what did you see under the basket?" Waada answered, "I don't understand the Fula language and I cannot say during the day what I saw at night."[8] So Sheikou Hamadou retorted, "Alfa Issa Sira Gatou must come here." Alfa Issa came. Sheikou Hamadou asked him what he had written. Alfa Issa then declared, "What Waada cried out was 'tabay,'—'hare' in Songhay, which is '*wodiéré*' in Fula. He cried out that it is an animal that possesses four paws, long ears, and very soft hair. He repeated it three times. He also added that a man with dark skin and another with light skin went together into the bush to capture it. You yourself noticed that these two were fighting. You asked they make a little cage for the animal, then you had it put under a canaris."

6. Koyïba is a village in the Niafunké region, thus in Songhay country.

7. Waada Samba.

8. Which means, "I cannot repeat in my usual state the predictions I made when I was in trance." It is known that the possessed, like all mediums, do not remember what they say or do in a trance state.

Sheikou Hamadou turned to the marabouts and asked them, "Did you hear what Waada said?" The marabouts answered, "We have heard." "What are your reasons for affirming that it is a bird?" "We saw that the animal moved." Sheikou then declared, "I have prayed God, thanks to whom I am installed to tell the truth in Hambdalaye, to make the animal in the image of a bird." After he said this, the men raised the covering. The hare stood up and quickly transformed into a bird, a bird that was a partridge. All the audience was rolling on the ground with laughter.

Waada watched the scene with his sombé in hand (the same one I still use). He wanted to throw his sombé on the partridge. Sheikou told him three times, "Leave it because of God." Waada cried out, "Sheikou!" "What?" "You favored the marabouts. Yet when you founded Hambdalaye, you asked God to destroy the city if lies triumphed there. This is the first lie today. You wanted to favor the marabouts, and love provokes lies." Sheikou asked him to stop speaking and added, "What Waada declared is the truth; if someone does not believe it, we have only to call Ali Fullani and Saïdou Mossi."

The people called them. Sheikou asked them, "What did you take in the bush to bring here?" Saïdou Mossi answered, "I took a hare in the bush." "Since the time you caught it, did it change into something else?" "No, it has always remained a hare." Sheikou turned toward the marabouts. "Did you hear what Saïdou Mossi has said?" "Yes, we have heard." "It is I who asked God for it to be a bird to protect you. If you go to a little woods where the partridge has alighted, you will see that it has once again transformed into a hare. If I had not done this, the Dina would have been defeated. Waada has many people behind him, from here to Timbuktu and Gao. He has many people. All these people would have revolted today. To vanquish them would have required causing many deaths. That is why I asked God to help us, so that it would go this way. Accept, Waada, that God gives you the truth." Waada said, "The truth is God's; the truth is also Waada's."

Sheikou Hamadou replied, "When they say Waada is a sheik, he really is—he is a real sheikou. Since the beginning of the Dina, I have had near me a shaytān named Ali Soutouraré—who knew it? No one. It is Waada who will tell people Ali Soutouraré's name from this day forward, in the name of the Dina, so that he is no longer unknown, and so he is not lost.[9]

"Last night, I told Ali Soutouraré to go take Waada by the hand

---

9. This passage refers to the fact that Sheikou Hamadou entrusted his personal genie, Ali Soutouraré, to Waada Samba, as Ghimbala tradition has it.

and to bring him here. Ali went. He found Waada in Séghé.[10] Ali came back and said to me, 'I was afraid of him and was not able to take him. He was seated; he had his beads in his hand. He was making his prayers. He saw me; he smiled at me.' Ali told me what had happened between him and Waada. I noted that he knew him well. Here is what he told me: 'Waada spent twenty-six years in the plains of Djenné. He sometimes took trips, but he always came back to the Pondori.[11] I saw him and encountered him all the time. One day we had to fight and I, Ali Soutouraré, had to sacrifice a white sheep. There is a djini named Baana whom I cannot dominate either.'[12]

"Here is what Ali Soutouraré told me. What Waada possesses, God gave him. We must take Waada into consideration, or else the people will revolt against us. Ali counseled me to respect Waada, to give him blessings, to ask him to chase away misfortunes that could happen in the country. May Waada be one of my allies! That is the only way to do things so that the people remain with us.

"I have not been able to verify all that I have been told about Waada. Men brought canaris here, full of red and white hen feathers. They had stuck cowries on the canaris. They said that they had seized all this from Waada's house and that it was a house of fetishes. I asked Ali Soutouraré if he was aware of all this, and if it were true or not. Ali answered me, 'I have never known Waada to have these things.'"

Then Sheikou turning toward Waada, said, "It seems that you slit throats [of animals] at the beginning of every flood season." Waada answered him, "That is true." Sheikou said, "I have also learned that you slit throats turned toward the west." Waada said, "That is not true. I make this sacrifice once a year. It is to God I address myself so that flooding goes well, the crops succeed, and the people eat well.[13] I slit only the throats of animals and do not mix the blood and grains. All those who participate in the sacrifice will eat of it. If flooding finds me here, I will do the same thing."

Sheikou said, "Is that how you answer me?" Waada said, "In all I have told you to the present, have you heard lies?" Sheikou replied, "No." Then Sheikou asked him, "Why don't you enter the mosque?" "If I go into the mosque, I will only be able to do one *rak'ah;* I will

10. Séghé is the place where the batou was to occur. Waada made his prayer before the ceremony began.

11. The Pondori is the floodplain situated between the Bani and the Niger.

12. Baana, the most powerful in the whole Ghimbala pantheon, was Waada Samba's personal genie.

13. But Waada neglected to say—and Oussou with him, reporting his words—that once the name of God has been spoken, the one officiating immediately addresses the local genii, first of all Baana, the most pagan among them.

faint away at the second. One who loses his wits cannot pray. One must keep one's wits to work, and when one cannot work, one can even less go to the mosque."

Sheikou exclaimed, "I do not agree! Tomorrow you will come to pray at the mosque." The next day, the call to prayer sounded. Waada went to the mosque with everyone. He prayed just one rak'ah; at the second he fell on the ground. He could not continue; he never did more than one rak'ah at the mosque of Hambdalaye.

Sheikou had warned Waada's men: "If he faints, get him out of the mosque quickly. He must not disturb the prayer of others." His men got him outside. They continued their prayer. When they returned to him, they found him slowly returning to himself. One of his companions then took the ring that was on his finger and put it in his mouth. It calmed him right away, and he went to sleep.[14] When he awoke, he said a word that every Muslim pronounces when he awakes. He said, "There is only one God."

He was given a goglet full of water. All the goglets that were in front of the mosque came from Djenné. He went to wash. He returned and sat down; he made his ablutions. People then said to Sheikou Hamadou, "He is not used to praying, but he is intelligent; when he arrived here, he observed us and he imitated us, but he does not know the prayer."

This speech shook Sheikou Hamadou. He asked Waada to come after his prayer. Sheikou asked him, "Waada, do you know how one must pray? Do you know the words of God?" Waada replied, "I think I know them." Sheikou said, "Take this goglet, prepare yourself, and make your ablutions in front of everyone so we can correct you if you make a mistake." Waada accepted. He made his ablutions in front of everyone; they all watched and verified everything. Waada faced the mosque. He called to prayer like the muezzin, and he said, "*Ali-gama*."[15] Everyone listened; everyone thought it was just right. He continued to pray. He went all the way through to the end. He spoke the *taḥīyah* out loud before getting up. Everyone heard. He did the *salām*. He asked the Muslims to do *al-Fātiḥah* with him.[16] Then he told those watching, "Today, I will sing you the poem Hambarké sang

14. On this use of the ring to stop unwelcome possessions cold, see the end of chapter 5. Could Waada have been possessed in the mosque? That is what this passage implies.

15. "Aligama" is the way he pronounced the last word a muezzin speaks before the beginning of prayer. [The standard transliteration and pronunciation are *al-jamā'ah*.]

16. Al-Fātiḥah is the act of thanksgiving one performs to mark the importance of a gathering, of a meeting, or of any other event that has come to an end before the actors of the moment separate.

here in Hambdalaye where he composed it."[17] [Here Oussou Kondjorou begins to declaim the poem, skipping a certain number of
verses, according to Almâmi.]

When he had finished the poem, Waada said to the Muslims assembled, "Let us ask God's grace." Sheikou Hamadou did al-Fātiḥah
with him and then turned toward the people. "Did you see? Did you
hear? You told me that I helped him, that I favored him. It was not I
who did it; it was God. He is older than I am. He has traveled much;
he has seen many countries; he has gone through Tindirma; he finally
settled in Doundé Al Kaya. Before, this island was home only to the
djini. He succeeded in staying there. No one else could have done
it. I, Sheikou Hamadou, I am not from Hambdalaye. I came here
through the grace of God."

Waada Samba stayed on several more days at Hambdalaye. Then
Sheikou gave him many horses and much gold. He added, "There
where my daughter was taken by the devils, two students from the
Koranic school were also attacked. Can you chase the devils from this
spot completely so that my people can regain peace?" "Yes, I will do
it. If you give me still more wealth, I will do it." Sheikou promised
him the gifts. Waada succeeded in removing the devils to a grove near
Kossi. The devils never went farther than that and refused to join
Waada in Doundé. The grove was near a branch of the river. When
Waada got ready to leave them, the shayṭāns all said to him, "You
exiled us from Hambdalaye; you led us into this woods. Be careful!
No one of your descendants will be able to enter here, or we will make
that one disappear."

Waada answered, "I agree with your prediction, but I am sure it
will be neither myself nor my son Abel, nor will it be Abel's son. We
will be protected against you."[18] [Oussou clarifies that this is the only
son Waada had all his life.] From this time on, no member of our
family goes into this grove. We can get close to it, but we are forbidden to enter it.

Waada stayed in Doundé a long while until God called him. His son
Abel replaced him. Abel was exactly like Waada was. Abel reached the
height of knowledge; he was brought to Bandiagara. God gave Abel
a great victory in Bandiagara. When he returned, he remained in
Doundé until God took him. He was replaced by his daughter, Adda
Abel. Adda did her time, and it is I who replaced her. Here is the end
of what I know.

17. Hambarké is Sheikou Hamadou's minister, who composed a mystical poem to
the glory of Hambdalaye, the Dina, and their founder, the emperor.

18. Oussou Kondjorou says "Abel." Most other gaw pronounce it "Abdel."

(Story told by Oussou Kondjorou, descendant of Waada Samba, in Doundé, 13 March 1986)

☙

This long tale, extremely detailed and alive, would merit long analysis. I have simply tried to recreate it here in the strength of its dramatic progression. One will nonetheless note that the interpretations of the descendant of the first great known gaw lean markedly in favor of Islam. Oussou certainly mentions the curative dimension of his cult but insists particularly on the divination episode, on all the points establishing that his ancestor was a pious Muslim. On the other hand, in contrast to numerous tellers of the Niger bend, he gives few details about the emperor's daughter's possession and healing and the importance of the genie Baana, barely evoked in passing. The genii (pronounced "djini," name closest to the Arabic) slip constantly toward the status of *jinnīy,* devils, even shayṭāns, those demons who are totally negative beings.

In other respects, one of the great merits of this witness is to establish that Waada Samba spoke Songhay, whereas his descendants speak only Fula.

APPENDIX 2
Moussa's Great Deeds

Moussa possesses seven homes: one in Gorongo, another in Birigna-doundou, another in Sendé, another in Nanga, another in Saganda, another in Balandanié, and the last in Taoussa.[1] Moussa, when he travels, sleeps in each place for seven days. The door is an iron one; when he wants to enter, he must crawl under this door. Inside there is a servant woman who massages him. When she says to him, "You have emptied my body, you have emptied my belly," Moussa stands up abruptly, gives a great kick to the door, which falls, and goes out.

There were seven genii who came from Awgoundou. They walked to Birignadoundou. They noticed that Moussa was not there, but a large genii village was established that bore the name of the waterhole. The village received the seven genii. Its inhabitants said, "We receive foreigners; we must treat them well." They made all the sheep they had kept in the water's depths come out. But those who came from Awgoundou took Moussa's sheep and Awa's sheep. "We and the genii don't have the same character; a genie can do ill to another genie who did him good."[2] The seven genii heard Awa's and Moussa's names but didn't know them. Each morning, they slit the throat of a sheep.

During this time, Moussa slept. When the news came to him, he stood up abruptly, screaming. He took his camel, he took his arms; he prepared himself for war, he took all his arms. Moussa said that he was going to see the foreigners who made all his sister's and his family's sheep come out and slit their throats. But before leaving, he seized his spear and stuck it in the ground. Then he got off his camel. Then he transformed himself into a kind of vagabond, with his hair a mess. He put on a very old, black boubou, an old pair of pants, an old turban. He took off his camel's usual trappings and set them on the ground. Then he got back on his mount. He took up his spear he had stuck in the ground.

---

1. Different holes in the river ranging from the region of Gaïrama, a village near Diré, to that of Timbuktu.

2. With this interjection, the gaw announces his personal opinion on the genii. Followers hold contradictory opinions: others say that the genii are more just than people, that they keep their promises, and that they recognize the benefits of doing so.

During this time, the foreigners ate, had a good time, amused themselves. Moussa went toward them. The village genii exclaimed, "Here comes the sheik of the genii!" Some said, "But it is his camel!" Others said, "It's not him; it is a vagabond who has taken his camel!" He was so transformed; he had made himself so unrecognizable. When he stopped, he had his camel kneel. The people were sure it was his camel, but they recognized neither their chief nor his way of riding nor the ornaments and jewels of the trappings he used. Moussa himself sat in the sun until he was dripping with sweat. Then one brave man among the seven foreign genii rose and asked that this man and his camel be brought out of the sun. Then he returned to his friends. Moussa said nothing. Another man rose and repeated the same thing as the first. Moussa did not answer. The seven genii came, one after the other, to ask Moussa to go into the shade.

Then Moussa rose, mounted his camel, and went home. He asked one of his wives to give him his spear, and he went back to join the foreigners. He stuck his spear very hard into the ground. One of the foreigners arose; he tried to pull it out of the ground to give it back to him; he could not. They all tried, one by one; they were not able. Then the seven all together tried to pull the spear. They strained so hard that their belts broke. Then Moussa put his finger on the spear and cried out, "I, Moussa, I stuck my spear in the ground, and those over there, the seven of them, can barely break their belts trying to get it out! But those seven there were not ashamed to take my sister's sheep!"

Then Awa brought the good food she had prepared for Moussa. He lay down on the mat and, propped up on one elbow, began to eat what his sister had prepared. And, still lying down, he put the cord around the seven foreigners' necks. Then Moussa led his seven prisoners to his sister Awa. He found her as she was crying to go blind.[3] When he grew close to her, he struck his camel to make it scream. Awa understood that Moussa was coming and exclaimed, "I don't want to go blind for nothing! The one who was to return my sheep is not dead!"

Moussa answered, "Big sister Awa, come! I am here!" He extended his hand to Awa, who took it. Then she opened her eyes again, and Moussa said to her, "Here are your sheep and those who took them." Moussa asked Awa, "Do you want me to dig a hole to bury them, or would you prefer me to shoot them, or to slit their throats, or yet again to throw them down the cesspool hole?" "Do nothing to them, just give them to me!" [Awa said.] Then Moussa departed, leaving the

---

3. Awa did not know the outcome of the confrontation and feared her brother had perished.

seven foreigners in Awa's hands. Awa then removed the cords and said to them, "Your throats will not be slit, you will not be killed, you have only to go home very quickly! You are merely children who went on a walk, but you are not hardened enough for war."

♣

One day Moussa said, "*W-Allāh, w-Allāh*,[4] if I die, I have no replacement. I have no more children. Who will take my place? Awa, you will lose all your sheep!" His captive, Baana, had heard; Awa had also heard. Moussa left, Baana came to Awa. One night, Moussa and Baana saw each other by a bolt of lightning. Each one got down from his horse. They began to fight. Moussa was stronger than Baana, but Moussa took extreme pity on Baana. Moussa's servant woman slipped between the two combatants. "Old one, you must not put your hands over your eyes," she said to her master. Moussa answered her, "It is risky, but I am covering my face with my hands!" The two genii fought. Moussa wanted to leave. Baana held onto him and stopped him. They fought all night, until dawn.

So when it was light, Moussa saw the trace of his saber in Baana's skull. He took him in his arms and said to him, "I am sorry, and I now take the risk of putting my hands over my eyes!" And he added, "If I die, there is now someone who could replace me." Baana left. Moussa left for his Taoussa home, where he went to lie down. (When he lies down, he must sleep for seven days before waking. His iron door is closed; he alone can open it. Instead of turning the key in the lock, he simply kicks it. Since he is strong, the door opens.)

Seven people to whom he owed a large sum came to see him and found him already awake. When he had gone to war in a nearby village, he had borrowed gold from these seven people to make sacrifices, and he had used it all up. The visitors told him they had come to claim their due. He answered them, "Sit down!" He went to get some little millet, he sowed it. He sowed big millet; he took rice, he sowed it; he sowed sorghum.[5] He sowed these four grains; then he sowed fogno, he sowed corn, he sowed wet rice. He sowed all this for seven days. Afterward he asked his guests to go see what he had sowed in seven days. They went to see: everything had grown, and the harvest was already done. He took out what he owed the seven people and paid back his debt. The rest he distributed to his family. "I,

---

4. "Alas, alas!"
5. The big millet alluded to must be an intermediary species between little millet and sorghum.

Moussa, I sowed little millet; I sowed big millet; I sowed all kinds of rice; I sowed fogno. I sowed corn and I was able to harvest! I paid my debt and I gave the rest to my family. Only I, Moussa, am able to do that. I pay my debts to seven people and I still have enough to feed the seven households of my seven residences." The seven visitors left and Moussa stayed on one more day.

♣

All the genii envy Moussa, but they cannot vanquish him; they can do nothing against him. He was married to a woman by the name of Mariatou. Mariatou had a child by him. His name was Beîtel Banni. He was still very small when Moussa left on a trip. So the genii, who had not managed to vanquish Moussa, took the child and slit his throat. They dug a hole and put the child's body in it, just under Moussa's prayer-rug. They added poison to kill [Moussa] when he came to sit.

When Moussa returned home, he understood everything. He understood that his child had been killed and put in a hole with poison in the place where he usually made his prayer. He deliberately sat where his child and the poison were buried. He gathered all the genii and asked them where his son was. Each one answered, "I don't know." He questioned Beîtel Banni's mother. She answered, "The child went out to play. I don't know where he went."

Among all the genii Moussa gathered, he had a nephew whose head touched the sky when he sat down somewhere. His name was Kokota Djini. This nephew was very disturbed by the death of his little brother. After Moussa had long questioned all the genii, Kokota Djini spoke to them and said they should get his little brother out of the hole immediately.

Then Moussa protested. "Attention! My own big sister Awa has had poison prepared in a canaris reserved for sorcerers! She wanted to kill me, but God was not willing. They slit the throat of my child and added poison in the hole so that I, Moussa, would die. But I will not die!" He told them all, "I am seated on my son's cadaver and on the poison, but it does not kill me."

Afterward, Kokota Djini declared, "We must revive the child that you have killed!" Moussa answered him, "Go away! Can you resuscitate someone who is dead? Where, then, is your mother who is dead? Where is your sister who is also dead?" The genii began blaming each other. "It's not me; it's you!" The genii were accusing each other. "You're the one who told me to do that!"

Moussa asked all the genii to go home. Since that time, certain genii have died, others still live. It's not poison that's going to kill Moussa! I will stop here in Moussa's story.

(Story by Bili Korongoy, Moussa's gaw in Gaïrama, 25 January 1985)

APPENDIX 3
The Heinous Crime of Komaïga
and Djini Maïrama

The young genii-men gathered to visit the young genii-women; they played the *batoulaanou,* which became Kodal Djini's song; afterward I will tell you why. The first young woman they went to was named Gassi Korey. Her mother was Djini Maïrama, her father Komaïga. When the young men presented themselves to her in order to know whom she loved, her mother, a great connoisseur of magic, said to her father, "I will slit our daughter's throat for them and make them a tasty dish, and when they ask to see the child again, I will tell them they have eaten her."

Indeed, the genii do not eat the genii. If one genii eats another, his or her nature will change; he or she will transform into an agama, an ant, a toad—into something worthless.[1]

When the young men arrived at Komaïga's house, Gassi Korey, Maïrama's daughter, came to greet them. They all saw her. When she went back into the house, her mother took her and slit her throat. She took a bit of each of the parts of her body (flesh, joints, blood, skin, hair), which she enclosed in a metal box. She dug a hole in the middle of her house and chanted incantations over it so no genie would find the buried box. Then she brought the young man the prepared dish. One of them, who had no master,[2] refused to eat. When the others began the meal, he told them, "Eat! And then you will pay for what you have eaten."

The devils only eat animals. plus incense, wakando, *ferré* [bastard mahogany], perfumes, fresh milk, etc.[3] The young men continued to eat until they encountered the head. When they saw the head, they understood that it was a woman, and they were all horrified. Among them there was a marabout named Samarrous Djini. There was also

1. Here Mahaman, the teller, changes the rhythm of his tale (and thus of the music with which he accompanies himself on the koubour) each time he interjects a remark parenthetical to the general flow of the story to clarify this or that detail.
2. That is, who was very strong.
3. In this second interjection, Mahaman enumerates some components of offerings and sacrifices—the genii's usual food.

Ali Soutouraré, who is very powerful because he is the captive of the
genii blacksmiths.[4] (Each time a noise of hammered iron is heard in
the night near a great tree, it is Ali Soutouraré.) Ali Soutouraré addressed all the genii present: "I am not ashamed because I am the
blacksmiths' captive, but you, you nobles,[5] you should be ashamed.
You must pay immediately for the girl you have eaten, or else by tomorrow you will change into toads, agamas, ants. . . ."

As for Samarrous, he tells the young men, "If you can find me the
five parts her mother removed, I will resuscitate her. I will reconstruct
her and I will put the soul back in her body because I am an educated
man." They delegated Ali Soutouraré to go see Djini Maïrama and
ask her, "Which are the parts you took from Gassi Korey's body?"
The mother told him, "I took nothing away; I simply slit her throat,
washed her, cut her in pieces, set her in the pot, and served her to you
that way. But I took away nothing!"

When he came back to the young men, one of them, Kodal Djini,
asked them if they would accept his becoming head of the meeting so
that this business would end without incident. "If you agree, very
well; if not, too bad for you." The young men answered, "We accept
you on one condition: the condition that you attack none of our society." (If the genii attack someone, the person is brought to a gaw.
Incense, plants, the animal—everything the gaw asks for is the share
of all the genii.[6])

[Kodal Djini replied,] "If you agree, I also accept what you ask of
me. It's agreed—I will take no one from among you!" "Who will you
take, then?" "It will not be from among you, but the one I will attack,
you will not be able to treat. He will never heal; he will remain stupid
until his death. I will take the ass, the dog, the cat, the tree. No one
can treat them. If I attack a tree, even a very large one, all the leaves
will dry up the next day on the side where I touched it." The young
genii fell into agreement with Kokotal Djini.[7] This was the cause of
the *laanou batou,* the order for the batou that was given to him.

Immediately, Kodal Djini called Ali Soutouraré and said to him,
"Go to Gassi Korey's mother. You will see a pillar supporting the
house. Dig a hole at the base of the pillar; you will find a metal box.

---

4. Samarrous Djini and Ali Soutouraré are usually considered old genii. In this tale,
they are included in the class of young men.

5. The genii's society, the double of human society, is organized on the same hierarchical model.

6. In this new commentary, Mahaman recalls some elements of the beginning of
the cure.

7. Kokotal Djini is a variant name for Kodal Djini.

Bring it back." Ali Soutouraré left. Without asking the mother, he unburied the box and brought it back right away. Samarrous took the marrow and put it back into the bones. He took the joints and put them back; he put back the flesh, he put back the skin, he put back the hair. He stood before her, he took his beads, and, telling them, he spit on the body until it became that of a sleeping woman. He asked the young genii to sing for her. If someone is sleeping, that person cannot awaken instantly.

One of them had no master in this world. Moussa had one, Baana had one before, but Kodal Djini did not have one. Before, all the genii had a malé, but Kodal Djini never had one. As he loved song, he called Gassi Korey strongly so she would get up. "Now you have only to return home to tell your mother that a wrap-skirt will never be like a pair of pants until the end of the world. We are men; we are not women!"

Here is the story of Komaïga, whose wife is named Maïrama, and the daughter Gassi Korey. The story took place on the Ndia Djun, a channel between Balla Mahoudé and Tindirma. Some call this channel Doyalgoro. In this place is a great gourgoussou planted with trees. It is here that the thing happened. Everyone must be told that it is Mahaman Tindirma who told this.

(Story obtained from Mahaman Tindirma, genii-griot, in Tindirma, 26 February 1986)

APPENDIX 4
Table of the Principal Plants Used in the Ghimbala

SONGHAY NAME	FULA NAME	SCIENTIFIC NAME	ENGLISH NAME/ DESCRIPTION
bosso	njabbi	*Tamarindus indica*	tamarind
diawa	djaawi		vegetal incense
diedie	ibbi	*Ficus sycomorus*	type of fig tree
ferré	kahi	*Khaya senegalensis*	bastard mahogany
horé	gigili	*Boscia senegalensis*	bush with indeciduous leaves
garboy	tanni	*Balanita aegyptiaca*	thorn tree; zachun-oil tree
kabé	boki	*Andansonia digitata*	baobab
kabou*	kooli	*Mitragyna inermis*	bush growing in flood zones
kobdié	ndunndeewi	*Ficus platyphylla*	tree with white latex, fat leaves, and a reddish trunk
turdia	turjaawi	*Calotropis procera*	
wakando	ghile		elongated, odiferous, black pods, used as a seasoning

My thanks to Christiane Seydou, who confirmed the spoken correspondences of the Songhay names and who told me most of the Latin names and French names.

*The kabou (*Mitragyna inermis*) is a small, bushy plant found in all the Sahelian possession cults from the Senegalese border to Niger. Among the djiné don of western Mali, it is called *djun*. It is the main cult plant because it belongs to Tamba, king of the djiné don, just as the wakando, Baana's black seed, plays a central role among the Ghimbala because of the importance of its owner, who dominates the entire local pantheon.

The kanji, which is also called *kangou* or *kangarou,* is done at the express request of a patient's family, which wants the patient to be attacked and possessed by the genie no more.[1] The family must furnish
a fine sacrificial animal. This is commonly a large kobiri with horns.
Initially the ritual resembles the yaré (head-against-head between the
patient and the animal; stepping over the animal; then, to close, the
postulant seated several moments on the animal). The animal then has
its throat slit. The sheep is thus stripped and its meat cut into pieces;
the genii's share is taken away and offered to them in sacrifice. The
skin is washed carefully at the river's edge. During this time, the participants in the ceremony consume the sheep's meat.

After dinner, the brotherhood begins a cult session to the sound of
the bomboutou, the water drums. When the gaw is certain that the
gangi have gathered around the ceremony, he has the postulant seated
on a mortar overturned at the center of the dancing area. The body of
the postulant has earlier been rubbed with the skin [of the sheep] and
a preparation of the genii plants. Three or four vigorous young men
then sit on other mortars, placed surrounding the mortar of the person
for whom the operation is destined. With one hand they stretch the
sheepskin over his or her head, holding it rigorously immobile with
the other. A last participant takes up a whip and places himself in front
of the group.

The interrogation then begins. The holder of the whip begins to
strike the stretched skin rapidly while the gaw and his or her assistants
tirelessly ask or ask again[2] the patient the name of the gangi possessing
him or her. As long as he or she does not cry out the name, the
stretched skin is hammered with whip blows. ("You would think it

---

1. *Kangou* and *kangarou* are the terms used by Kola Gaba and correspond to the
terms in use in the northwest of Ghimbala. "Patient" [*malade*] is the exact translation of
the Songhay word used by Kola Gaba, *wirtikom.* The patient's family includes, first of
all, the husband or wife, but also the head of the family or the one who represents the
head locally.

2. According to whether the kanji is organized to prevent integration into the cult
(as was the case for Sheikou Hamadou's daughter) or whether its target is already part
of the brotherhood and wants to disengage from it.

was thunder," Kola Gaba tells me.) As the limit of the insupportable end of suffering is reached, the patient reveals the name of his or her genie and the genie's characteristics. But the interrogation continues: "Do you still love your genie? If you love him still, you must divorce him. Otherwise we will continue to hit." As long as the "beneficiary" of the treatment refuses to abandon the genie and does not explicitly say that she or he no longer loves the genie, the whipping continues without letting up.

When the disavowal has been wrenched out, the ritual enters into another phase, enumerating all the circumstances that might cause a wild possession in the patient. It is pursued during blows: "If you hear thunder in the sky, will you be mounted?" "No!" "If you smell the odor of a rag burning, will you scream?" "No!" "If you smell incense or perfume, will you be mounted?" "No!" "If you smell the odor of a woman giving birth?" "No!" "If you smell the perfume of kabé flowers that surround the newly wed?" "No!" "If you have a fight with your husband (or with your wife), will you scream?" "No!" "Will you be mounted if you get upset?" "No!" "If you are on a pirogue that overturns?" "No!" "If you see a house burning down?" "No!"

Throughout the entire time of the renewed questioning, the skin remains stretched over the postulant's head and the strapping man holding the whip continues to strike. "You must tell us that you really no longer love your devil, that you have divorced, and that you consider him forbidden to you like alcoholic drink!" "I will not follow him anymore; I will abandon him forever; I will not scream again until the end of my life!" After this the gaw addresses the audience to ask if she or he has forgotten anything, and the spectators of the separation ritual can then complete the interrogation with questions.

Finally we enter into the kanji's final phase. The gaw make his patient say, in Arabic, the first verse of the Koran: "There is but one God and Mohammed is his prophet." The patient picks up in Songhay: "There is but one God; I have returned to my Lord. I have abandoned the genii; I have abandoned the shaytāns." Then the patient repeats seven times, accompanied by the whole assembly, "I have left the genii and the shaytāns; I have returned to God and to my malé."

It is only at this point that the skin is removed. The patient appears to all with a swollen face, eyes shot with blood, in a state of advanced exhaustion.

(Taken from a story obtained from Kola Gaba, gaw of Dabi, 2 March 1986)

BIBLIOGRAPHY

Abitbol, Michel. *Tombouctou et les Arma*. Maisonneuve et Larose, 1979.

———. *Tombouctou au Milieu du XVIIIe Siècle*. (After the chronicle of Mawlay al-Quasim.) B. Mawlay Sulayman.

Ba, A. Hampaté, and J. Daget. *L'Empire Peul du Macina*. NEA-EHESS, 1984.

Caillié, René. *Voyage à Tombouctou*. François Maspero–La Découverte, 1982.

Desplagne, Lieutenant L. *Le Plateau Central Nigérien (Une Mission Archéologique et Ethnographique au Soudan Francais)*. Larose, 1907.

Dupuis-Yakouba. *Les Gow ou Chasseurs du Niger (Légendes Songhaï de la Région de Tombouctou)*. Ernest Leroux, 1911.

———. *Essai de Méthode Pratique pour l'Etude de la Langue Songoï*. Leroux, 1917.

Gallais, Jean. *Hommes du Sahel*. Flammarion, 1984.

Gibbal, Jean-Marie. *Tambours d'Eau (Journal d'Enquête sur un Culte de Possession au Mali Occidental)*. Le Sycomore, 1982.

———. *Guérisseurs et Magiciens du Sahel*. A.-M. Métailé, 1984.

Hourst, Lieutenant de Vaisseau. *Sur le Niger et au Pays des Touareg (La Mission Hourst)*. Plon, 1898.

Konaré Ba, Adam. "Sonni Ali Ber." *Etudes Nigérieinnes*, no. 40. Niamey, 1977.

Monteil, Charles. *Une Cité Soudanaise, Djenné*. Anthropos, 1971.

Rouch, Jean. *Essai sur la Religion Songhay*. Presses Universitaires de France, 1960.

Sardan, J. P. O. *Concepts et Conceptions Songhay*. Zarma, Nubia, 1982.

———. *La Société Songhay*. Zarma (Niger, Mali), Karrala, 1984.

Stoller, Paul, and Cheryl Olkes. *In Sorcery's Shadow*. University of Chicago Press, 1987.

INDEX